In a time like our own
the only WWII female
of war, Pat Hartwell ic
US military, and the troops awaiucu ....
painting from Hitler's study. Really?

She was the only woman in the CBS news room, assistant to the head of the Office of War Information, VP of one of the largest public relations companies in the world, third in command of UNICEF where she convinced Matisse to provide artwork for free, editor of her own Arizona newspaper where she hustled naïve art on the side, and eventually head of the Hawai'ian arts council, a state of extremely complex political and social stake-holders, where she left a legacy of preventing art fraud. Her story is a fascinating journey through history, art, and deception.

The memoir delves into the art of invention and the shapeshift-ing of memory and truth, interwoven with humorous yet pro-found moments. It examines the comical Soviet efforts to conceal Hitler's death, McCarthy's investigations, and the author's own struggle to compete with both her mother and her mother-in-law. Threaded throughout are insights into organizations that ma-lign the word "mother" and, of course, plenty of mother-in-law jokes.

With meticulous research and a unique perspective, *Hitler and My Mother-in-Law* challenges the boundaries of narrative hon-esty, offering a powerful exploration of propaganda, identity, and the personal reckoning that defines the art of memoir. It's a gripping mix of history, family, humor, and a biting reflection on the politics of truth—past and present.

Hitler &
my Mother-in-Law

Hitler &
my Mother-in-Law

A MEMOIR

TERESE SVOBODA

O/R

OR Books

New York • London

Published by OR Books, New York and London

Visit our website at www.orbooks.com

All rights information: rights@orbooks.com

First printing 2025

The manufacturer's authorised representative in the EU for product safety is Authorised Rep Compliance Ltd, 71 Lower Baggot Street, Dublin D02 P593 Ireland (www.arccompliance.com)

Typeset by Lapiz Digital. Printed by BookMobile, USA, and CPI, UK.

paperback ISBN 978-1-68219-651-9 ebook ISBN 978-1-68219-652-6

Cover image: Movie still from *Berchtesgaden at liberation, 101st Airborne Division; Goering's art collection moved* (May 1945). Accessed at United States Holocaust Memorial Museum, courtesy of National Archives & Records Administration

The first time you tell a story, it's fact, the second time fiction.
—Hegel

Truthiness: the misuse of an appeal to emotion and
"gut feeling" to reframe factual reporting.
—Stephen Colbert

The Trumpian lie is different. It is the power lie or the bully
lie. It is the lie of the bigger kid who took your hat and is
wearing it while denying that he took it. There is no defense
against this lie because the point of the lie is to assert power, to
show I can say what I want, when I want to.
—Masha Gessen

For Steve

Contents

Hitler 1

Writing the News 12

Influence and Interference 30

Smoke 48

Souvenirs as Proof 59

Truth 68

Mayor of Berchtesgaden 84

Censorship 96

True Love 107

Abuse, Begetter of Lies 119

Mother 126

Invention 143

Evidence 153

Propaganda or Promotion 167

Mothers-in-law 185

Witch Hunts 197

Addiction   213

Truth in Art   223

Stories   236

Artifice and Erasure   250

Fake   263

Polio?   276

Silence   286

Truth to Fit   296

Belief   304

Acknowledgements   321

About the Author   323

Endnotes   325

Index   392

1

Hitler

Very funny, *Hitler and My Mother-in-Law*. Mothers-in-law are supposed to be dictators, harridans, women who brook no compromise. *I haven't spoken to my mother-in-law for eighteen months. I don't like to interrupt her.*

But no, not so funny. The title refers to a 1945 photograph in which my twenty-nine-year-old future mother-in-law, Patricia Lochridge, dressed in a burly coat and a headscarf, points to a pile of ashes. The photo is black and white, 5"x7", promotional size. A year earlier, she had been recruited from her position as assistant to the head of the US Office of War Information to cover the war as a sort of poster girl-reporter. The military chose her to stand beside the ashes because she was a civilian, she said, and they desperately needed someone outside their purview to verify Hitler's death. Look, says her outstretched hand.

*

She didn't just find a pile of ashes on the street and decide it was Hitler's, I say to my husband Steve. Who said they were his?

The military, he says. Anyway, that's what she said.

*

Pat knew how to control information. Hired by CBS radio as the only woman in news on its re-launched network, she was one of a team of five that included beetle-browed Edward R. Murrow.[1] In a 1995 interview, she said, "Because Hitler always did his deeds on a Sunday, and as I was the only woman and therefore the slave of the department, I was always on duty—fortunately for me—because I had an opportunity to begin to make major decisions about what would or would not go on the air, and how we covered it, and so on, because it was always very early in the morning."[2]

Ever quick to turn a negative—"slave of the department"—into an opportunity, she was in her early seventies when she gave this interview; enough time had passed that she understood the social forces of the forties that oppressed her, and now she showed her experience to her best advantage.

*

In the photo I remember, disbelief creases Pat's face as she points to the ashes. That face was also buck-toothed like my mother's—and like her friend Eleanor Roosevelt's. One side was pinched from polio, with no-nonsense hair tucked under the scarf, and a decent figure below, yes, but also—as revealed in home movies—a limp. She projected "feisty." Good looks might have been a disadvantage in her line of work anyway, as men in power often assume an attractive woman's only asset is ornamental. At the time Pat was embedded—what a suggestive term!—with the 101st Airborne in Berchtesgaden, a town very near Hitler's hideout.

But Hitler shot himself in his Berlin bunker; that's where Eva Braun took the cyanide. Berlin was where his remains were burned. Everyone knows that. The photo could have been taken anywhere, the ashes at her feet could be anything, a smear of black on the ground, perhaps several handfuls of whatever was left in the grating of the closest fireplace.

*

Mom, says my husband, didn't like answering questions. She was good at asking them.

*

In 2015 a British poll of 2,000 people suggested that women are twice as likely to lie as men.[3] They lie because it is useful. The children don't need to know their father's at the bar, her mother would be better off ignorant of her diagnosis, her husband will delight in her good mood without knowing whether it has to do with her trip to the hairdresser, or the track. White lies say more about expedience than evil. Family lore might just be lore, what the family wants to hear.

But Hitler?

*

The Allies didn't know for sure if Hitler was dead, but they wanted to reassure the public—and the Germans—that the war was over. Declaring him dead would convince them to lay down their weapons. And if he wasn't dead, well, it was only the opinion of a woman. The postwar ethos had already arrived, the voices of women again discounted.

*

Two weeks after the war was over, Pat was en route to Buenos Aires to track down rumors of Hitler supporters fomenting revolution in Argentina. She told her editors that there was good reason to believe that the country harbored a large group of Nazis, and she spent a couple of weeks in Buenos Aires and more time elsewhere investigating. Those she met "had a great story to tell about how they had been trying to save the world for white Anglo-Saxon Protestants."[4]

The story she told her family, however, was that she was looking into business opportunities for women in South America.[5] Years earlier, she had traveled that far south with her father, then in the oil business, who had taken the whole family on a tour. This time she visited seven countries, a two-month trip with many contacts, an itinerary like a Bond movie. Having supposedly pointed at Hitler's ashes, she was the obvious person to look for those who still believed him alive, but she published nothing about her findings. Did she file a story with someone other than her editors, or was there no story in the chase? Or did she file a report?

As soon as Pat returned, she, along with 250 other correspondents, watched the Nuremberg trials that convicted the leaders of the Nazis. The female correspondents slept on camp beds; their single filthy bathroom was equipped for men, with two urinals. But they were not without amusement. Janet Flanner, reporting for the *New Yorker*, made everyone choose which Nazi leader they would have sex with.[6] A woman with Pat's hairstyle, a thick pageboy, passes through the courtroom, her back to us, in footage released to the public in 2013.[7] So much about this period is coming to light only now.

*

For reasons of propaganda, the Nazis had a practice of keeping their heroes alive. The sixteen brown shirts who died in the 1923 Munich Putsch were for years celebrated by Hitler and the country as immortals who continued to fight for the soldiers. "For us they are not dead," said Hitler. He cast himself as an immortal by surviving a number of assassination attempts, and by suggesting in a radio speech that it was Divine providence that protected him.[8] Because the populace had no body to mourn after his suicide, it was as if Hitler had been assumed straight into heaven. In 2000, Chief of the US Secret Service Brian Conrad conceded that "the only decisive evidence ... would be the discovery and positive identification of the corpse."[9]

*

I am resurrecting Pat, who died in 1998, to learn the truth about her in the context of her times, her haunting of her sons; of course some truth about me, since I suspect Steve's attraction to me has something to do with my similarity to his mother, both of us professional writers and women who made a few foolish decisions in love, and, above all, to sort the peculiarities of what truth means today. The impetus behind all memoir is always about getting to the truth.

*

I am traveling in that famously WWII-era mode of transport called a jeep, even more famous for its lack of shocks, so every dip in the road produces a terrible jolt. Forty years from now, a new jeep will be introduced, and the military will complain that it's too cushy, with drink holders and actual shock absorbers, but in 1976 this ride is a luxury because most of the time we— my soon-to-be-ex-husband and I—have had to travel through Sudan largely on foot. Now big trenches left in the road during the rainy season have hardened to rock. Every time the jeep wheels hit them, our heads smack the roof, our backsides thump the seats, we hold on to our teeth. I fear the jeep will fall apart the way it did yesterday, when our driver had to collect spoons from our stores to melt down and refashion the broken part from scratch. But for now, we've hit a stretch that is flat and smooth, and our driver accelerates.

He starts to sing as he speeds along, we get downright giddy with the singing and the thrill of moving through the late afternoon so quickly, hoping to arrive at our next village before dark, where we might bathe while it's still light enough to see oncoming crocodiles. Our plan is to ingratiate ourselves to the brother of the last person we met in the previous village who endured our presence long enough to document the lives of Nuer women. A few years ago the ex had partially shot and finished editing a beautiful bestselling documentary about the Nuer for the Harvard Film Study Center. Meant to be inclusive, it mostly neglected the women. Since this is the mid-seventies and women have been rediscovered, he is making a sequel. I'm the sound person. The film will not be finished, though I will write and win grants toward its completion. Instead, he will become the subject of my first novel, which takes fifteen years to write and is called *Cannibal* because he was eating me from inside out.

Nuer village near Jikau, 1975

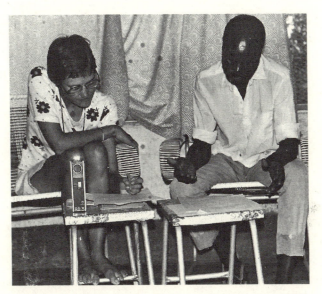
Author with Philip Machar Ruoc translating songs, 1976

I had already won a grant to translate the songs of the Nuer from Columbia University. My naivete with regard to song collecting and translating—my idea that a twenty-something poet unschooled in Africa, let alone Sudan, anthropology, or the Nuer, could make sense of any tiny fraction of this great river of oral tradition that celebrates every aspect of life here: not only marriage and worship but politics, cannibals, even a smooth road—was vast, as it had to be for me to dare to undertake such an impossible project. The grant favored poets over linguists, and fortunately the application did not ask how well I did in college French. I am dutiful and diligent, and the translations will be published ten years before the novel the trip inspires.

Now, with the morning sun almost overhead but still bearable, the breeze of our speed drying the inevitable sweat, my dysentery on hiatus because of a nice little pill in my water bottle, out of some big crevasse of a dry season ditch unfold three soldiers who scramble into the middle of the road, each waving a gun.

Our driver stops.

The tallest Nuer—the Nuer are among the tallest people in the world, and this man, the one wearing shoes, is probably nearly seven feet—gestures for us to get out. His face is grim. Don't you know that I am a soldier? he says. That these are the shoes of a soldier? You must stop for soldiers.

Never mind that we couldn't see any of them hiding in the ditch, let alone their shoes or their weapons. A border war is being fought nearby in starts and stops, wherever someone decides where the border is. We had no idea we were so close.

The other two soldiers grin and nod and point their guns at us, but don't step away. Why? Nuer pours out of our driver far faster than I can translate, all three soldiers interrupt and everyone gets very excited. My ex is taking stills, which annoys the soldiers further, which makes them shake their guns at him until he points his camera over their heads. Stop that, I say. They think it's surveillance. Even I can tell that.

They don't have any bullets, not to worry, he says.

The tallest Nuer soldier, smiling, points his gun at me, and says in very clear English, We will kill you.

We all look at each other, the three soldiers with this curious smile on their faces, the driver with his What?, my ex-to-be dropping his camera to his lap, me flash-thinking *run* but to where? We're surrounded by totally empty flat vistas in all directions. Our driver talks even faster, all three of the soldiers start to argue and gesture angrily back toward where we had come, and one of them aims his gun at the horizon as if to pick us off.

Right-o, says our driver. He starts the jeep and pulls away with a jerk, the soldiers now waving goodbye and smiling.

I understand nothing. I turn to my future ex who shrugs in bewilderment. The driver, his hands shaking on the wheel, shouts it was all a mistake, that what the soldier meant to say was "We could have killed you" since we had driven up so fast, but the soldier had been educated only to the second grade, he didn't know how to say that.

My Nuer is kindergarten, I say.

A tense situation.

*

Descartes loved facts. He burrowed deep into rationality to explain the self as fact: I think therefore I am. The 18th century skeptic Hume went further: I'm just a collection of facts: height, weight—only the sense data. Just because it happened in the past, doesn't mean that it will happen like that again. Hume believed that the real world of fact, whatever "real" is, is unknowable, and that this real world of fact—even hearsay, but not fake news—has a physical presence that can, at least, be corroborated. He also believed that we are more influenced by our feelings than by factual reasoning. Propaganda, for instance, is all about leveraging feelings. We find an idea nice or threatening and, on that basis alone declare it true or false, and reason comes in only later. It is necessary, however, to presuppose that the future will resemble the past, said Hume.

We will kill you.

*

A veteran of two marriages by the time I met Pat—one more divorce than her—I appreciated her skepticism about whether I made an appropriate mate for her son. We had just announced our engagement when Dickson, Steve's estranged stepfather, died, not unexpectedly, as he was an alcoholic in poor health. We decided to fly to Hawai'i to see how she was getting on. I was jet-lagged and had barely emerged from the bedroom when she assigned me to write an article on local basket weaving for *Cultural Climate*, the journal she wrote and edited for the Hawai'i State Foundation on Culture and the Arts. I hesitated. Later, I would write about stars for the *New York Times*, about chemical sensitivity for *Spin*, Negritude for *Guernica*, jewels for *More*, dogs for *Harper's Bazaar*, divorce for *Redbook*, and sex with your ex for *Vogue*, but just then all I'd written were rock'n'roll reviews for a Vancouver magazine. Here was my chance to make a good first impression.

I sat under a banyan tree and talked to a basket-maker. Since I'd spent six months on a film shoot in the Cook Islands before going to Sudan, I knew enough to ask about the relationship between the basket patterns and Cook Island cosmology. Pat published the piece, with a few edits, and paid me.

*

My husband tried to earn his mother's love by fixing everything, every toaster, every broken lampshade, every frayed cord. I am extremely grateful—we seldom call a repairman. Pat's second son had a number of serious relationships but did not marry until he was sixty. The third son became a journalist in the hope of more direct maternal acknowledgment. Her youngest moved far away and took a pill to avoid his father's drinking problem.

*

Just before we ended our first visit, Pat talked about having tea with Eleanor Roosevelt, and displayed her war trophies—and that photograph—perhaps to impress me, as well as to bolster her link with Dickson, whose expertise in public relations had earned him a bronze star and the rank of lieutenant colonel during the war. I was anxious to be accepted but being young and ignorant of just how impressive Pat's accomplishments were... Like many others, I found the stories that went with the artifacts hard to believe—Goebbels' silverware, Goering's Minox camera? I was also a little resentful of her treatment of her son—why wasn't she as enamored of him as I was?—and even a touch scornful. A fairly typical first mother-in-law encounter.

*

Now my husband can't find that photo of his mother with the ashes. He looks everywhere, he calls his brothers for validation.

She was always telling stories, says the youngest.

*

Carolyn M. Edy, author of the definitive *The Woman War Correspondent, the U.S. Military, and the Press: 1846–1947* opens her essay "Trust but Verify: Myths and Misinformation in the History of Women War Correspondents" with "We [journalists] all know, too well, the saying 'If your mother says she loves you, check it out.' But what if your mother is a journalist, or even a historian? The short answer is you approach her statements the same way."[10]

2

Writing the News

Pat always claimed Eleanor Roosevelt was a friend. Like fellow journalist Martha Gellhorn, Pat also said she stayed over in the White House suite now and then.[11] Mrs. Roosevelt wrote for *Woman's Home Companion*, the same magazine that employed Pat. During her twelve years as First Lady, Roosevelt also held more than 300 press conferences solely for women journalists, where she defended low-cost housing, the subsistence homestead program, equal pay for equal work, old age pensions, and the minimum wage. Pat isn't listed as attending in the official accounts. She's also not listed as being formally invited to tea. Mrs. Roosevelt, she insisted, would invite her for tea to talk about what it was like in the real world. Because Pat traveled quite a bit, she said she was "one of two dozen people, half of them women, whom Mrs. Roosevelt came to rely on for their informal reports."

Steve recorded his mother saying that she corrected FDR's table manners—but the president wouldn't have been invited to Eleanor's all-female press conferences.

We were all having lunch at the White House . . . there must've been eight of us . . . and the first course was consommé I looked up and I saw the president putting Saltines—bunching up his fingers—and putting them in his jellied consommé. Since I was a well brought up young lady who had never been permitted to put my crackers in a soup, much less a jellied soup, out came the words: "Hey, boss, this is jelly!" And he looked at me, he said, "Yes, I know, I know . . ." What a faux pas, having lunch informally with the president and reminding him of his table manners![12]

She is not listed as having had lunch with FDR either, but the FDR archives reveal that some luncheons had no guest list. Does the specificity of the anecdote clinch its truth? The only tangible proof of any relationship is a letter to Eleanor setting up a civil defense broadcast for CBS; Pat writes that she's looking forward to working with her again.[13] Little brother Lloyd marched in the Eagle Scout honor guard for FDR.[14] Perhaps that's the best evidence.

*

My husband is downcast. Eleanor Roosevelt held over three hundred press conferences for all those reporters and my mother's not on the list?

I nod. On record, anyway. And no invite to the White House either.

He pretends not to hear me, he holds dear the vision of his mother with pinkie lifted, sitting across from Eleanor in the White House parlor, chatting about what she was doing at CBS, with FDR pouring tea and crunching up his soup crackers.

He fusses with his glasses. I heard Eleanor had a lover, but did they confirm it?

Lorena Hickok's journalism made the front page of the *New York Times,* I say, glancing up from my computer. She looked a little like Eleanor and your mother: homely and friendly. Maybe that's what it took to be a good female reporter then—a non-threatening appearance. She may have been why your mother was invited to the White House. If she was.

Not everyone's mother talked about having tea with her, he says. He's looking out our window onto the backsides of buildings on the Lower East Side.

Look, my writing this memoir might entail rewriting your memories of Mom. Better stop me now.

No, he says. Let's have it.

*

Pat's other three sons are skeptical and roll their eyes when they are confronted with their mother's accomplishments. Was she decorated by General Eisenhower for reporting in the European theater, as she claimed in an interview?[15] There is only a commendation by the Secretary of the Navy for outstanding performance, probably for her reporting at Iwo Jima. Sometimes her sons say she lied, or at least stretched the truth. She was Texan, what could you expect? Born in Austin in 1916, Patricia was meant to be "Patton," a family name so beloved that it was adopted as "Pattie" for females in earlier generations.[16] She would be no Pattie. In her birth announcement, her father crowed, "At the rate the suffrage movement is growing, she may be President yet."[17] A well-known editor and onetime publisher of the daily *Austin Statesman,* Lloyd Lochridge lost the newspaper before she was born, and by then held a position at Sinclair Oil.[18] "A very jolly man who was undercapitalized," said Pat.[19] Her mother, a graduate of the University of Texas, gave up her teaching career for the home. By 1926 they had moved the family to Forest Hills, a residential neighborhood of Queens, where Lloyd climbed the ranks of the oil industry. At age fifteen, Pat spent a year at the University of Texas, where her grandfather had been comptroller, then went to Wellesley, where she majored in political science. She claimed to have been accepted to Harvard Law School in 1936 but the law school didn't take women until 1950.[20] At the time, she could have gone to the Harvard School of Public Health or its Graduate School of Education, both of which accepted women. Maybe she was considering her mother's teaching career? She followed her father's, graduating in 1938 with a master's from Columbia's School of Journalism, a program that had begun just a few years earlier. One alum of that year described his sixty classmates as "including a Catholic priest, a German baroness who enunciated each word with the precision of a Swiss watch, a retired editor from Ohio, and several Yale and Harvard graduates."[21]

Her first job was on the *Daily Intelligencer* ("Isn't that a wonderful name for a newspaper?" she enthused in an interview), published in Mexico, Missouri, where she "reported on county politics, murder, softball, church socials; swept the floors; wrote advertising and learned to run a Linotype machine."[22] The newspaper had run *No News Today* in a banner headline across a front page the year before.[23] The prank, reported nationwide and in *TIME*, indicated that the editor had a sense of humor, which may have been what attracted her to work in a town with a mere 9,000 residents.[24] But she only lasted a few months. In another letter home, she writes that she lost her job in Mexico because she was suspected of being a private investigator in a local murder case.[25]

She must have asked too many questions.

"Went on to the *Kansas City Star*," she writes, "but before I could get really started was offered a job in New York." Her true reason for leaving the *Daily Intelligencer* was much less

Pat at top and her family c. 1926

dramatic. A letter from her father reveals that the newspaper was lowering the wages of those who were exempt from the new tax law so as to pay better wages to those who were not, and this rankled her.[26] Under this truth was another reality: she wasn't happy in small town Missouri, and after she went home for Christmas, she finagled an interview with another Columbia grad at CBS.

That all checks out: Columbia, the *Intelligencer,* CBS, even the part where she boasts of knowing Philip Hamburger, the *New Yorker* writer. He turns up in her class at Columbia. Steve's "old baby carriage mate," says a letter from her in 1971, was his son Jay Hamburger who, she comments, had just written a song for the Broadway musical *Godspell*.[27]

*

Jay is the name of Pat's second youngest son, Steve's half-brother. Tense yet quick with a quip, geeky yet graceful like the surfer he used to be, he's just retired after forty years of teaching journalism at the University of Hawai'i. The bulk of his mother's papers is stuffed in assorted file cabinets around his lanai. I decide to research as much as I can before asking if I might read them. Like her, he went to Columbia's School of Journalism, he's written a book of his own, he's only recently said he doesn't have the bandwidth to write one about her.[28]

*

Pat kept her first paycheck from CBS in 1939. It totaled $35.[29] H.V. Kaltenborn was her first boss, famous for his 14-day nonstop coverage of the Munich crisis, delivered with such intimacy it set the stage for the panic surrounding Orson Welles's too-realistic "War of the Worlds" broadcast a few months later. Kaltenborn could simultaneously translate Hitler's speeches while on air. He and others turned CBS into the premier radio news network in an industry that was just emerging.[30] Before 1939, broadcasters read from the newspapers, but by then, according to Pat, "the newspapers had decided that radio was an enemy and they would no longer furnish news."[31] By the end of the war, radio reporting had become the country's chief source of information. The team that Pat joined included not only Edward R. Murrow but Robert Trout, Eric Sevareid, and William Shirer, and linked journalists in New York with on-the-scene reporting in Europe.

Pat with Bob Trent broadcasting from London, 1945

She started as their shortwave news editor and wrote four broadcasts a day for Europe and South America that were translated into five languages.[32] Her enthusiasm for the job must have been palpable. In 1941, after she gave a talk to Columbia's School of Journalism, her hostess gushed: "You were an adventure story, an electric shock, and a beauty treatment rolled into one, in your appearance here yesterday morning."[33]

In *Radio Girl*, Pat's unfinished memoir of the time, she writes that on her first day she had to convince the elevator man to let her off on the 17th floor. No woman had ever before been employed in those offices. "The newsroom had been a broom closet in its better days [with] just room for two desks and 4 teletype machines. I lost 10 pounds the first month to squeeze in." She had to wait three hours before someone let her know she had to prepare five minutes for the six o'clock broadcast. "Nobody ever tells you anything—until you make a mistake."

She outlines her procedure: "First you take some yellow copy paper . . . This you put it into a crotchety old typewriter . . . Then you write your opening sentence: 'Here is the latest news,' then you stop and light a cigarette." During the election of the pope, the reporters ran a betting pool about which cardinal would win. She had five bios prepared but had a hunch about a sixth and ran down the hall to consult with a "Church of the Air"' writer who called St. Pat's to get more information. She still lacked a final detail on this candidate—which American last entertained him—but extracted who from her boss's secretary, a good Catholic and, she said, sharp with names. It was the sixth that was elected, Pope Pius XII, and she won the pool.

She was not always so successful. One of her early leads was the tongue-twister: "Today Frankie Frisch made short shrift . . ." About that gaffe, she writes: "I was an extremely unpopular young lady for some time." But she recovers: "the most fun that we have is . . . sitting down with the late city edition of the *New York Times* and seeing how many of their page one stories we hit twelve hours earlier in our six o'clock show."[34]

All of America waited to hear the nightly news at "eastern wartime"—as reporters put it—crouched around their big radio sets: farmers just in from the field, businessmen who've hurried home in their Pontiacs, mothers still gripping their cooling casseroles, and the kids on the carpet, shushed and solemn. War news affected all of them: the price of grain, the shoe store's stock, the availability of milk, the kids soon to be drafted. The radio bulletins provided plenty of excitement, transforming their living rooms into towns turned into rubble under strafing bombers. Stories had to be written so that people "saw" the faraway war as clearly as possible in order to drum up support and buy bonds, sacrifice their livelihoods and, eventually, their children.

*

I too wrenched copy from the teletype, but I didn't rewrite it. By 1967 it came ordered and concise, with the local news reported by someone else in the office. I spent two years as a radio announcer for KOGA, the hometown station in Nebraska, shoving cassettes of special reports into playback slots, and spinning country music records when I wasn't Tongue-Tied Terrible Terese Telling You the Time and the Temperature. The job had its pitfalls. Sometimes the simplest words suddenly turned foreign. Late one Saturday night *asylum* looked, to my bleary eyes, very much like *as-ee-lum*. By late Monday morning my high school English teacher made sure everyone in the school knew the correct pronunciation. Mostly I played the top ten in rotation and dedications: *Molly wants Tom to know this is how she feels*. In college, I spent a few nights as a disc jockey on a paddleboat on the Hudson until I found out the place was involved in a lot more than just drinks and gambling. No way would I have discussed my experiences with Pat.

*

In her three years at CBS, Pat rose to producer of "The World Today," the weekend edition of Edward R. Murrow's record-breaking "World News Roundup," was on the news staff set up for the Foreign Service Division that ran regular wires to the American press associations, Reuters and Tass, and received reports via radio from neutral capitals. She also tracked secret information from the OSS and had a line into the war department."[35] Her boss was Paul White who visited her class at Columbia and later met her parents.[36]

Flying to Washington and returning to New York at 2 a.m., Pat often found herself working 33 hours at a stretch.[37] The toughest hours she put in for CBS were December 7 and 8, 1941.

"We worked for two days with little sleep, trying to make sense of the little news we were receiving. And every time we put on a musical interlude, we'd receive a lot of phone calls wanting to know what happened to the news."[38] But it wasn't all bombings and troop movements. She covered both the Democratic and Republican conventions, submarine sinkings, the King and Queen's visit, World's Fair, Boy Scout Jubilee, American Legion convention and horse races.[39] In March 1940, twenty-four-year-old Pat flew to Hollywood to cover the track at Santa Anita. Her self-assessment at the time: "I am forthright and charming in spots and a little hard, as all career girls have to be, but not cute" (emphasis in original).[40] "Rather underpaid," she accepted the collection that her colleagues at CBS took up for the purchase of a mink coat to impress the Californians. *Broadcasting*

Pat Lochridge, CBS Correspondent, 1939

announced her trip as part business, part pleasure.[41] She was there long enough to use Warner Bros. stationery to plead for mail—after only two and a half days!—and mentioned that she was wearing her fur.[42]

*

When persuasion counts, send a young woman: that was true in the 1980s too. In 1981, I flew to LA to persuade the actor Donald Sutherland to be the spokesperson for the 13-part PBS poetry series "Voices & Visions." Even more compelling, I was freshly turned platinum—I'd just volunteered to be part of *Real People*, a proto-reality show that turned normal people into punks, and a bleach job came with the opportunity. It was an out-of-the-body experience, turning blonde, not your "true" self. People, particularly men, reacted differently. This new me could do anything.

Author in TV series *Real People,* 1981

From a mutual friend, I knew Sutherland loved baseball and poetry almost as much as he did acting, and he had already appeared in over a hundred films, recently stunning audiences with his performance in *Ordinary People*. Did I dare to mention my brush with *Real People*? All I remember of the business part of that first hour was the way he quoted Auden while skating his long fingers over his desk—not as an arpeggio of show-offy emphasis but unconsciously following the cadence. I was impressed. He needn't have auditioned—if that's what it was—because we were barely paying scale. He called in his manager, they thought something could be done, and he suggested lunch. Which vehicle to drive? A white Cadillac convertible appeared and with great flourish—*should I wear a tie?*—he drove us across the street to the restaurant.

We must've eaten something. I must have talked about my time in Sudan, translating Nuer song, because he told me a story about a Peace Corps worker who was summarily hanged by Afghanis after she accidentally killed a child. I included the incident in my first novel *Cannibal*. I also must've told him about my brief stint as McGill's rare manuscript curator because we visited a rare book dealer after lunch. He was a good listener. With that talent—rare in men—and those huge, expressive eyes and bourbon-honeyed voice, that hitch in his posture that remembered the polio he'd suffered as a child, and height—what other Hollywood actor was as tall?—well, I was mesmerized. We stood in the stacks and slid out books and exclaimed over titles, but only he made a purchase. The dealer said he'd drop it off at his house. Actors do not carry parcels.

*

Kaltenborn was working in Europe in August 1939 and Elmer Davis, Pat's second boss at CBS, filled in. He soon commanded an audience of 12 million listeners. When he mentioned on air that the government should coordinate war news, FDR created the Office of War Information (OWI) and appointed him head. Pat followed him to Washington in 1942 as his assistant. "They used to call me Elmer Davis's tiger woman because I tended to protect him from other reporters who would ask questions that weren't necessarily very useful. In the war effort you forget about truth in journalism. You are writing to tell your country's story of why really, in those days, we should be in the war, and not simply supporting Britain."[43]

"You forget about truth in journalism" is the phrase that reveals she's understood the ethical conflicts of her trade, especially with regard to war. But how far does the truth have to retreat? The OWI disseminated propaganda and disinformation as well as information.[44] A lot of prominent people were faced with this question. The OWI staff of 30,000 included historian Arthur Schlesinger, Jr., sociologist Jane Jacobs, director Gordon Parks, even musicologist Alan Lomax. Another colleague, the poet Archibald MacLeish, assistant director of the OWI, declared that "the principal battleground of this war is not the South Pacific. It is not the Middle East. It is not England or Norway, or the Russian steppes. It is American opinion." He subsequently put together the CIA.[45]

"A correspondent is at best a busybody and at worst a potential spy," says Edmund Stevens in *War Correspondent: Thrills, Danger and Boredom*.[46] Pat reported later that she was "exposing enemy propaganda and running counter-propaganda."[47] Ed Sullivan, who was then writing a column for the *Daily News*, whistled in her direction: "Be sure to read that OWI release sent along by Patricia Lochridge, the story of the Nazi man-hunt for slave-labor . . . it is spellbinding."[48]

Pat Lochridge with Office of War Information head
Elmer Davis c. 1942

A photograph of her with a bow in her hair, offering a sheaf of papers to Davis, does not disguise her aura of competence. Another photo of her as a new hire was also featured in the center of a syndicated pastiche "Our Photo-Flashes." She is surrounded by other noteworthies: comedian Don Ameche, a tame fawn, a piece about placemats, the ubiquitous female soldier in a swimsuit, and Esther Williams, the swim champion who's about to star in a movie.[49] Her boss lunches at the White House some forty times while she's his Tiger Woman. Perhaps that's when she tagged along and corrected FDR's table manners?[50]

Pat was also writing magazine articles on the side. This turned full-time when she was hired away from the OWI by *Woman's Home Companion* and assigned long cover stories.

Another reason for her move might have been what instigated her friend Philip Hamburger's resignation from the OWI: "They [the OWI] possess a fundamental contempt for the American people" and "carefully produce a steady stream of fully contrived propaganda wholly unworthy of a great democracy at war." He worked under MacLeish.[51]

In February 1944, Pat published "Startling Facts about Black Market Revealed by Shopping Tour of Nation," an article on the abuse of rationing across America. Traveling 11,000 miles, crisscrossing the country with no ration stamps but a pocketful of money, she found everyone—rich or poor—buying goods on the black market. Doctors wrote prescriptions for meat, drunks exchanged ration stamps for liquor, a bank president kept a drawer full of $5 black market nylons in his desk for the best depositors. After paying for dozens of black market hot dogs, she had trouble dumping them at a canteen run for veterans. They were very suspicious of anyone having so many.[52] More newspapers commented on the article than anything else she ever wrote; she appeared on NBC to talk about it, and was threatened with jail time.[53]

A month later *Woman's Home Companion* arranged for Pat to become their reporter as an accredited war correspondent. Accreditation meant that the Army or Navy would transport her into war zones, feed and shelter her, and send her dispatches home. In return, she had to follow military law and censorship. Each magazine could have only one accredited reporter, which meant that at the end of the war she was pitted against Hemingway who wrote for *Colliers*.

Her CBS colleague Robert Trout wrote her a long letter of winking congratulations. In a few months he would provide live coverage of D-Day for the nation, but here he can't resist ribbing her about her new job.

Pat talking about the black market on NBC, 1944

To some "Companion Washington Correspondent" may suggest an honor conferred by H.M.; to others it may contain a vague hint of the Crusades, with the Companions valiantly battling the knights of Collier's; still others may be reminded of the band of pleasant comrades whose activities are recorded in Mr. J. B. Priestley's most popular novel; but there are others, I fear, for whom the Companion Correspondent will mean, simply, "Oh, you kid!"[54]

Pat ordered boots from Abercrombie and Fitch, had a uniform made to order at Saks, her photograph taken by Warner Bros., and her new career as a war correspondent promoted as "the *Companion's* Fearless Girl Reporter."

My stories were, from the advertising standpoint, more promotable than Gellhorn's. They used to take out full page ads in the *New York Times* for my stories. They would give me a luncheon at the Waldorf for three hundred and I would do a star turn and come in my uniform and dazzle them with examples of what stories I found."[55]

Patricia Lochridge press
photo, 1944

She spent enough time in L.A. that she was "glamourized"—a free makeover by cosmetologist Perc Westmore, a photo session with *Life* photographer Gjon Mili, lunch with Ginger Rogers and "Roz" Russell, and dinner with Bogart, at least according to her letter home. Somehow the last two items about her dining partners ring less true than her confession that she lost $12.75 playing gin rummy. She was an inveterate poker player, what was she doing playing gin rummy? She ends her letter by saying she must run to lunch with the latest heartthrob Paul Henreid, recently starring as Victor Laszlo in *Casablanca* who, she says, "has a boil on his left cheek."[56]

After Trout's razzing, she does not dare breathe a word of this to any other reporter.

3

Influence and Interference

Pat's first assignment was to write for CBS radio in the Pacific. "I was the first woman war correspondent to come out here to the Pacific, the idea being that the war in Europe was heavily covered and this was the neglected war."[57] Admiral Nimitz gave her permission in August 1944, and she was in Guam by October.[58]

The Pacific theater was neglected? That was also the conclusion of Tom Hanks and why he worked with Steven Spielberg to produce "The Pacific," a 2010 ten-part documentary series. A more nuanced and murkier affair than the fighting in Europe, the Pacific war was poisoned by mutual racial hatred and a dreadful level of barbarity—it was a war about terror and racism. The Pacific theater was also a very foreign place. Unlike in Europe, few of the locations were familiar to Americans, the distances between them were often enormous, and clean uniforms and regular food were scarce for journalists as well as soldiers. Besides, the military didn't need much propaganda from reporters after Pearl Harbor.

*

"Be sure you're the first woman somewhere," an editor in New York advised reporter Dickey Chapelle early in her career. Chapelle switched from journalism to photojournalism when she discovered that the Navy had thus far accredited no women to take photographs in the Pacific.[59] Twenty years later in Vietnam, she had the misfortune of being the first female reporter killed in action.[60] With only 180 or so credentialed women during WWII, the odds were fairly good that some first would turn up for most of them.[61] Sometimes this first business bordered on the ludicrous. After Peggy Hull from the *New York Times*, Barbara Finch from *Reuters*, and Pat were accredited in the Pacific (with Pat being the first to be sent out), Hull filed a story with the headline: "First Woman Reporter Files from Pacific Area by Telephone to the *New York Times*."[62] Pat was the first Caucasian woman to set foot on Guam after its recapture by US forces, the first woman to be accredited by the Navy to the Central Pacific war zone, the first woman magazine correspondent accredited by Nimitz (though perhaps that is the same as the previous?), the first woman reporter to land with troops in the Pacific, the first woman reporter at Eagle's Nest, the first woman reporter at Dachau, the first (and only American) woman appointed mayor of a German town, and the only woman to cover both theaters of war.

Many in the military weren't so pleased to have female reporters at all and often made logistics difficult. Latrines were always a problem, as illustrated by the British headline "300 Men Unmoved for Three Days."[63] The women were all more or less WASPs, often from very privileged families, but deprivation and danger didn't stop them. Tellingly titled, Martha Gellhorn wrote "Only the Shells Whine" for *Collier's*.[64] The women examined war as representatives of a gender removed from violent conflict but they had to force their way into dangerous situations and then be invisible so they wouldn't be raped or held hostage. While the American brass barely tolerated the women, the British strongly discouraged them. General Montgomery declared: "I'll have no women correspondents with my army."[65] Male correspondents were also not helpful to the women. After covering both the first and second world wars, the fighting on the Mexican border and in Siberia and China, Peggy Hull stated: "Our freedom is ephemeral. Our presence in various fields is bitterly resented by the men we compete with."[66] Authorities also feared that women would break down under fire or would influence soldiers to take risks to protect them. The women themselves were divided about their role. Dorothy Thompson, known at the time as the First Lady of American journalism— her opinions in the 1930s and 1940s as important to the public as Eleanor Roosevelt's—believed that women "would only be happy if they were securely married with several healthy and loving children."[67] Her husband, novelist Sinclair Lewis, resented her career as a reporter, and her neglect of their son.[68]

*

Before filming in Sudan, my ex and I worked for the Smithsonian's National Anthropological Film Center (now part of their Archives). As I have mentioned, we first traveled to the Cooks, a group of islands located between French Polynesia and American Samoa, to document dance. Our job was part international goodwill, part science, and a lot of experimenting with film, as visual anthropology was still a nascent practice. Margaret Mead, one of the founders of the Film Center, firmly believed that cultures were disappearing and the faster they could be documented, the better. After six months in the Cooks, we island-hopped to Africa, where we planned to film in Sudan. This was something you could do back then with cheap round-the-world tickets, and, in our case, without a Smithsonian expense account.

The Solomon Islands, an early stop, were terrifically hot. Locals were eating fish 'n chips in the nude on the dock when we arrived, their full body tattoos eerily similar to the newspapers wrapping their snacks. We foolishly preferred more privacy for a swim and had to trudge quite a long way out of town and then fight through thick mangroves to get to the water. Against the sky rose razor sharp lava-black mountains, where one of our hostel-mates was hiking, a bobbing dark dot against the intense tropical sky, shirtless but not bootless. We were glad to have resisted the temptation to climb the crags ourselves, though the ocean had the temperature of sweat. We paddled and dove until one of the local East Indian children who had gathered at the shore shouted: Don't swim. The war, she said.

Guadalcanal was not far away. The little girl told us the sharks came in that terrible battle, that her grandmother said not to even wade into the water. You should not be bathing, she said, with such a charming accent.

My ex showed them his disappearing thumb trick and the children screamed and raced back through the thickets of the mangrove. I dunked and backfloated and tiptoed on the bottom as if that would somehow deter a shark. *Jaws* would debut in Hollywood only a few months later, but for now we experienced only this Guadalcanal fear, secondhand from grandmother to the children to ourselves. Thirdhand? We didn't see any sharks. Maybe she was trying to scare the children out of the water because they hadn't learned to swim? We paddled around for a while but not very far out, the water was so dark and the effort too much against the tepid, unrefreshing waves.

The children returned and the eldest offered us two waxed paper parcels. Peering under the wrappers, I found pear and chutney sandwiches, our reward for not being eaten. I thanked her. My ex ducked underwater and poked up his hand like a fin. They screamed again and ran off.

We gobbled our treat and made our way through the mangrove to thank our benefactors personally. A house on stilts hid at the edge of the dense foliage, where the children waited for us with their parents. You are tempting them to go into the water, scolded their mother.

You are so kind, I said, with your sandwiches.

Their father told us that, like us, the sharks will eat anything, why some nights they even put out offerings.

Surely, said my ex, the sharks swam here before the war?

The father shook his head emphatically. Only after the big boats went down. Then they never left.

*

Pat's first assignment from *Woman's Home Companion* as a war correspondent was to write "Flight for Life," a piece about the air transport of the wounded from Saipan to Honolulu.[69] No flying over the Pacific this time—she took a triple-loaded troop ship. She bunked with the nurses and played poker with the Air Force officers. First she disembarked in Guam. Fifty years later, she talks about the sexual harassment that must've been constant throughout her tour: "One night someone tried to crawl into the bunk with me. I was surprised. I was camped beside the commanding general's tent . . . I still to this day do not know whether that was a PFC or the commanding general." She stayed only a few days. "I was courted by the various servicemen of rank because I was a woman and not necessarily because I would write how glorious they were."

Once in Saipan, she boarded a C-54 with 31 wounded soldiers, a nurse, a pilot, and a flight surgeon for a 23-hour return flight to Honolulu. On take-off, she looked out at the Saipan hills, now dark, where "several thousand Jap soldiers are waiting too, waiting for a chance to come down out of their caves and kill."[70] The first refueling stop was 1,500 miles away on Kwajalein, a tiny island. A few hours aloft, she and the pilot took a cigarette break, and he told her that one bullet could bring down the plane, and shortly thereafter half of the plane's engines broke down. They flew back to Saipan. Offloaded in the middle of the night, she was awakened four hours later by local Chamorro children singing hymns; she bemoaned the missionaries' zeal.[71] The plane boarded again shortly—no dawdling with the wounded—and the brigadier general they'd taken on as a heart patient told bad jokes to help ward off the shock that the most serious cases often suffered. Consoling a patient who'd lost an eye, Pat was surprised by the soldier's jocularity: "You mean to tell me they could fix me up with a glass eye that has my old wolfish gleam?"

The plane refueled a second time on Johnson Island, the tiniest dot in the Pacific, where the soldiers were given hot boiled eggs and ice cream. Pat played cards, this time "nickel-a-hand blackjack." She lost twenty cents right off the bat. Before disembarking, she located shoes for a crippled soldier who valiantly resolved to use them again, foreshadowing the offer of "lucky boots" from a soldier in Iwo Jima a month later when she became the first woman reporter to take part in a landing.[72]

*

"I have to fly the plane alone to Saipan," the Qantas pilot told us, drinking his coffee with our fellow passengers while a cyclone raged outside. He had just landed the plane sideways on the

Darwin, Australia runway, en route to Bali, which was to be our next stop on our journey to Sudan. Darwin had no hangar big enough to house the plane. We were evacuated to a local hotel that turned us out after only a few days. East Timor was now in turmoil, and it would take weeks to get a ticket out. We had wired money to Bali and had little left and nowhere to stay. Walking through town feeling dejected, we heard rock music we liked and turned into the yard. Five Australians and a pet dingo on the porch welcomed us. We stayed three weeks while I worked as an architect's secretary for cash. The dingo turned out to be ailing, forbidden by his hippie master from running down prey and instead fed shrimp, and he died one night. A lesson, said my ex.

Not to eat shrimp?

No, you have to be flexible. Stay loose, he said, eyeing one of the Australian girls.

I did and divorced him a few years later.

*

Pat didn't fly off to Iwo Jima right away. She returned to Washington and waited for a few weeks until "a request came through from the Navy that she be sent back to the Pacific for 'a big story,'" nothing she could talk about. She was flown out "in winter in an unheated plane with a temperature of 103, arriving in Pearl Harbor on Christmas Day."[73] She says they drank eggnog all the way.[74] In her chatty January 26, 1945 letter home, she confesses that she was seeing two men on alternate nights and "all of my colleagues expect to take my money at poker." Her letter goes on to boast that she played tennis with Admiral Nimitz and his wife but that it was "not my idea of activity for a forward area." But how did she manage to get the game in the first place? Perhaps his Texas ranger grandfather knew hers?

Nimitz's tiny hometown, Fredericksburg, included a Wendish branch of Pat's family who had arrived at the same time in the mid-19th century seeking religious liberty.[75] Pat also mentions that she "saw General Willis Hale the other night and he asked to be remembered to your Mother." Perhaps her mother knew the Major General, the Commanding General for the Air Force in the Pacific, a James Stewart-ish looking man, from his flying school and courtship days in San Antonio in the 30's? Perhaps he was also a connection to the Admiral? But no tennis was ever played with Nimitz's wife, who never set foot in Hawai'i. Did Nimitz have a mistress? No, or at least not one as well documented as Eisenhower's.

Pat's last note in the letter is that she's gone to a "very fancy party" thrown by the "president of Paramount Pictures, and head of Red Cross here." Then she signs off: "My [new] assignment is quite thrilling, but if I wrote you of it the censor would simply scissors this letter so you'll just have to await developments."

Not just any censor, but the head of the censors in the Pacific, as it turned out.

Waiting to travel to the frontlines, Pat writes "They Call It Passion City." The story is the result of "being pursued by high-ranking wolves," but rather than write about her own experiences, she tells what happens "when the AAF imports 1200 American civilian gals from the mainland to work here in the air depot and they are marooned on this relatively small island with 500 thousand lonely men."[76] These women lived in Quonset huts and worked "the same kind of assembly lines that women were doing in Nebraska or New York." She adds in her letter home: "Who would have been interested in what they did with a screwdriver? I told about their hard work and how they lived in these lovely Quonset huts and what they did on their off hours."[77] The women would also visit Waikiki Beach, making them a hazard to "home and hearth." If her editor "doesn't sweeten it up too much, it ought to give you a lot of laughs," she writes her friend Peg. Convinced she wouldn't get "They Call It Passion City" past the censors if she tried to file in the normal way, she "prevailed upon a friendly air force colonel in public relations to pick her up at her hotel at 2 a.m., and take her to the night censor who was believed to be more lenient."[78] The colonel, head of public relations at Hickam Air Force Base and above all the censors, was Dickson Hartwell, her second husband-to-be.

*

Dickson received the Order of the White Rose from Finland for his services to that country in 1941.[79] The Order won't reveal why he was accorded the honor, and no one in the family knows anything about why he received it. One would have thought he'd have boasted of it. The year of the award Dickson was a member of the public relations firm Hartwell, Jobson, and Kibbee, with offices in Chicago and in Rockefeller Plaza in New York, a firm which he helped found as a young man in the 1930s. As for Finland, in 1939, the Soviets invaded it two months after Hitler invaded Poland. The Soviets wanted to display their military prowess to Germany and were hoping to secure their defenses at the vulnerable Finnish border, not unlike the 2022 Russian invasion of Ukraine. Finnish proximity to Leningrad and other strategic points made the country an obvious test case. The Finns, vastly outnumbered by the Soviets, determined that their best battle ploy was delay, to give the not-yet-Allies time to come to their aid, or at least hoping to buy time for diplomatic proceedings that would result in Finland retaining its independence. Thus the world had to be persuaded that this small Scandinavian nation was worth protecting in the face of the Soviet juggernaut and, in turn, the Nazi threat.

The response was not overwhelming. Brazil sent 10,000 sacks of coffee, Denmark a wagonload of food aid, Norway seventy medical professionals, the French obsolete arms, the Uruguayans 10,000 cans of corned beef, the English anti-tank guns, the Americans two million dollars, the Swiss Medical Association and the Swedes, a cadre of volunteers. Norway's Nobel prize-winner Sigrid Undset donated her medal and Hungarian winner Albert Szent-Györgyi offered to do the same. The Hungarians chartered a special train via Italy and Yugoslavia labeled "tourists going to ski-camp," filled with armaments and a trained battalion that arrived too late to be of any use. The Pope, for his part, condemned the invasion.[80]

The Finns did their best. They poisoned wells, positioned amazingly accurate snipers, blew up lake ice, and invented the Molotov cocktail to destroy Russian tanks. The cocktail was named after the Soviet Foreign minister Vyacheslav Molotov, who told the Russian public that bombing missions over Finland were actually airborne humanitarian food deliveries. The Finns deemed the bombs "drink[s] to go with the food parcels."[81] If it were not for the brave Finnish ski troops who repeatedly stymied the Russians in their frozen white world with guerrilla tactics, the country would have been wholly swallowed up. As it was, the Finnish "Winter War" was over in 105 days, and Finns were forced to negotiate a peace treaty that gave away a portion of their land that exceeded Soviet pre-war demands.

Had Hartwell been part of the public relations effort to stir up world support? Why would you use public relations in this case instead of diplomats? And why an American PR firm? Nineteen Americans received the award between 1941-1944.[82] Photojournalist Thérèse Bonney, an American, was given the honor in 1940 for her images taken on the Russian-Finnish front, and she returned to Finland a year later to work as a spy.[83] Hermann Goering, an international arms dealer, and two Nazi generals also received the award the year Dickson won.[84]

Dickson's firm had a reputation for being able to influence international policy. Between 1939-1941 Hartwell, Jobson, and Kibbee worked with the American Committee for Non-Participation in Japanese Aggression (ACNPJA), an organization that aimed to stop the provision of war materials to Japan. Together they "delivered 2.3 million pieces of literature in eleven kinds of publications between August 1938 and February 1941, targeting selected individuals and groups of significant influence in American society."[85] The ACNPJA failed to register as a foreign lobbying agent although they had opened an office in Washington explicitly to develop a close relationship with the State Department. The question remains whether they were conducting espionage or a public relations campaign, straddling the gray area between influence and interference, information or propaganda. In the wake of Russian interference in the 2016 presidential election, the ACNPJA was cited as an early example of this less-than-legal behavior.[86]

*

Hardly novel, foreign interference in American politics has ranged from transferring foreign money to various political entities, journalists from abroad spreading less than truthful stories, and meddling public relations professionals. Influence works both ways. Even prior to WWI, Americans conducted "regime change interventions" in Cuba, Mexico, Haiti, the Dominican Republic, Nicaragua, Honduras, Panama, and Costa Rica.[87] More recently, Trump simplified the complexities of foreign influence during his first administration by providing little news and few diplomats.[88]

*

Moving to Saipan to await the invasion of Iwo Jima, Pat was housed in the ubiquitous Quonset hut "furnished with a thick concrete floor, and that was about all . . . At the end of the row of cots a tiny space in a corner had been screened off from the men with a blanket." She and Barbara Finch slept in shifts on the single cot.[89] In *Love Goes to Press*, a postwar play written by reporters Martha Gellhorn and Virginia Cowles, the two correspondents mock the military's negligence: "I wouldn't dream of troubling you, Major," says the woman who plays Martha Gellhorn. "I'll be quite happy rolled up in a blanket anywhere." The other female correspondent says (airily!): "The floor, the gutter, just anywhere."[90]

On Pat's off hours, she lost her shirt.

> Ten minutes after the game started, I had lost over $400 in cash and traveler's checks [about $6,000 in today's money] and had only about $50 between me and New York, eight thousand miles east, and I was wondering just how I was going to explain to Bill Birnie, my editor, that he'd better cable me some more dough. Then I caught a lucky couple of pairs and, while not rich again, I was close to breaking even. I wanted to get out of the game, then, but fast – but gracefully. There seemed no possible way when I got a break. I had asked the B-29 boys to let me know when planes were returning after a strike so that I could be down at the control tower when they came in. At that moment a B-29 PRO officer tapped me on the shoulder; I must rush right out to the field. I never played poker with foreign correspondents again.[91]

She was playing with John Lardner (son of Ring), Percy Finch, *Life*'s Bob Sherrod, Bill Whipple, and Keith Wheeler, the last soon to be critically wounded at Iwo Jima. You can imagine the scene: overturned supply boxes or buckets for seating, the lousy lighting, men hunched over their cards, chewing on cigars, and Pat, sweating, the only female in the game, doing her best amid the jeers and glee of her male competitors. Did her failure to win prove that Pat found men hard to read, or that she was a lousy poker player?

*

After waiting six weeks—some of it in serious flirtation with the head censor in Hawai'i—and the rest of the time in Saipan, Pat finally boarded the hospital ship *Solace*. It arrived in Iwo Jima four days after the battle began. Photojournalist Dickey Chappelle arrived February 28, five days after her, but did not land, unlike Pat who saw the battle firsthand and without a camera to shield her.

A hellish volcanic island stinking of sulfur and without potable water, Iwo Jima hid 21,000 Japanese in its bunkers and tunnels. An alliance between the American navy—which wanted to outflank the army—and the air force—which wanted to show off strategic bombing so that they might form part of an independent air service after the war—cut the Marines out of the attack planning. However, the Marines suffered the most: some 7,000 fatalities and 20,000 wounded, ending the first day alone with 2,400 fatalities. Although they far outnumbered the Japanese, more Americans were killed by the end of the fighting, making it one of the bloodiest battles in the whole war. Writing in *Newsweek* not even a week after the fighting was over, Admiral Pratt summarized civilian feelings about the outcome: "There has been a certain amount of public criticism over this expenditure of manpower to acquire a small, Godforsaken island, useless to the Army as a staging base and useless to the Navy as a fleet base."[92] But the island was the first that was actually Japanese territory.

Anchored within several hundred yards of a black sand beach littered with abandoned gear and wreckage and bodies, the *Solace* was quickly swarmed by ambulance boats. A surgeon handed Pat a bottle of smelling salts to use "if things get too rough and you feel faint." Filled with dread—it was her first experience of actual combat—she was deemed "water tender" and received an insignia painted on an arm bandage with mercurochrome. The first of the wounded she met claimed to have been one of those who raised the stars and stripes in that famous picture, proudly pointing to where he said he'd been just an hour earlier. She said she could just make out tiny figures struggling up Mt. Suribachi, "and then we saw it, an American flag on the peak, snapping in the wind."[93]

The *Solace* was filled in short order and quickly put out to sea to protect its four hundred patients. With seventeen doctors, thirteen nurses, and 175 corpsmen working all night, blood was everywhere, on shoes, railing, discarded uniforms. Doctors performed the minor surgeries right in the beds or on the mess tables. Sixty-eight patients used over four million units of penicillin that night. Six died. Pat stowed away her bottle of ammonia after meeting a wounded man who asked for the same nurse who had fixed him up in Saipan a month earlier. The battle was "worse than his wildest nightmares." Robert Sherrod reported that "nowhere in the Pacific war had I seen such badly mangled bodies. Many were cut squarely in half."[94] Everyone on the ward went quiet when someone announced that a Congressional Medal of Honor-winning veteran of Guadalcanal, whom they believed was invulnerable and had refused safe billet back to the US, had been killed.[95]

*

Men writing about Iwo Jima mostly delivered exciting stories about maneuvers and manpower, with lamentation for the dead pushed aside for the language of glory and the mechanics of conquest. "The ship to shore movement worked to perfection;"[96] "Eight thousand troops stormed ashore on their designated beaches right at H-hour;"[97] "The Mark I system could spew burning napalm at a range of 150 yards with a duration of more than a minute;"[98] and especially the use of the particularly gruesome term "mopping up." As a correspondent for a monthly, Pat had time to avoid cliches and to write more broadly about the experience of war. Every so often, she slipped a few grim details past the censors, like the "wildest nightmare" comment. Since censors read everything the reporters wrote, they had an informed opinion about who had the best copy. A censor in North Africa wrote, "Only the women really understand these GIs."[99]

*

"She's More of a Woman than Ever" reads the *Woman's Home Companion* ad for Pat's article about her landing at Iwo Jima.[100] The magazine wanted to reassure its readers that Pat was not at risk of losing her femininity as the result of her brave reporting. None of the women war correspondents aligned themselves with feminists. Although Eleanor Roosevelt's first book while at the White House was titled *It's Up To The Women,* women of that period associated feminism with the outmoded politics of the suffrage movement and their stridency and suffering. The closest Pat gets is in her speech to her alma mater Wellesley in 1957: "There is much evidence that the American woman is stronger than the American male."[101] Female correspondents simply wanted to be on equal—or, let's face it, better—footing with the men. Pushed to cover the human side of war, they indeed often outdid the men in engaging their audiences.

*

Pat understood about death. When my first son died in an accident at age four, she was consoling, although when she first heard that a small boy came with the engagement, she wrote to her sister that this was "not quite the way I'd hoped to have a grandchild." But Deng, named after a Nuer god, was a towheaded darling, very charming, an apparently genetic trait that caused me to make the mistake of accompanying his father around the world. While Pat did not dote on Deng, she did ask after him, and sent him lovely presents. After his death, she was kind enough to name a little skiff *Deng*, sent us tickets to mourn in Hawai'i, and greeted me with a hug. It may have been my only hug from her but it was one more than I got from my own mother, who said by way of comfort, on the way to the cemetery, that she'd soon be dead too.

Deng, 1980

For decades, that hug had been proof of Pat's understanding of what I had been through in experiencing the extreme grief of losing a child. But those decades have also proven to me that no one who has not experienced such a death understands what a crushing defeat of motherhood and even selfhood it is, especially after an accident. Surely I could have prevented it. Pat knew plenty about death en masse but nothing of death on her lap. She might have felt guilt for leaving her children for weeks at a time as a result of her later UNICEF travels, but that is a burden that many professional women bear. I understood that guilt too. I tied my firstborn in a scarf around my neck like the Nuer to do secretarial work for an older female writer and kept typing for as long as he slept. Should I have been staring into the child's eyes while the two of us starved? The female body spends nine months reorienting itself to merge with another creature and then must tear itself away for food, for other children, for love. The extent of this physiological-emotional flexibility is buried in the genes for survival, but when a child dies, all this compromise is tallied.

Death close up is different from viewing thousands of corpses of people you've never met. But I can imagine the horror.

*

"On the second day the ship began to smell of blood, disinfectants, gangrene and death," writes Pat at Iwo Jima. She doused herself with perfume, which the patients fully appreciated, and made her landing ashore to see how the doctors and corpsmen operated under fire. Before she left, she volunteered to find the sergeant's lucky boots, and another asked that she find his bag on the beach with photos of his family.

> I had a very strange idea of what the shore would look like. I just went down the gangway and caught the next landing craft that was going to shore . . . Nobody had any

responsibility for me . . . I had no conducting officer. I was just looking for Joe's boots. Why they meant so much to him, I don't know.

She failed to find them: "the confusion ashore was incredible."[102] Japanese mortar was falling everywhere and sometimes killed the wounded waiting for help—and threatened reporters. She also didn't retrieve the bag. The *Solace* soon became so full that the crew moved out of their quarters, and cots were set up on deck. One corporal was cursing because he'd lost one of the two bluebirds tattooed on his crushed chest, and a twenty-one-year old was furious because he'd been hit on his birthday. But "they thanked you for nothing: a kind word, a smile, a cigarette, a glass of water," Pat writes. Those who could walk worked alongside the nurses. Finally the *Solace* began to pull out. One of the wounded Marines left behind in the ambulance boat cried out, "Come back! If I had my rifle I'd shoot you! Come back." But by then they could take on no one else.[103]

*

Sometime during April 1945, "*Solace* at Iwo" was read on the radio by one of the greatest leading ladies of 20th-century theater, Helen Hayes, who played the part of Pat.[104] "Lochridge shared with Martha Gellhorn a capacity to write with such compassion of the wounded that her readers would weep forty years later," writes Julia Edwards in *Women of the World: The Great Foreign Correspondents*.[105] Pat's boss at *Woman's Home Companion* sent her a congratulatory telegram with regard to the broadcast, although her article wouldn't appear in the magazine for another month.[106] By then she'd be standing in Hitler's Eagle's Nest.

4

Smoke

But first, Dachau.

In 2013, seventeen years after Pat's death, she's referenced in a pro-Nazi, Holocaust-denier conspiracy blog that takes great offense at her article "Are Germans Human?" and insists that a woman couldn't have written it.[107] Concerning her coverage of Dachau, the article was published in *Woman's Home Companion* in July 1945.[108] No longer the precinct of Willa Cather, Jack London, and John Steinbeck, the magazine was now known as the "fighting lady," and featured controversial journalism, including Pat's "VD: Menace and Challenge" and "Abortion is an Ugly Word," a pro-choice article she published in 1947.[109] [110] [111] With regard to her assignment in Dachau, she told her family: "I'm bending all my efforts to find a brand new chamber of horrors which hasn't been visited by Rep Clare Luce or a junket-load of publishers."[112] Writing to Bill Birnie, her editor at *Woman's Home Companion,* she said:

> I received your cable about doing a concentration camp piece at Wiesbaden. Had a tipoff on Siegburg and so took off immediately for Bad Neuenahr near Remagen.

Siegburg didn't live up to its reputation—it was an old prison where typhus was killing one hundred a day, but the deaths were due to medical negligence rather than systematic planned destruction. Decided therefore to hop off to Buchenwald altho as I'd cabled you, its story seemed a little worn out. While I was up at Weimar, we received word that Dachau had been taken.[113]

She got in with a tank division of General Patton's Army and arrived with photojournalist Lee Miller on April 30, the day after the camp opened.[114] Lee had already visited Struthof, which housed interned German civilians, and featured a small improvised gas chamber and "meat hooks for holding the victims in place."[115] Raped as a child, Lee was saved from being run over by the publisher of *Vogue* who then made her famous as a model. She became a prominent photographer, specializing in combining journalism with art. "Believe It" was the title of her photo essay about Dachau, containing such images as a drowned SS guard, prostitutes who'd worked in the camp brothel, and a Viennese doctor with a Gypsy woman under her care.[116] She shot photos while Pat stood in the middle of the chaos, observing the responses of the residents of the town of Dachau. Local kids "ran around these prisoners to see if there was anything to take. I've often tried to think why they did that, and all I could say was that these prisoners really didn't look human anymore." She accompanied the town's leading citizens, men and women, while they were forced to tour the camp.[117] Three weeks earlier General Patton had made this standard practice. Some of the townspeople found it hard. After the mayor of Ohrdruf and his wife had to visit the camp beside their town, one of the earliest to be freed, they returned home to kill themselves.[118] So did the mayor of Weimar and his wife after viewing Buchenwald.[119] But they were the exceptions.

At the time of its liberation, Dachau held more than 30,000 filthy and starving surviving prisoners, crowded into a camp designed to house 5,000. It was also the location of forty boxcars overflowing with the decomposing human corpses of more than 2,000 men, women and children. Most had suffocated or starved to death while being evacuated from Buchenwald to Dachau several weeks earlier. Pat reported that the townspeople looked straight ahead during the tour, pretending to be unconcerned, until they reached the crematorium. The Gestapo had run out of coal, so most of the rotting dead were stacked in front of it.[120] Footage of their tour shows the townspeople burying their faces in their handkerchiefs, more likely from the stench than from tears, judging from Pat's interviews.[121]

When asked about what happened, the townspeople displayed little contrition or even awareness of the atrocities. Pat questioned the baker on how it was possible that he would not have spoken to his customers about the camp. "If we did not deny it," he said, "we would have been killed." The town's most prominent doctor said: "The business at the camp was none of our affair," and "we were shamefully deceived, there was nothing we could do." The one woman who did cry over a stack of bodies said that "nothing more terrible could have been done than was done at Dachau. But most Germans weren't involved. The Fuhrer couldn't have known about it. He would never have permitted such suffering."

The Fuhrer's propaganda had been very effective.

The next day, a "proud Hitlerite," once the official barber for the SS, told her, "You Americans are such sentimentalists." Pat reported that "no voluntary offers of food, clothing or medical aid had been made . . . The common citizens and the town of Dachau were completely indifferent."[122] The first to report on the German's protestations of innocence, Pat later discovered her

Pat surveys the Dachau dead, 1945

colleagues Margaret Bourke-White, Martha Gellhorn and Lee Miller all experienced the same level of denial from the German populace.[123] Interviewing the citizens of Cologne, Miller was convinced they were trying to curry favor with the Allies, their new masters, by denying their involvement.[124]

Over a period of five days, the people of Dachau were forced to bury the victims, thirty corpses to a cart, five carts a day.[125] They objected but the US Army gave them no choice. Lee Miller noted that the walls of the camp were situated right beside the town, and surely they would have smelled the burning human flesh, and also that the railroad tracks for the cattle cars ran right beside a number of beautiful villas.[126] Pat wrote to her editor: "I was physically sick from what I had seen first in the camp and then in the townspeople—their utter indifference and selfishness. I felt totally incapable of translating this to our readers. I hope somehow it got across."[127]

Years of willed ignorance encouraged by the powers-that-be, of not enough news, of suppressed news, news that just didn't make the news, blatant censorship about the persecution of Jews, Gypsies, homosexuals and dissidents by the Third Reich—why weren't the horrors of the concentration camps known about earlier? If German citizens had known, why couldn't they have prevented it? And more than just the Germans were implicated. "We are not entirely guiltless, we the Allies, because it took us twelve years to open the gates of Dachau," wrote Martha Gellhorn. "We were blind and unbelieving and slow, and that we can never be again."[128] She arrived a few days after Pat.

*

Those on the conspiracy blog go so far as to suggest that psy-ops at government headquarters wrote the article for Pat. Psychological operations have been around since WWI, and flourished as part of the Office of War Information, Pat's employer in Washington for two years. They were experts in distributing select information worldwide to influence the emotions, motives, objective reasoning, and the behavior of whole countries. One might say that Hartwell, Jonson, and Kibbee executed a form of freelance psy-ops with its work for the American Committee for Non-Participation in Japanese Aggression. Did Elmer Davis, Pat's old boss at OWI, direct the writing of her article? More likely Pat's training at OWI led her to that particular slant on the subject, and certainly her editors at *Women's Home Companion* approved.

The bloggers believed that only dedicated psy-ops would pose those questions, interview those people—someone with an agenda, a holocaust to confirm rather than deny. Because Pat published nothing about the showers, the bloggers believed the omission was hard evidence that they didn't exist. It would be two more days before the famous photo of Congressmen standing beneath the shower heads would be taken. Perhaps her copy was cut? And surely her editor chose the headline: on the same page that the second part of her article appears is an advertisement for war bonds with "Are Japs Human?" in large type. She does mention a crematorium, but the bloggers insist that all the corpses were the result of a typhus epidemic.[129]

No one denies that there was a typhus epidemic.

*

What did the residents of Ohrdruf and Weimar tell themselves after their mayors and wives committed suicide? How did the surviving relatives explain the desperate acts to their children? Complicity is the shrapnel of suicide, everyone is guilty, no matter what the circumstances, but in this instance the motive was available to all.

*

The Sudanese suffered 2.5 million casualties in their two almost concurrent civil wars, the highest number of any country since WWII, including the half million dead as a result of the genocide in Darfur.[130] The second civil war lasted twenty-two years, almost breaking another record for the longest civil war in the world.[131] In contrast, fewer than half a million Americans died during ours, and about the same number during the six years of our participation in WWII. The horrors of the Sudanese civil war were mostly invisible to the rest of the world beyond a shot on the screen in the hour's news or a minute's worth of reporting on NPR. Not much was at stake for other countries except who was getting their oil, which is still considerable. Two years after gaining independence in 2011, South Sudan had its own civil war, and another 400,000 citizens died before it was resolved seven years later. War broke out again in 2023, with one general fighting another over Khartoum, the capital of Sudan. Yet another estimated 150,000 Sudanese had died by June 2025—over 15,000 people were killed in a single city—and over eight and a half million displaced, eight times more than Gaza, though death and displacements in Gaza continue to go up.[132] [133] [134] Displacement camps have replaced concentration camps, with the simple weapon of starvation.

While I was working in Sudan, I heard many rumors about "ghost houses" where soldiers and political figures were taken and tortured.[135] After I left Nasir, the guest house I lived in was taken over by the government and used in this way. The walls and floors were cement, easy to hose off. My Nuer friend Nyagak Pinien fled Sudan for Ethiopia and is now a Canadian citizen. She spoke to her husband, the governor of one of Sudan's southern provinces, just before he died from the effects of torture that the army had inflicted. All he could say was A-B-C-D on the telephone, she told me. Reciting the alphabet must have protected him from revealing too much during torture.

*

Harold Marcuse, grandson of the radical German philosopher Herbert Marcuse, wrote *Legacies of Dachau: The Uses and Abuses of a Concentration Camp,* a book about postwar German responses to the atrocities committed in their name. He cites Pat's article, saying that "the statements she records prefigure so precisely the protective subterfuges documented for later months and years that it is unlikely that she made them up." He also assesses that "her interlocutors were not inhibited by his [her translator's] presence" and so talked freely.[136] Footage of the tour she participated in is still shown daily at the camp for visitors.[137] Marcuse notes that for decades after the war, local and regional officials tried to make the camp difficult to find, and that in 1955 they wanted to tear down what remained of it in order to discourage tourists.[138] No new memories must be made.

*

Past or present, people believe what facts they want to believe. "It is unlikely that she made them up," writes Marcuse.

*

Lee Miller suffered from PTSD for decades after her visit to Dachau and Buchenwald. When Margaret Bourke-White photographed Dachau, she blocked so much she couldn't remember having taken the photos after she printed them.[139] Martha Gellhorn said what she saw in Dachau entered her soul and she was never again free of it.[140] "It was as though I fell off a cliff at Dachau, and suffered a form of concussion ever since."[141] In Hawai'i, thirty-six years later, Pat mutely pointed at the 5"x7" photos of the camp she kept as souvenirs, with the limbs and bodies of the prisoners stacked in a boxcar a foot away. Nancy Sorel, the author of *The Women Who Wrote The War*, told Pat that women correspondents "seldom put their real feelings in print."[142] Certainly no one wanted to publish them at that time. To suggest that war was hell was unpatriotic. *The Man in the Grey Flannel Suit* starring Gregory Peck was one of the few films immediately after the war that managed to depict the psychological suffering of at least the soldiers.

Journalists are still given less preparation than soldiers to cope with the inherently dangerous situations or life-threatening incidents they are expected to cover. A macho ethic pervades the practice. Witnessing trauma is regarded by the public as routine for the job, a notion reinforced by the media itself. A recent study of the experiences of journalists in South Africa during its most violent era of apartheid showed a preponderance of people unable to cope, partly because they tended to rely solely on dissociative strategies.[143]

*

Steve remembers his mother as very distant—and never home. This was not a case of Mom going to bridge club every Tuesday night, and an over-sensitive son. By the time he was eleven in 1959, Pat was visiting fifteen countries twice a year, along with yearly cross-country US tours for UNICEF as Director of Information.[144]

*

The most common images of Dachau are found in a series taken by an unknown photographer and published as propaganda postcards, part of Eisenhower's campaign to publicize the atrocities. The US Army circulated a pamphlet of these images throughout Germany so that "ordinary citizens become aware of the crimes which were committed in their midst, in their names, and with their permission."[145] An instance where truth is used as propaganda, with facts disseminated widely to force a populace to confront their guilt.

Seven months after Dachau was liberated, the Nuremberg trials began, a way of forcing the whole country to face the truth of its degradation by trying the main instigators. The Khmer Rouge Trials, the International Trial Tribunal for Rwanda, and the Truth and Reconciliation Trials in South Africa are other examples of such showcases. Their effectiveness is inconclusive. The United Nations, the premier institution in the peacekeeping business, was "not created to take mankind to heaven," according to Dag Hammarskjöld, "but to save humanity from hell."[146]

*

Hitler and Eva Braun's bodies were doused repeatedly with forty-seven gallons of gas and burned throughout the afternoon and into the Berlin evening of April 30, 1945. No one mentioned the smell.[147][148]

*

Captain J.D. Fletcher wrote of pre-liberation Dachau: "Of all the horrors of the place, the smell [of the burning], perhaps, was the most startling of all. It was a smell made up of all kinds of odors—human excreta, foul bodily odors, smoldering trash fires, German tobacco—which is a stink in itself—all mixed together in a heavy dank atmosphere, in thick muddy woods, where little breeze could go."[149] Staff Sergeant Malachowski, at Nordhausen with the 329th Medical Battalion, recalled that "the smell [at Dachau] covered the entire countryside ... for miles around.[150]

*

Consider that summer in Dachau, when the owners of the elegant villas lining the nearby river would have had to close their windows, take their dinners inside instead of eating on the terrace. The children would have said something about the stink, the maids or the governesses using handkerchiefs to cover their noses. Since the camp ovens were used frequently, perhaps the townspeople coined euphemisms: *the devil is farting*. The wealthy ate their roast pig, while the other roasting went on and on, the smoke clouding their view. Did dogs snap and moan at such smoke? Were there cupboards that never lost that smell so that years later, looking for an old coat, they'd open a door or a drawer and that lost time would come back, the sense of smell being the most potent holder of memories?

*

Among Pat's Dachau interviewees was the town matriarch who was surprised that Pat should be at all interested in the town's involvement. "The state put them there," she said. "They weren't good Germans."[151] She was of course putting herself in the category of good. Good Germans didn't kill Jews, the Holocaust deniers argue. The question then remains: who did?

*

Alas, genocide has been a (in)human trait from the beginning, since Moses annihilated the Canaanites. Are Germans human? We are all Germans. As a response to the carnage under Hitler, the Germans lied to the military to stay alive, they lied to each other so they wouldn't be betrayed, they lied to the Americans so they would be treated well, they lied (or omitted the facts) in their history books in order to encourage a kind of amnesia about what had happened. It is human to lie in response to the enormity of such a crime.

5

Souvenirs as Proof

Pat was the first female reporter to arrive at Eagle's Nest, a glorified mountain hut with a stupendous view, traveling with the first wave of military, the Third Infantry Division. It was the end of April 1945. This chalet, three thousand feet up, was the second seat of power outside of Berlin, where Hitler planned his conquest of Europe and hosted heads of state as well as intimate retinues of party cronies. A few miles below sat the Berghof, where Hitler lived about a third of his twelve years in power, supposedly only feeding the deer and kissing toddlers in the perpetual sunshine of the Alps.[152] Below that lies the town of Berchtesgaden, an upscale Bavarian resort town surrounded on three sides by towering mountains. Pat's climb wasn't easy. Elizabeth May Craig, arriving just after VE Day, agreed: "I didn't think I'd ever make it up that tiny, slippery path."[153] Fires were still raging out of control, lit by SS officers.[154]

"Have been meaning to write you about climbing an alp," Pat writes to her mother, "not just an ordinary one, but Hitler's private Ober Salzberg. Was the first gal reporter to make his Eagle's Nest and it was certainly well worth it altho I picked up a miserable cold wading through snow hip deep for the last 1,000 feet."[155]

She picked up far more than a cold. A couple of months earlier, when the war was just winding down, she wrote home that she had already scrounged a number of interesting souvenirs and would continue to work hard at it so there would be enough to go round for everyone.

So far I have two German pistols, the small size; two Nazi flags, the small size, one Hitler jugend dagger, one beer mug, one early 18th century original engraving, one alarm clock, several propaganda books, one case champagne, several dozen German postcards, and a good camera with a 3.5 Schneider lens.

"Does this sound like I have been on a scavenger hunt?" Pat asks her family in her June 2, 1945 letter. By June 4, she queries her boss at *Woman's Home Companion*: "How can I ship to you several volumes of symphonies by the Munich and Berlin orchestras which I acquired informally from Messrs Hitler and Goering's music library at Berchtesgaden?" On June 13, she has a book published in 1610 from Hitler's library.[156] By June 17, the Texan newspaper *The Monitor* reports that she now has a small Belgium .25 pistol "a/k/a a husband-killer," table linen "complete with Der Fuehrer's monogram," a camera once the property of Herman Goering, a practically new red convertible Mercedes Benz that belonged to the universally despised von Ribbentrop, and Eva Braun's bedroom curtains—and she has already broken "one of the 14 bottles of a priceless brandy stolen from France by Herman Goering."[157]

*

The insistent reassurance that Pat gives in her letters of bringing home the spoils makes me curious about the reasons behind the pocketing of souvenirs in the world of conflict. Are they like

Pat displaying her souvenirs, 1945

delivering the ears of the vanquished? You'd take the enemies' guns to be certain they weren't to be used against you, but as a noncombatant, why not destroy them? Perhaps the victors three thousand miles away wanted the enemies' guns as some kind of good luck talisman, or to display like heads on a pike. But taking Hitler's napkins—why would anyone want them? To touch celebrity, or to wipe their dirty faces against his linen?

*

As Dickson Hartwell states in *Off the Record*, "Correspondents went after souvenirs second only to their stories; they weren't fussy. Anything would do. More closets of more correspondents are probably piled with more junk than the Collier brothers' mansion." Jonathan Leonard, the science editor of *Time*, kept radioactive metal from Hiroshima in a lead-sheathed desk drawer, and Harold Smith of the *Chicago Tribune*, known as "Packrat" Smith, amassed a huge collection of Japanese swords, guns, and clocks.[158] Clare Hollingworth brought her five-year-old nephew a dagger, some watches and a military cap, which she looted from North African battlefields.[159] While photographing the Berghof, Lee Miller took an ornamental silver tray.[160] The (secretly) Jewish reporter Sigrid Schultz, whose hand Hitler had kissed, looted books from the same library.[161] Helen Kirkpatrick stole a frying pan from the kitchen.[162] Pat modeled a turban she had made in Paris from Goering's military sashes, in particular his Knights of the Iron Cross medal, in an article she wrote at the end of the war.[163]

Pat modeling the turban and large purse made from Goering's military sashes, and holding his Minox spy camera, 1945

The looting of the Berghof was particularly frenzied, with both journalists and soldiers ransacking the premises. "It was like a very wild party," wrote Lee Miller.[164] "Of course it all had to fit into the knapsack on my back because I had to crawl back down the mountain," says Pat.[165]

*

I go through all the file drawers and boxes of old papers in our apartment, but I can't find the photo of Pat pointing at Hitler's ashes. Surely it's in the basement. I'm fortunate as a New Yorker to have this additional storage, unfortunate to have filled it. Steve will have to help me there. A serious packrat himself, he has developed systems for storing everything: heavy objects on casters, paintings on edge, all boxes labeled. But the labels are old, some have peeled off, and worse, seldom represent what's inside anymore. Everything has to be taken out and gone through in the narrow hall.

We must have missed something.

*

Souvenirs represent proof of your existence elsewhere, and that difference exists. My stop in New Hebrides (now Vanuatu) on our way to Sudan presented a temptation I couldn't resist. Leaving my ex-to-be to negotiate a place at a hostel, I toured Port Vila, the capital, eventually investigating its only art gallery. I very much admired the Big Namba sculpture on display. A bulbous object woven out of reed and mounted on a black wooden cube, it had an attractive mix of minimalist and primitive. The French dealer told me that the Nambas in Vanuatu were divided—like the island itself, which was ruled then by both the English and the French with double bureaucracies—into Small Nambas and Big Nambas. I knew my ex scoffed at souvenirs: we had no room to transport them en route to Sudan, we had very little money to buy them, and politically, if they were any good, to take them home was like stealing the Elgin marbles. I had vowed to keep only objects that were given to me, but here I admired this one so much I overlooked all my objections and bought it, paying a considerable amount to ship it home. I never told my ex, but in the end that didn't matter—the souvenir never arrived. Perhaps the dealer is selling it again today.

Now, googling, I see that nambas are penis sheaths.

*

The history of looting is as long as the history of genocide. After smiting the Canaanites—that is to say, killing them all—Moses collected their possessions. Rome was sacked by Gauls, Goths, more Goths, Normans, the Spanish and Lutherans, the French, and of course, the Nazis. Cortes looted the Aztec gold. Three quarters of all the Italian art in the Louvre came to Paris via Napoleon. Are there objects of inestimable cultural value that should not be looted? "May [the military] not seize and appropriate to his own use such works of genius and taste as belong to the hostile state, and are of a moveable character?" debated scholars during the US Civil War.[166] The Lieber Code, the first modern codification of the laws of war, was enacted under Abraham Lincoln. It specifically exempted monuments, places of worship and works of art from looting. It also says: "Neither officers nor soldiers are allowed to make use of their position or power in the hostile country for private gain"—all the plunder should go to the victor's government.[167] But the temptation remains. So many children of WWII vets are now trying to cash in on their parent's loot that Antique Roadshow insists on strong provenance for every object of the period they consider. "The 'Mona Lisa,' as it were, appears in just about every city we visit," says Daile Kaplan, their long-time photography expert.[168]

Four years after the end of WWII, the Geneva Convention made the looting of civilian property a war crime. It obliges the military not only to avoid destroying enemy property, but to protect it. How has this worked out? In 2003 CNN reported that US customs seized fifteen paintings taken from one of Saddam Hussein's presidential palaces after the invasion of Iraq. Among the suspects were a former Fox News employee and other returning journalists.[169]

*

"In other countries through which the war carried me, looting never became the big-time obsession it was in Germany," writes photographer Margaret Bourke-White. "We correspondents and officers often talked about the looting fever, and wondered if we would drop our looting habits when the war ended. We talked about whether we'd have to nail down things in our own houses, if any of us visited each other."[170] It was a common joke in Germany that 'USA' was an acronym for 'Uhren stehlen auch', or 'They steal watches too,' according to historian Seth A. Givens.[171]

*

After our swim in the shark-infested waters of the Solomons, my ex took Polaroids of the parents who were so generous to us on the beach. Their children lined up beside them, shoulders thrown back, their eyes laughing at something I said. Thanking us, the parents offered to return us to town on their motorbike, sparing us from the very long hot walk back to the hostel.

The bare-chested hiker had returned and lay collapsed in his room. We befriended the only other visitor, a curator for the British Museum who was trying to negotiate the loan of an artifact from the local museum, a shield covered with tiny squares of nautilus shell. "They haven't the means to keep the wood from rotting in this climate, and these are priceless," she told us.

Nefertiti, the Rosetta Stone, the list is long, said my ex. To collect is a projection of power and of British imperial desire.

I remember his words easily, he said something similar often, being a sort of anthropological scold. I remember his canting of his head with every assertion. I also remember how she did a double take at his lengthening the word *desire*.

There is loot, and there is loot, she said. The British Museum doesn't charge, the Acropolis does. The BM is at the crossroads of so many more travelers. Many of the treasures wouldn't have been discovered at all if the Europeans hadn't funded and organized the expeditions or the digs that located them.

So? he said.

The shields were used as a ritual gift of exchange with Europeans in the mid nineteenth century, she answered. They were actually made for us.

But she didn't succeed in getting them, not even on loan.

*

In June 1945, an Austrian builder told the Allies that Hitler had actually been shot by an army general in March 1944, and the corpse could be found in a crypt below Eagle's Nest. No wonder the military needed a photograph, and Pat was—or was about to become—mayor of Berchtesgaden, and would have been the perfect person to verify it. Later American investigators found no evidence to support the Austrian's claim.[172] They were left with the question: Who would have taken the body?

The final souvenir.

*

We were given a sketch by the little girl on that beach in the Solomons: two stick figures and something poking out of the water behind them: the shark, the last looters. Where is that picture now? Tucked away somewhere safe, like the photo. A gift is porous, it unites the giver and the receiver as a bridge over time. A souvenir is frozen, a mere transaction. *I have been in this location long enough to exchange money*, not *I am part of your country now, as real as this gift of a talisman.*

Souvenirs of conflict often end up destroyed or at least locked away to prevent more conflict. The set of eight-foot long Nuer spears and a huge hippo hide shield that I brought home from Sudan belong to that category. They were going to be burned after being used as evidence during a trial about a fight over a hippo. The magistrate feared they would be used to enact revenge for the conviction. My ex and I rescued them from a bonfire behind the courthouse.

6

Truth

We own the last shellfish shucking shack in Long Island. Tiny, with a view of the water in every window, it's built on sand. The floor slants so steeply we are always battling gravity and even the Murphy bed that folds into the wall has to be slept in backward, foot-to-head, the sand has shifted that much. Built in the 1870's, the house has no joint that runs perpendicular, a marble dropped in the kitchen rolls to the front door, and no window hangs straight.

Yet it stands, nothing "true," but a structure built to last.

*

Hitler's bunker in Berlin was first an air raid shelter, customized with a roof of cement ten feet thick. Unpleasantly damp and leaky, from January to May 1945 it was home to about fifty people, including Joseph Goebbels' six children. The dog trainer Fritz Tornow walked Hitler's German shepherd Blondi underground, with at least nine other dogs. They howled at night.

Hitler let it be known that he slept with Blondi, propaganda that was supposed to prove that he was an animal lover. Before shooting himself, Hitler tested his cyanide on the dog. The experiment was a success. After Hitler's suicide, the trainer shot Blondi's five pups, Eva Braun's two terriers, and his own dachshund, but not himself. Blondi and a pup were buried with the burnt corpses of Hitler and Braun in a shell crater in front of the bunker.[173]

Their ashes were only theoretically in Pat's pile.

*

The term fact-checker was first used in 1938 by *Colliers,* although the *New Yorker* employed the earliest fact-checkers in 1927.[174] Since only women were hired for the job before 1973, they were always being pitted against the male authors to keep them accurate, a sort of grammatical gender war. It was not easy. The editors of *TIME,* noted for its very thorough fact-checking, bemoaned the "constantly moving target of fact-checking and its impossibility."[175] Reporters make statements about facts, and these statements invariably—and hopefully—involve ideas. With Trump's unrelenting dishonesty and the fragmentation of the media due to technology, fact-checkers have become even more important in present day reporting. Trump, however, has triumphed over fact-checkers by creating a new reality, "post-truth," in which they are irrelevant. "Repeat a lie often enough and it becomes the truth" is attributed to Hitler's Minister of Propaganda, Joseph Goebbels, not Donald Trump, its contemporary practitioner.

In January 2025 Mark Zuckerberg and Elon Musk "de-truthed" social media in the name of Trump's First Amendment by firing their fact-checkers. This decision allows the 5.5 billion users of Facebook, Instagram and X to push any kind of truth they want—and repeat it, with paid bots and fervent followers.[176]

*

My husband's hundred-year-old Uncle Lloyd confirms that he and Pat bicycled through Germany in 1936 before the war broke out. "We were invited to see how innocent the Germans were," he said. "And they were not. Everywhere we could see them preparing." Martha Gellhorn visited Germany on invitation three years earlier with a delegation of young peace activists. It took only a week of her observing the Hitler Youth to understand what was really going on.[177]

*

I studied truth at Oxford in 1969. My parents had befriended a geography don and his family camping near my hometown, and he volunteered to arrange to have me study between semesters my sophomore year in college. This was long before formal semesters abroad. I proposed several subjects, witchcraft in England being the one that most embarrasses me now. Since I was majoring in philosophy, we settled on A.J. Ayer and his positivist classic, *Language, Truth, and Logic*, which argued (among other things) that only statements that are empirically verifiable are cognitively meaningful. The paper I wrote for my tutor, the Australian Elizabeth Reid, later the world's first government advisor on women's affairs, explored whether a person whose head had been transplanted from someone else was the same as the person before the transplant.

*

Denton A. Cooley performed the first successful heart transplant in the US in 1968, and a year later, Dickson hired him to work on his heart—but not a transplant. When Cooley was asked at a trial if he thought he was the best heart surgeon in the world, his answer was in the affirmative. "Don't you think that's being rather immodest?" said the lawyer. "Perhaps," said Cooley. "But remember I'm under oath."[178]

Ah, the truth.

If Dickson had gotten a heart transplant, would someone else's heart have made him a better stepfather?

*

Pat claims to have witnessed the arrest and surrenders of both Goering and Kesselring, numbers two and three of the Nazi military hierarchy. Confusion swirls around when exactly the first happened since Eisenhower's order to arrest Goering was the last top-secret mission of WWII's European theater. David Lesjak, an American guard at Fischhorn Castle where on May 7, 1945, Goering spent his first postwar night with Americans, said that part of the confusion stems from the American division commander deciding to go after him without telling XXI Corps Headquarters or the Seventh Army, causing inaccuracies in the staff journals. The division in question was "probably in the 101st Airborne Division's area," the 101st being Pat's group.[179]

The roads around Fischhorn Castle are narrow and winding. In another account (which dates the events to May 5), Goering's entourage was stalled at Radstadt behind hordes of Germany's retreating soldiers and hundreds of released Allied prisoners of war. Goering wanted to be rescued by the Americans, as the SS was eager to silence him. Official reports have only three American military meeting him, although one account has a limousine showing up.[180]

> When we were in Rosenheim one day, Goering decided to give up and he loaded his vast open car with fried chicken and wine, and I suppose the usual things as souvenirs and he was driving around trying to figure out who he should surrender to, so he surrendered to the press. We entertained him overnight and we ate his chickens and he

told us how it had all been a terrible mistake and he was so sorry, he was such a good guy...

said Pat. "Of course the daily press had quite a story about this captured Hermann Goering being a houseguest of a division, so they hurried down to take him into custody and treated him not so handsomely."[181] She never mentions the exact day.

According to Lesjak, the military brought in Goering and an entourage of about thirty other Germans to the castle at 11:30 the night of May 7. He arrived with "everybody in splendid humor... Goering is cracking jokes with the American soldiers," according to another witness.[182] A drinking party ensued, complete with someone shooting through the roof. Interviewed forty years later, Lesjak twice commented that it was lucky no newspaper photographers were around.[183] But that didn't exclude reporters, says my husband. Pat told both of us—and his brothers—that she was in the car that intercepted Goering's en route to his surrender, and that she danced with him that night while feasting on the bounteous provisions he brought along in his car, custom-made to hold his huge bulk and lots of supplies. While I suppose Pat could have been part of that strange celebration, dancing with all three hundred pounds of Goering, his wife looking on, the room filled with angry defeated German military brass, it doesn't seem likely. To dance with him would be crossing a line—although as a reporter, she was expected to cross lines. Indeed, there was some documented fraternization: at least one account has the US soldiers drinking with the SS that night.[184] And Goering was indeed a ladies' man. If she did dance with him, she didn't include the anecdote in anything I've seen, and she doesn't mention the story in *Off the Record*, the book about correspondents' war stories Dickson put together with Andy Rooney for the Overseas Press Club eight years later. But when the *Chicago Daily News* interviewed her a few months after the end of the war, she said she was indeed present when Goering was captured.[185]

A day after Goering turned himself in at Fischhorn, Pat was in Berchtesgaden, about 90 minutes away by car, dining with General Iron Mike O'Daniel, who had taken the town a few days earlier.[186] Peace had just been declared and the enemy disarmed. That night "squads and details passed each other with sidewise stares of interest, attempts to maintain step and rhythm which pleased the more drill-minded officers on both sides," according to the 101st historian.[187] Pat writes:

> Outside of town is Hitler's fabulous gasthaus for distinguished visitors [Berghof] and on the actual night when hostilities ceased, four of us were guests of General Iron Mike O'Daniel's Third Division. At midnight they fired everything in the area and I'm sure the Austrians thought the war was just starting.

In a letter to her editor, she writes: "I even contributed a blast from my trusty .25."[188]

*

In an interview in 1995, Pat says: "I believe I was in Paris on VE day." That would've been May 8, 1945 when she was to have been with General Iron Mike O'Daniel. She goes on to say she can't remember exactly "because it was so in my mind when President Roosevelt died, and I felt very close to him." Roosevelt died April 12. Perhaps it is the memory of a guilty conscience. She was not supposed to be in Paris at all.

> I was on the streets of Paris having fun with fellow correspondents and we heard the news . . . Someone writing

about the news of the president's death mentioned that one woman correspondent had broken down and cried on the streets of Paris when the news came, and gave my name. My editor telegrammed: What are you doing in Paris? [189]

*

The ex-publicity director of CBS, Louis Ruppel, also noticed she'd been caught out in Paris in that stateside column. They had exchanged several flirtatious letters when he was driving a tank for intelligence. "When I get home I'm opening a tank park at Coney Island – more fun than the Tunnel of Love – give you a ride."[190] After the war Ruppel became editor of the *Chicago Herald American* and then *Colliers,* for whom she wrote a 2-part story about emergency rooms.[191] Maybe it's through him that she knew the Roosevelts' since he and FDR were friends, and he became Deputy Commissioner, Bureau of Narcotics for a year.[192] Pat answers his letters crammed full of the names and doings of journalists as if nervously fending him off.

*

With regard to the third ranking German general Kesselring, Pat writes: "Dick Johnston of the *NY Times* and Howard Cowan of UP—had a hot tip on Kesselring . . . So we hied ourselves down to Kitzbuhel and helped capture the good General. Had dinner in his private railroad car—the works."[193] In *Tracking the 101st Cavalry,* (then attached to the 101st Airborne), Melaney Moisan writes that

a train with Kesselring arrived at Zell am Zee and guards were set up around it and the platoon stayed in the hotel across the street . . .Three reporters showed up the next morning [May 8] by 9 o'clock. They requested an interview with Kesselring but were denied.[194]

A major arrived that afternoon to make arrangements for Kesselring and certain members of his staff to be taken to 101st Airborne headquarters at Berchtesgaden. The three members of the press were still there, and they had not had an interview.[195] By May 10, the Americans had his railroad car and Kesselring had surrendered "with newspapermen camped around him."[196] [197]

Goering was moved to Kitzbuhel on the same day that Pat began chasing Kesselring. Kitzbuhel had been untouched by the war. Many Nazis spent their vacations climbing the Alps nearby, and fishing in the river running through it. Goering had a chicken dinner at its Grand Hotel that later led to fraternization charges. Was that when she danced with him? His picture was taken in front of the Texas flag at that location, as the 36th Division that was occupying Kitzbuhel was from Texas.[198] Pat says in a letter to her mother that "there aren't any Texans in it any more," so she could have popped in on Goering while waiting for the Kesselring interview.[199]

She had one more opportunity. Statecraft and propaganda require ceremony for an official surrender. The next day, Goering was flown to Augsburg to formally present himself to the Chief of Staff Seventh Army.[200] The pilot recounted that Goering spoke English to him briefly en route, and then stopped speaking it, exactly how Pat describes her conversation with him. Augsburg was a two-and-a-half hour drive from Kitzbuhel, easily accessible to Pat. "Several days later [after Goering's capture] headquarters called a press conference and in the garden, Goering, who theoretically spoke and understood no English, was given an interpreter and by then everybody had arrived, all the correspondents, including Margaret Bourke-White." Goering met with some fifty reporters and footage of the official surrender shows a number of women among them.[201] Did she dance with him then? The nature of the event makes it somewhat unlikely.

*

Quibbles, you say. Can't a woman stretch the truth a little? After all, she was in the neighborhood, with the means. What does it matter? It matters deeply to those who want to know what kind of woman she was, living in this era of violence and compromise and privilege, and why she would want to boast of not only meeting the second most evil Nazi, but dancing with him.

I believe her. There's just enough detail in her account, and just enough confusion on everyone else's part to shift the incident from "somewhat unlikely" to "likely."

*

It's July 2011. I've just finished teaching a class in creative writing in Nairobi, the closest I've come to Sudan in 35 years. What makes me think I can fly to Juba and see Riek Machar, soon to be the vice president of what will be, in another twenty days, the newest country in the world? I want to give him my coffee table version of *Cleaned the Crocodile's Teeth: Nuer Song* as an expression of my solidarity with the future South Sudan. I'm optimistic: he's Nuer, and they will make up about thirty percent of the population of the proposed new country. He's also something of a ladies' man, dubbed the Bill Clinton of Sudan. Deborah Scroggins wrote *Emma's War* about his romance with Emma McCune, a wild British girl whom he married in the bush during his dashing guerilla days. (Tony and Ridley Scott optioned the film rights).[202] Now he's married to a Sudanese woman who for five years was in charge of the country's bounteous oil. I'll play the white woman card and mention my last academic appointment was with Columbia University, and also the book was selected as a "Writer's Choice" by the *New York Times Book Review*.

As soon as I land, I reach Mario Jackson Mareng, Minister of Information, Public Relations, Culture and Protocol. Mario is staying one hotel away, in one of its many well-appointed air-conditioned cargo containers. When I ask him about the relocation of the millions of displaced South Sudanese for oil drilling, he laughs and says the government can't provide housing for its ministers—he's been living here for the last five years. Educated at UCLA, he ran the country's TV station and spent two years in a Khartoum jail as the reward for his writing.

"Your Excellency," I say into Mario's cell phone after he introduces me. What else did I say to the Vice President? Something acceptable, because right away he asks to speak to Mario. We take off for the V.I.P. Lounge at the airport where Machar is waiting to greet the president on his return from last minute negotiations in Khartoum.

I see no guns at the V.I.P. Lounge, no bodyguards, no soldiers. Machar is no Goering, but he is second in command and a serious veteran of violence. A thousand people will die when he is dismissed two years later, and thousands more up to 2025, with thousands already dead in earlier battles he's led, some share of the two million fatalities in South Sudan's road to independence. But Machar and other officials are seated in huge leather armchairs inside mere ropes, the kind that keep the riffraff out of NYC clubs. He rises and kisses me like an old friend. He's at least six-five, still powerfully built and cute, with a gap between his teeth. I flirt as best I can with the book of translations as our subject. "I attended the funeral of a paramount chief last week in Fangak," he says. "The men sang our history for four hours." I ask whether he still knows any songs. He smiles. "They are the ones from when I was a very young man. I composed them myself." We exchange a laugh. They would be songs in praise of himself, advertisements for the girls, hip-hop with spears. But at the time he was at university getting a PhD. Most young Nuer men court instead of study; he had to learn other wiles. Songs

Riek Machar reviews *Cleaned the Crocodile's Teeth,* 2011

are still important to his position. Contemporary Nuer prophets use them to unify local troops and have promised in song that the ashes the young soldiers smear on their chests will protect them. An often-performed 19th-century song predicts this year's overthrow of Arab rule. They're not Yankee Doodle.

Machar leaves to greet the president—"Stay, stay," he insists—and when he returns, he pats the seat for me to sit next to him, smiling a guileless smile that can't be real or he wouldn't be alive today. I write a dedication in the book while he practices pronouncing my name. "We should start a book club," he suggests to Mario, and the interview's over.

I don't dance with him.

*

Flying into London's Dorchester Hotel a week after Kesselring's capture, Pat woke the sleepy night clerk who insisted he had no rooms available. She was not deterred. "But it's for Madame Hemingway," she said, "and double-talked the sad character a bit until he wasn't sure whether I was Madame, her sister-in-law or whatever, but the name was Hemingway. And sure enough, I was given a delightful suite, complete even to a bowl of fruit and towel-warming racks."[203] Martha Gellhorn, Hemingway's wife at the time, was the correspondent's diva: blonde, daring, articulate, an excellent writer and a veteran reporter of the Spanish Civil War, a daunting figure among many talented women. By then she had lost her military credentials for having stowed away on a hospital ship on D-Day, and soon she would have her magazine job stolen from her by Hemingway himself, but being his wife played at least some part in her subsequent reporting opportunities—and comforts. When Pat claimed her suite, however, many in Paris knew Hemingway was living at the Ritz with Mary Welsh of *TIME*.[204]

*

Hitler wrote of telling a lie so "colossal" that no one would believe that someone "could have the impudence to distort the truth so infamously."[205] People would believe the lie only if it were big enough. Hitler's big lie was that Jews had begun a "war of extermination" against Germany, and so Germany had a duty and a right to "exterminate" and "annihilate" the Jews in self-defense. This bit of propaganda closely matches Putin's claim of the Ukrainians attacking the Russians in their country. Trump's losing the 2020 election has also been termed by him "the Big Lie." The bigger the lie, the bigger the test of allegiance. Will he be rebuked? Hitler's goose-stepping troops and Trump's much reviled tank parade reinforce the most unsubtle of propagandistic memes for the populace: the lie that you are not hungry, your stomach is just angry, march with me and you will be filled. Both the psychologist and the anthropologist have been known to join hands to amplify the myths needed to sanctify the dark corners of propaganda.

*

Erosion of the truth equals confusion. This is easy to see in those 2020 elections, with fake news, doctored videos, mashup photos and the bewildered disenfranchised electorate, and even more so in 2024. Russians are considered the experts in sowing confusion, having used it to turn the Glasnost—"openness"— of the Perestroika movement into the closed bureaucratic oligarchy of Putin's reign. Or is singling out the Russians as the culprit just another expression of my own nationalist prejudice? How much have Americans cyber-meddled to influence Russians? Does the *New York Times* commit the same crime by burying articles about Elizabeth Warren and putting Michael Bloomberg on the front page? The manipulation of the truth can be pervasive and sometimes even unconscious. Why does your mother mention your sister's grade point average so often? Is truth just a matter of who is the better persuader and who's listening when?

*

Margaret Mead's credo for visual anthropology was that the camera doesn't lie, and that if you just let it run, you'll capture what is true of a culture. That is naive: someone decides when to turn the camera on and where to point it. The Heisenberg Principle—that by looking at something, you change it—is also at work. Or, as anthropologist Clifford Geertz theorized, the eye of the viewer sees what it wants, what it has already seen.[206] His book, *The Interpretation of Cultures,* launched an attack on *The Nuer,* written thirty-three years earlier by E. Evans Pritchard and foundational in the discipline of social anthropology. Geertz accused the study of being truer to the eye of a British anthropologist than to Nuer culture. But what if the proud Nuer did sometimes act like British imperialists? Geertz had not lived with them, not even the brief nine months of my stay.

Believing that editing, effects, and voiceover falsifies footage is a variation on assuming that documentaries contain no truth. Uncut footage is unwatchable to all but the most diligent scholar—whose job it is to create meaning. Scholars and editors interpret, just as journalists, eyewitnesses to unfolding events, choose their words. To paraphrase Geertz again, culture is made up of the meanings people find to make sense of their lives and to guide their actions.

The making of dramatic film is very manipulative, using every means possible to convince its audience that what they are seeing is not over-dubbed or blue-screened. In contrast, documentary film is often shot without synchronized sound and the sound inserted later. The addition of audio provides a possibly contradictory narrative layer: voiceover, sound, or effects that can enhance rather than illustrate. Or contradict what is seen. In other words, when you see the bear going over the mountain, the narrator does not say: "The bear is going over the mountain" but something more like: "It is spring when males will travel long distances to mate." That gap between what you see and what you hear is always there. When the words "These are Hitler's ashes" are spoken over a photo, the viewer must create his own truth, interpreting the intent of the voice, the possible tampering of the photo, and the circumstances of its presentation.

While producing the *Voices & Visions* PBS series in the eighties, I interviewed many video artists about how they would approach using moving images against spoken poetry or on-screen text. The discussion centered around how each medium could support the other and avoid the redundancy of illustration. It was difficult, although French filmmaker Chris Marker's *Sans Soleil*, an essay film released around that time, was narrated by a woman reading a letter over travel footage that not only avoided illustration but created a metaphorical connection between the footage and the audio. Inspired by his work, I subsequently made fifteen videos exploring that connection. *To See or Not to See* was the result of footage I collected in Papua New Guinea of giant walking sticks crawling on my tripod. The strangeness of the insects created a cognitive dissonance against the voiceover that I used to suggest the leap viewers have to make to really see the Other. But one could simply falsely label the footage and invoke the paradigm of the documentary—that it's nonfiction—to make the link to an assumed truth. A few years later, I co-curated a show in 1993 for the Museum of Modern Art called "Between Word and Image," featuring a selection of videos that took advantage of the separation of sound and image to create media positioned between documentary and dramatic narrative.

Culture has its own way with truth. After the Cook Islands dance festival, my ex and I waited six months for a boat to take us to Pukapuka, a remote atoll of the Cooks. Touted as having a perfect democracy, the one hundred or so Pukapukans had recently elected someone to choose which program to watch on their single television. *National Geographic* wanted a photo essay. But the boat never arrived. We waited all those months until I realized I had misinterpreted our government liaison. Every time I asked him when the boat was coming, he promised it was on its way—but raised his eyebrows after each reassurance. I didn't know that the eyebrow raise meant no, the boat was not coming, but that culturally he couldn't refuse us. He wasn't lying.

*

If you're looking for truth, you'll find it, one way or another. Or reframe the facts to fit. *Mom did love me.* To her credit, my mother tried to talk about how I felt about my son's death over the five days I spent with her at Mayo Clinic while my father was undergoing a difficult surgery. It had been two years since my son fell from a window, and I was still too hurt by her initial response to take her seriously. Or was she looking for me, as a veteran of terrible calamity, to parent her through my father's illness?

*

In the past, a photo was supposed to clinch the truth, despite possible distortions such as the telling angle of the shot, the time the photo was taken, or the positioning of corpses, as in the manipulations of Civil War photographer Mathew Brady. Now, in the age of Photoshop, images are even less persuasive because the possibility to manipulate them is endless. Hitler's ashes? Easy.

7

Mayor of Berchtesgaden

In June 1945, the American military appointed twenty-nine-year old Pat mayor of Berchtesgaden. Although Hitler's Eagle's Nest was three thousand feet up, the little town below had to adjust to a defeat that was very personal. The very cream of the German military hierarchy had strolled its fairytale-like streets and taken in the sites—and planned their conquests. "It is the intention of the Allies that the German people be given the opportunity to prepare for the eventual reconstruction of their life on a democratic and peaceful basis," wrote the Allies at Potsdam.[207] In Germany, this was a nuanced and difficult task, with the conquered angry populace on the brink of starvation.

"You can be the first American woman in the military government of Germany. I warn you, however, it's a tough assignment," said Lieutenant Colonel Robert S. Smith of the 101st Airborne Division, according to "I Governed Berchtesgaden," the article Pat published in 1945 July's *Woman's Home Companion*. "No gag, honest" reads the headline.[208] Fifty years later, she reported that "Being a combat unit, they didn't have a G-5 or a person who was trained to run government. I said, my goodness, at Wellesley my major was political science so of course I am well trained to run a town."[209] The first and only civilian to be given such authority, she was to show to her readers the human side of responsibly governing a country in surrender.

You can imagine "the enormous inlaid desk" with not-so-tall Pat seated in a sturdy chair behind it, military cap straight, hair over her ears, a stack of documents, a sharpened pencil and Captain di Piero at her side, a "tough paratrooper" who "wigwagged the right answers whenever a problem came up."[210] There were problems. During and immediately after the surrender, German guerrilla units worked to sabotage facilities, Nazi agents in US uniforms raped and murdered to incite rebellion against Allied troops, and new German recruits, some women, but the majority teenage boys, pillaged and robbed the many homeless.[211] In France, women who'd slept with Germans were put on parade but had to be protected to prevent the crowds from tearing them to pieces.[212] And the occupying forces had to be kept out of trouble. Leonard Rapport, the chronicler for the 101st Airborne, a unit particularly known for their fighting during the Battle of the Bulge, was also noted for its penchant for a good time. "Indeed, it was a social error to be caught without a corkscrew in Berchtesgaden," writes Rapport.[213]

At 9 a.m. Pat received the burgomaster, "who bowed so low I thought I heard his short Bavarian leather pants crackle." She ordered all able-bodied Germans to grow vegetables, then requisitioned food supplies for 600 displaced persons, including starving formerly enslaved laborers. She issued a proclamation requiring Nazi insignia to be removed from street signs and buildings and was photographed burning them. She then began requisitioning necessities for the 101st Airborne Division's quartermaster: "mess tables and chairs were needed, and also blackboards for the special service officer." One of her prisoners, SS Lieutenant General

Berger, "reluctantly surrendered" several million dollars in marks which he had buried under the floor of a barn. She ordered workers to report for duty to repair the railway line to Munich, which was needed for the transport of 55,000 prisoners of war. And so the day went. She dealt with problems ranging from forestry to the fate of the local church's 15th-century cannon. She admitted she was "not ready to tackle the futures" of two hundred orphaned babies, the product of Lebensborn, an SS-sponsored breeding program, abandoned not far from Berchtesgaden.[214] She ordered that any Jews who were found were "to be given additional food since they had long starved," and then appointed the only one they located as interpreter for the US Army.[215]

Pat assumes her mayoral duties in Berchtesgaden May, 1945

As "Fraulein Kommandante," she'd scooped her classmate Philip Hamburger with a far more important assignment than his, a mere correspondent for the *New Yorker*. He too had worked for the Office of War Information but under Pat, as she was the assistant to the head of the whole organization; he too had plowed through the snow up to Eagle's Nest on the day of its liberation with the doyenne of female correspondents, Dorothy Thompson; he too picked up souvenirs: he found Goering's engraved calling card on the living room floor and brought it to Harold Ross, the *New Yorker* editor, who framed it for his office wall. He describes the Bavarian Alps as having a beauty "of a magnitude touching the threshold of pain" and the architecture of the Berghof "the guardhouse of a state penitentiary" in an article he wrote about visiting Berchtesgaden fifty years later for the *New Yorker*, where he was still employed. Pat doesn't mention him, although he was staying with other reporters in a chalet where John F. Kennedy was also billeted.[216]

She was supposed to have governed the town for a week, according to a letter she had written to her family and one of her interviews, but after she liberated the bank so women could get money to buy food for their starving children, General Patton was so annoyed he shortened her term of office.[217] She said he was already furious with her for leapfrogging ahead of him at Dachau, and she had annoyed him further by using a hotel toilet in a Schweinfurt hotel before he arrived and could clear it for mines—a favorite way to kill Americans. One of her last acts as mayor was paying off the midwife of an Italian girl who had just given birth. In gratitude, the new mother wanted to name the boy after her. Instead, Pat suggested the child be christened with Patton, her family name—and, of course, the general's.[218]

*

Among Pat's responsibilities during her short reign was Goering's art collection. He had amassed more of the world's art treasures than anyone in the world over the last ten years, acquiring, on average, three priceless works a week. Laurent Fabius, the French foreign minister, described Goering's collection as "an odious hunting trophy, the fruit of the villainous plundering of jewels of European art."[219] In May 1945, soldiers discovered a gargantuan salt mine concealing more than 10,000 pieces of confiscated art.[220] More art was hidden near Berchtesgaden. After Goering's private railroad car was ransacked by locals, discarded picture frames suggested that further investigation was necessary. Chipping through the eighteen-inch-thick wall of a local air raid shelter, soldiers found five Rembrandts, a Van Gogh, and a Renoir—among many other paintings.[221] More were hidden in nearby caves, a monastery, and a garage beside a grocer's. All had been moved from Goering's estate Carinhall six months earlier. Pat, as mayor of Berchtesgaden, gave an order to dispatch equipment and firemen to protect the collection immediately, and they were to remain on duty around the clock.

*

Goering not only collected more of the world's art treasures than anyone else, he also collected medals, far too many to wear all at once. He loved them, and there were rumors that he slept with them pinned to his pajamas.[222] The last question Edda, his eight-year-old daughter, put to him before his suicide was "When you come home, will you please put on your rubber medals in the bath like people say you do?" [223] Such a remark from his own child revealed the humiliations he would've faced had he not taken his own life. He was wearing all his military crosses on May 9 in Augsburg for the photographers at his surrender, probably the last time he wore them. The officer in charge of

Goering's interrogation, Major Paul Kubala, said he had all the Goering medals he could find melted down, but Kubala left the service barely having escaped his own court martial.[224] Pat herself walked off with quite a few.

In mid-June, after troops liberated Ribbentrop's excellent wine cellar (he had been a champagne salesman prior to foreign minister), a wild party ensued.[225] Irv Kupcinet, the legendary gossip columnist of the *Chicago Sun-Times,* reported that some drunk GI pinned a whole lot of Goering's medals on Pat's blouse, and she subsequently slipped out past the MPs. "I'm saving out one of Hitler's medals," she writes in a letter to Ruppel.[226] How the medals came to be at the party is unknown. She certainly took possession of at least one of Goering's two Iron Crosses, or perhaps even the Grand Cross, for I have seen a scribbled receipt for its sale to a radio auctioneer for $150 (about $2,500 today). Goering was the only recipient of that cross during WWII. She also went away with a Swiss Minox, the tiny spy camera that accompanied the award of the Iron Cross because Steve remembers using it. Quite a few of Goering's medals seem to be left over, judging from various displays on the internet, and an article on the fakes. [227] [228] [229]

*

Pat gave me an iron cross set with an amethyst our second visit. Not junk from a disused vanity drawer but heavy silver, quite beautiful, strung on a silver chain. I was touched and wore it frequently before I suspected it might have less-than-positive associations, given her history. Had she been waiting for some innocent person to come along and relieve her of it? The iron cross has been a German military decoration for centuries, although this one lacks the swastika in the center that the Nazis were so fond of. Mine could have been worn on a ribbon.

Unterstein, where Captain Anderson stored the art, is located four kilometers south of Berchtesgaden. A placard reading: "Hermann Goering's Art Collection through the courtesy of the 101st Airborne Division" identified the gallery. It had taken three days to move the 1,375 paintings, including the five Rembrandts, and works by most European masters, such as Gerard David, de Hooch, Van Dyck, Rubens, Canaletto, Boucher and Courbet, into the building, yet these constituted only a very small sampling of all the art Goering and Hitler had amassed.[230] Pat certainly visited Unterstein at least once, during a press conference mid-May, since there is a photo of her holding "Christ with the Woman Taken in Adultery," a painting supposedly done by Vermeer.[231] She told us the officers suggested she take her pick of the art as a souvenir. Instead of the Vermeer, she chose "Cupid Complaining to Venus" by Lucas Cranach. Had she some intuition that the Vermeer was a fake? It was then valued at half a million dollars.[232]

*

Pat had to have visited the 101st Art Gallery sometime after May 21 when the Monuments Men found the fake Vermeer wrapped around a stove pipe at Fischhorn Castle, but before August when "I Governed Berchtesgaden" appeared in *Woman's Home Companion* with the photo of her holding the fake painting, and the inventory at Unterstein no longer included "Cupid Complaining to Venus."[233] [234]

*

Pat told her children both that the Cranach was given to her at the warehouse and also that she took it from Carinhall, Goering's own home. She could only have visited his home between Iwo

Jima in February of 1945 and before he blew it up on April 28, 1945. It is highly unlikely that Goering would have had time for any American reporters then. Yet Pat opines in an interview that "[Goering] was perfectly capable of organizing Germany for another war," describes Frau Goering as "a Broadway chorine down to the last mink coat," mentions that their basement held enough food to last another year and "several hundred" of Goering's toy trains, and that Frau Goering had kept a few masterpieces "to tide her and her daughter over a straitened period."[235]

She says she interviewed Goering twice.[236] She could also have interviewed just the Frau after June 11, when, after nearly a month in residence at Fischhorn Castle, the 101st escorted the Frau to Veldenstein Castle, a property Goering inherited from his godfather and his mother's Jewish lover.[237] But Pat couldn't have seen the train sets—they had been blown up earlier at Carinhall. Was her familiarity with Goering due to an interview during his capture, that night she said she danced with him? En route to Veldenstein, Goering's trailer overturned on the road, and quite a bit of champagne and rum and cigarettes fell out, and perhaps also more of the fourteen bottles of brandy that Pat boasted of taking with her.[238]

She was right about the Frau hoarding the rest of Goering's masterpieces. American officials confiscated them after the jailed Goering requested one be given as a bribe to his interrogator.[239]

*

Or did she win the painting in a poker game? An American tank commander, Maj. William S. Oftebro won three paintings by Old Masters in a game and mailed them home. Seventy years later, his heirs handed them over to the German ambassador, but not without some soul searching. "I'm sure as heck not giving anything back to the Germans," said his son, debating what to do with them. Then he watched George Clooney's *Monuments Men* and changed his mind. [240]

A 2014 buddy film based on the true story of a bunch of artsy officers trying to round up looted art treasures at the end of WWII, *Monuments Men* has all the elements of a blockbuster: death, warfare, intrigue—Cate Blanchett as the real life museum curator with a secret—and art with a capital A. Actor John Goodman huffs and puffs through basic training, part of the real Monuments Men's preparation for removing and hiding artworks quickly near the frontlines, and the chatty German dentist who fixes Bill Murray's toothache did indeed introduce the Monuments Men to his son-in-law, a former SS officer who knew which treasures were where. "Eighty percent of the story is still completely true and accurate, and almost all of the scenes happened," insists director Clooney who also acted in the film.[241] During the war, three hundred and fifty art historians, curators, museum directors, artists, architects, and educators, men and women from thirteen countries, not only recovered looted art and tried to return it to its rightful owners as a sort of band of militarized Robin Hoods, but also worked to dissuade Allied bombers from destroying enemy targets of cultural importance.[242]

But not even Clooney with his famous grin could save the film. Made about people wanting something other than money, its premise questioned whether art is worth putting lives in jeopardy and endangering military strategy. Was saving the Mona Lisa more worthwhile than saving a soldier? Faced with this serious conundrum, Clooney decided to inject humor and delayed the film's premiere by two months to re-edit.[243] The result is stiff and contrived.

The film never addresses the temptation of the military to pocket the art themselves.

*

At the end of the war, four American soldiers offered to return a number of paintings stolen from the Schloss collection in exchange for $40,000, not a bad price. The whole collection consisted of 333 paintings, including Dutch and Flemish masters like Rubens, Rembrandt, and Ruysdael. It's one of the best examples of acquisition for Hitler's Führermuseum by forced sale during WWII—and was heavily looted by both the French and the Americans.[244] "My father told me the story of how he kicked [the soldiers] out, telling them they should be ashamed to be wearing US army uniforms," said Alain Vernay, grandson of the collector Adolphe Schloss.[245]

*

Pat's painting, "Cupid Complaining to Venus," is a little over three feet tall. Surely the 101st wrapped it up for her and shipped it, the way the Army did for Margaret Bourke-White's "tall green metallic nude from Hitler's study," which the 42nd Infantry Division suggested she take. It wasn't qualms of conscience that prevented Bourne-White from getting it home—the statue disappeared en route into the hands of some other art lover. "Somewhere between the airfield at Munich and the airfield at Paris, my Hitler souvenirs evaporated," admits Bourke-White.[246] Even if the art were offered by the military, Bourke-White and Pat had a moral responsibility not to take possession. Art is not a confiscated weapon. Pat doesn't say a word about taking the painting in her letters home.

It would change her life.

*

Letters are a fairly reliable source of information. The sender is apt to convey immediate impressions and relate events as they unfold. Though the writer shapes the material with an eye toward the reader, a letter delivered is not subject to the revisions of hindsight. But there is self-censoring, just what Byron Price, head of censorship insisted on.

*

Errors were made by US military officials with regard to the distribution of booty. Lieutenant Wallace L. Stephenson begged for the recovered diamond-encrusted Reichmarshall dagger so he could buy a chicken farm, and his commanding officer handed it over.[247] One of the Monuments Men, Thomas Howe, later President of the Association of American Art Museum Directors, trustee of the American Federation of Arts, a member of the Fine Arts Committee for the White House and the Smithsonian Art Commission, and Chairman of the National Collection of Fine Arts, not to mention Director of the California Palace of the Legion of Honor for decades, determined that a sword given to Goering by Mussolini was not a "cultural object" and allowed the troops to take it home for their clubhouse.[248] This casualness with regard to the definition of "cultural object" emphasizes the laxity of the immediate postwar period. The Cranach would have definitely been a "cultural object."

*

In 2015 it was discovered that some of the paintings in the Goering collection recovered by the Monuments Men were given to the families of Nazis instead of being returned to the families of the looted Jewish collectors. German officials left to the task of returning the art found it much easier to identify the ex-Nazis than to find the original Jewish owners.[249]

*

As many as five thousand works of priceless abstract art were burnt in Berlin by the Nazis, piled in bonfires in 1939. "No picture gets mercy," wrote Propaganda Minister Joseph Goebbels in his journal on January 13, 1938. He had modern art labeled degenerate—Kandinsky, Picasso, Chagall—and seized it from museums and private collectors. It was put on exhibit in an effort to educate the public on its ugliness, but ironically, the show was very popular and seen by a million Germans. The most valuable pieces were exchanged in the black market for foreign currency, arms, and supplies. But now and then, art, once listed as destroyed, turns up.[250]

Maybe it was a fake burning, for propaganda reasons, and dummies burnt.

*

The 101st Airborne gallery was only open for a short time and then someone finally realized the security risks and closed it down completely, refusing even three-star generals a viewing.[251]

8

Censorship

Lieutenant Colonel Dickson was known as "The Whip" in Hawai'i to those who served under him in the censorship office.[252] In a chapter on the subject in *Off the Record*, he and Andy Rooney write that "by its own nature censorship often attracts censors who are petty authoritarians." They also wrote: "The most flexible word in the war was "security."[253]

*

Press censorship began after the Crimean War when it was realized that journalists were giving away intelligence that the enemy could use against them. During the Civil War, correspondents' coverage on meager wages led to bribery that resulted in inaccurate and falsified reports, and imaginary deeds were reported to the masses. At the highest level, when Churchill proposed that the *London Times* encourage British enlistment by downplaying the horrors of the trenches, Roosevelt protested, believing that such coverage would discourage Americans from considering the situation serious enough to join the fight. The British even created "traveling censors" to follow the reporters around and squelch stories before they could be filed. Thirty years later, with

Lt. Col. Dickson Hartwell c. 1943

Vietnam an undeclared war, reporters finally had the freedom to go anywhere and talk to anyone, and became much feared by the military.[254]

Byron Price, head of censorship during WWII, was convinced that instead of forcing reporters to comply, or jailing them for ignoring censorship rules, as in WWI, journalists should self-censor.[255] "War might not be worth winning if the First Amendment had to be sacrificed."[256] More than thirty US government agencies, however, were involved in tracking this self-censorship, especially regarding the newsreels that more than 50 million Americans watched every week. The result was a cheerful gloss over the conduct of soldiers who had to be trained as killers and faced unimaginable horror. As John Steinbeck wrote: "There were no cowards in the American Army, and of all the brave men the private in the infantry was the bravest and noblest . . . and that the truth about anything was automatically

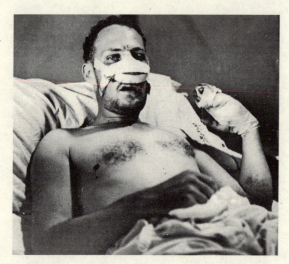

Censored photo, 1944

secret."[257] He said journalists felt they had to protect the home front or it would panic, and avoided criticizing servicemen or "they might retire to their tents to sulk like Achilles."[258]

What did the military not want those at home to see? The horrors of war, dismembered soldiers in particular. After all, war is essentially about the killing or maiming of more young men than the other side, the terror of every mother. Diplomacy and nationalism aside, the sight of every dead or wounded soldier on your side screams defeat. It took nearly two years into the war before a photo of a single dead soldier was published, and only because government PR decided Americans needed to be shaken out of their complacency to better support the military's efforts.[259]

After censorship and self-censorship, there is turning the bad news into good. As a reporter in the field, Pat was to keep up morale by accentuating the positive. In her article "I saw the wounded come home" she plays ping pong with a young man in a cast and loses, and sees someone kick a crutch out from under another vet "for their own good."[260] A few of the injured she interviewed seem to be enjoying themselves. She writes: "Some even learn to dance a little."[261]

*

When the German populace were required to remove all signs of the Nazi cult, they painted or chiseled away the swastikas to resemble edelweiss.

*

In our search for the Hitler photo, we go through dozens of 5"x7" blowups of WWII photos, mostly Dickson's, aerials of planes dropping bombs over what was probably too clearly enemy territory and thus censored and unpublished. A few of the saved photos show soldiers and reporters with ghastly wounds sitting or lying under the Pacific's palms.

But no photos of Pat standing over ashes.

*

Historiographer Bertrand Roehner reports that by May 1945, the Allies forbade all means of public communication and information in Germany "except as directed or otherwise authorized." "We [the Allies] now control 37 newspapers, 6 radio stations, 314 theaters, 642 movies, 101 magazines, 237 book publishers, 7,384 book dealers and printers. [We] publish one newspaper with 1,500,000 circulation, 3 magazines, and operate 20 library centers." A newspaper that complained of the conditions had its pages reduced from eight to four by the military government. Roehner notes that information about retaliation, for example, a British Army captain killed by automatic gun fire on May 31, 1946, appears only in the *North*

China Daily News, suggesting that postwar, the Western media continued at least some form of censorship. This included attacks on German trains in 1946 found reported only in the Shanghai papers, and a Japanese report that by August 19, 1945, waves of suicides had engulfed Germany, with whole families dying, 1,200 people in Berlin alone. However, this last was published only ten days after Hiroshima, and could have been Japanese propaganda.[262]

By April 1946, 500 rape cases per week were being reported to the Judge Advocate General of American forces in Europe but certainly not to the American public. During May and June 1946 there were five instances where young German women were found dead in American barracks. Americans also did not hear about incidents of German pedestrians being run over almost daily between 1945-52.[263]

*

"I get so tired of being a cherry chap, friend of every G.I.," Pat admits to her family. "Haven't spoken a cross word or had a temper tantrum in so long now that I'm probably building up for a terrible storm."[264] She didn't lessen the dangers of her profession for her family. Describing a typical day, she writes: "...arriving at camp anywhere from 8 p.m. to 2 a.m. with the roads being strafed occasionally and the worries about motor accidents from blacked-out convoys." Not only does she show up too early before the hotels are cleared of ordnance but sometimes she would lose her way.

It was pouring rain and we got lost. Suddenly we found ourselves in a village where there were no American troops – this about 5:30 p.m. On a dark rainy evening is a mite unpleasant. We (Louis Lochner of the AP, Sid Olsen of *TIME*, and our driver) made a quick turn around when a sniper fired and a few miles back found an infantry company CP. They didn't feel even this town was a good spot for three unarmed correspondents so we turned off and found a battalion CP.[265]

"Warfare here is much like the Pacific, i.e., you can get killed with no trouble at all," she wrote them on April 29, 1945, the day before she arrived at Dachau.

Maybe the family did worry about her, but no one hinted that was the case. Self-censorship on their side? Maybe Pat included these hints of danger because she wanted a little credit for her bravery as a woman. At the time her brother Lloyd was stationed in DC as a lieutenant commander in charge of procuring petroleum products.[266]

*

Or is the reason I can't pin down the exact dates of her Goering interviews because she censored her letters home and in the press, alluding to her accomplishments but leery of being too exact for fear her reports and letters would not get through? Although she wasn't reporting on the spot, dateline tomorrow, she had to be careful.

*

I screw up my courage and email Steve's brother Jay to ask if I can read Pat's letters. To my great surprise, he agrees. I am ecstatic. But he says they are too fragile to ship. Does he mean it's too much trouble to put them all in boxes, or sending them to me represents a loss of control? It would be great to talk to him at length because he was close to his mother, especially in her final days. He was her executor, he threw things out, he suffered most under seventeen years of the jealous guardianship of her last lover, the guy next door who served under Dickson during the war.

I have to fly to Hawai'i to really talk, and of course, to read the letters. While I mull how to afford the airfare, Covid sets in. An eleven-hour flight to Hawai'i? No way. I convince my brother-in-law to scan her correspondence. "There are so many letters," he says. "She kept duplicates of every letter she mailed for sixty years." He will make the selection.

*

Civilians don't realize how carefully the military controls its image. It must constantly monitor civilian perceptions of its efforts in order to promote, at the very least, the orderly conscription of citizens. "It's only public opinion that translates into the soldier's mind the things to win wars with and makes them want to fight," according to Dwight Eisenhower.[267] Propaganda props up leadership from the top to the bottom, censorship blinds civilians to all but the positive.

Today the military insists on nearly complete control of information, especially in this era of instant transmission. Voila, within seconds, everyone in the entire world—including the enemy—are able to view a report. Unlike WWII, Korea, and Vietnam, it is now possible for the press to broadcast directly from the battlefield. Without censorship, and its close friend propaganda, the military can't plan strategy or be assured that some loose-lipped reporter won't compromise its efforts.

*

Unexpected is the pairing of a censor and a journalist. The correspondents write, the public relations officers (PROs) censor. Is it proximity, the intimacy of someone carefully going over your every word that's attractive? In Martha Gellhorn and Virginia

Cowles' play, *Love Goes to Press*, one of the women correspondents falls very hard for the PRO, but at the last minute chooses the battlefront over the staid country living he has in mind for her as his bride.[268]

*

After Pearl Harbor, the FBI covered for the country until the censorship office was fully implemented.[269] For example, the press reported that Pearl Harbor lost only one (old) battleship (eight were sunk) and a single destroyer (there were three, and seven more ships either sunk, capsized or were heavily damaged) and made no mention of the 200 planes that were lost. The Japanese knew exactly what had happened, but the Americans didn't want the public to know how badly they'd been surprised. Hawai'i immediately went under military rule, no media at all was allowed.[270] There was plenty not to talk about: over 2,000 Hawai'ians of Japanese descent were interned and sent to the mainland, and the Allies in the Pacific suffered quite a bit of defeat in the ensuing months, in the Philippines, Singapore, the Dutch East Indies, Wake Island, New Britain, the Gilbert Islands and Guam. Even weather forecasting was censored to "little change in temperature" or "much cooler."[271] When the US Army Air Corps assigned Dickson to Hickam Air Force Base in Hawai'i to oversee public relations for the Pacific, he had plenty of work to do.

*

Recently, censorship has made startling inroads on the American concept of free speech, a prime example being the banning in Tennessee of the graphic novel *Maus* about a son learning about his parents' experiences during the Holocaust, with animals as characters. That even a minority of the American public want no reminder of the tragedy of the Holocaust means that they long to forget history and human decency in an embrace of antisemitism. That longing is also an admission of guilt that they share the same hatred, the root cause of such violence. And then, of course, the book banning in Florida and elsewhere, focusing in particular on the history of Black Americans. The legislative push for banning critical race theory that amounts to whitewashing the importance of slavery in our history destroys any notion of responsibility and paves the way for rampant and continued racism. If the history of six million Jews under the extreme cruelty of the Nazis and of four million enslaved people of color in America can be forgotten, who's next? As the famous quote by Lutheran pastor Martin Niemöller, ironically an early supporter of Hitler, lays out: First they come for the Communists, then the trade unionists, then the Jews, and then you.

Replace "Communists" with "immigrants."

*

If the government doesn't want the truth reported, the media doesn't want the truth reported, the reporters don't want to report the truth, and the public doesn't want to hear the truth, what is the role of the journalist? Entertainment? Perhaps Fox News has it right.

*

An oblique and seldom recognized alternative for those refusing to self-censor is the subversive writing of poetry. Few read it, making it a safe venue for difficult disclosures. A kind of telling and not-telling, poetry has always been particularly popular in repressive regimes, including Iran and Russia and many South American countries under dictatorships. The genre often contains all the truth that can be found, and in those countries, poets are often jailed despite their "telling it slant." Even Plato said that poetry is "nearer to truth than history." Maybe it will become more important in the US.

Poetry can compress equivocal truths to create succinct, emotionally-driven messages that affect readers more than pages of statistics or long speeches. These messages lie very close to the engine of advertising, although poets seldom go into that trade. Hart Crane was employed by the J. Walter Thompson agency in the twenties and hated it: "I got so I simply gagged every time [sic] I sat before my desk to write an ad."[272] Much-lauded US poet laureate James Dickey hustled Coca-Cola in the seventies and excelled. "If you work for the Coca-Cola Company," he said, "the first thing you're told is how many people's jobs and lives depend on the drink and how old and venerable and honorable the company is."[273] He also worked for Armour Fertilizer Works, a firm that produced toxic fertilizer as well as uranium from phosphoric acid, a process that permanently contaminates the environment.[274] His biography, *The World as a Lie*, depicts a man who made lying a literary strategy and a protective camouflage. With regard to his poetry, he believed in the "creative possibility of the lie."[275] Even his family and closest friends didn't know what was myth and what was true about him.

Journalist Paul Hendrickson interviewed Dickey about his arguably most famous poem, "The Firebombing," from *Buckdancer's Choice*, a book that won the National Book Award in 1966. With great bravado, the poem delves into the sense of power pilots feel when flying missions high above targets while detached from the destruction and death they cause below. Dickey boasted that he'd done one hundred flights over the Pacific during WWII when he actually flunked flight school on his first try at soloing as an aviation cadet. What he became was the onboard radar operator, seated in the back of the plane, often not even facing the direction of the target. Why did his lie to Hendrickson matter? Hendrickson's father had flown the same plane that Dickey claimed to have flown seventy-five times on similar runs. Hendrickson felt the lies belittled his father's accomplishment and cheapened the risks he had taken in the war. But didn't the poem deliver a succinct emotionally-driven message to everyone else? Dickey once said: "To have guilt you've got to earn guilt, but sometimes when you earn it, you don't feel the guilt you ought to have."[276] That tortured explanation is what "The Firebombing" is really about. He'd managed to write a poem that touched readers because he was guilty of its lies, not because he felt guilty about dropping napalm on innocent civilians from his perch in the sky. Hendrickson forgave Dickey anyway. Dickey's son, a friend of Hendrickson's, told him that he'd found his father's baby book after his death. His mother had stuffed it full of childhood clippings dating all the way up to his young adulthood. She'd wanted too much of him.[277]

9

True Love

Just a few months after Pat "identified" Hitler's ashes, four newspapers, including the *New York Times* and the *Washington Post*, announced her betrothal to Henry Bull, a Lieutenant Commander who spent the war expediting the delivery of refrigerators critical for plasma and other perishables. No combat did he suffer. Not terribly handsome, perfectly nice and bland, he loved parties and held plenty of them in Washington. He was from the West, with a grandfather who had been a doctor at the Oklahoma Land Rush, a man who fixed someone's broken leg rather than stake a claim. Perfectly nice. Very reliable.

*

Boyfriend Dickson cabled her in October 1945 while she was supposedly chasing Hitler in South America. In a Connecticut hospital for some unspecified ailment, he was awaiting discharge from the military, and wondering why he hadn't received the "long, long" letter she promised she'd sent from Guatemala.[278]

By then she'd been engaged to Henry for over a month. "I'm really the last madchen left now," she had written to her family in June, her siblings all married off.[279] All her friends were getting married too. The pressure must have been intense. Pat wanted to please her father who was now international vice president of Standard Oil, working in Washington to organize fuel supplies for the Marshall Plan.[280] However, he was perhaps not the best example of marital contentment as he was living the high life with his secretary and soon to die from cirrhosis of the liver.

She flew to Oakridge immediately after the bomb dropped in Japan, and then to Washington for Henry's victory party, which must have been when he proposed.[281] She'd known him since 1943, when she was working for the Office of War Information and freelance for magazines. A "chum and gin rummy partner," he suddenly converted into a suitor and started courting "with food, drink and theater tickets" for Pat, and steaks and bacon for her mother. He was "a very lovable character and a good companion" and ten years older—like Dickson.[282] The description does not sound like passion. D.C. was filled with thousands of "government girls," as the women workers were called, ready to go home and make babies at war's end, and an equal number of exuberant GIs. The two-day party must have been quite intoxicating.

*

"Over my dead body" is the term used to describe a situation impossible to accept, like Dickson's who found out about the engagement through a third party. A month later, he was featured in a full-page ad in the *New York Times* touting *Colliers* as the place to put your post war advertising dollars.[283] He would bury himself in his work.

Yet he himself was still married to someone else.

*

In one of the Fuhrerbunker's warren-like underground rooms, Hitler told his secretaries over lunch that his dead body must not fall into the hands of the Soviets.[284] Two days after his suicide, the Soviets were first on the scene in Berlin, and shortly thereafter they started the rumor that Hitler had fled to Argentina. Stalin wanted to be sure that certain people knew he was dead, but was equally concerned that this fact be hidden from England and the US. Why is unclear. His soldiers had already disposed of the body when, in a show of pure theatrics, Stalin berated his own commander-in-chief Marshal Georgi Zhukov over his failure to find it. In an additional twist, Pravda insisted that rumors that Hitler's body had been found were a fascist provocation, and that Hitler was alive and well and being looked after by the treacherous Americans in their zone of occupation.[285]

*

In Pat's wedding photo, her tuxedoed father looks quizzical, as in *Where's the champagne?* but perhaps all fathers do at their daughter's wedding. After all, he's giving her away. The bridesmaids walking before the two of them do not look joyful but downcast, even a little sorrowful. Do they feel this is less of a joyous occasion than it should be? Pat's big smile is aimed at them, as if to convince them of her happiness. Do they suspect the marriage won't last? Or are they bored by all the weddings, one after another during this postwar period, and why not them? Or is it that their off-the-shoulder gowns are slipping? They are wearing very fashionable tilted-back turbans and carrying what appears to be, in black and white, decorative cabbages. They can't be cabbages. Pat is trying to hold onto her father, but his white glove does not quite clasp her. It is December 7, 1945. The war has been over barely eight months, and most of the time Pat has been traveling all over South America and Europe.

"The idea is...for her to stop trotting around the globe," writes Henry to his parents. "I am a very happy person."[286]

*

Pat's first wedding, 1946

Propaganda was Pat's stock-in-trade, as well as Dickson's, as a public relations expert. Pat was soon hired as a vice-president at Carl Byoir & Associates, then the largest public relations firm in the world. Like Edward Bernays, Byoir had been very involved in establishing public relations as a recognized profession. He led the US propaganda effort in WWI, and afterwards landed a contract with the Cuban dictator Gerardo Machado to promote Cuba's image. Skirting the issues of widespread poverty and organized crime syndicates that turned Havana into a haven for prostitution, brothels and gambling, Byoir doubled tourism in a year, and made his company profitable.[287] Pat specialized in magazines at the firm and hired Dickson as a freelancer to plant articles for clients. At the time, Dickson also had a syndicated column, perhaps facilitated by Pat's old CBS friend, Louis Ruppel who by 1952 had become head of the first newspaper syndicate in the US. Pat and Dickson must have scheduled a few business lunches.

*

The kidnapping of Steve and his brother Jeff, aged four and three, by their mother, occurred sometime at the end of 1952. I say sometime because the bulk of the story comes from Louise, Steve's stepmother's sister-in-law, and is perhaps broadly censored—but also backed up by the FBI who were investigating Dickson at the time. At least once the two boys were sent to live in Harlem with Shawnee, their part-Cherokee nanny, while their parents worked on their relationship. Henry argued that he did not want a divorce, he was willing to forgive Pat her indiscretions. Carpe diem was the lesson of Pat's time at the front: she had her life to live and Dickson, was determined to wrest her away. "I think...that it would be best for some people to feel this was a decision taken on your own and not with a specific guy in mind. Then when I do the whirlwind courtship it will be considered romantic instead of a plot."[288] Schemes were hatched, liaisons took place (the FBI interviewed the bellhop and clerk at their hotel) and surely tears were shed. She went in and out of the hotel with Dickson for nearly a year, until she did what her lawyer suggested, and told no one when she took the boys to Florida, where Dickson was establishing the required ninety-day residency for his own divorce.

Steve remembers only arriving at a barren crab-grassed Florida backyard. The FBI interviewed the landlady.[289] They were investigating Dickson, part of a McCarthy sweep of UNICEF.

When Pat didn't return with the boys for Christmas, Henry broke down under the tree. Good friends rescued him and told him to give up, she wasn't coming back. Henry finally signed the divorce papers. He never wanted to see the boys again. After all, they looked like her side of the family, and he would be reminded of her every time they visited. Besides, he considered them brainwashed co-conspirators, having spent all that time with Dickson in Florida. His antipathy regarding the boys was only overcome through the intercession of his mother-in-law, Franklyn Lochridge.

At college, Pat had some kind of breakdown around her relationship with her mother, and saw an analyst almost daily, so the mother/daughter bond must have been very fraught.[290] Of course her mother would've argued that a daughter needs a proper husband, not an affair with a married man. But over the seven years of her marriage, Pat had fulfilled the wifely role: she'd borne two children, de rigueur of the period and presumed sufficient to seal and bind the union. Children or no children, seven years is a long time if you're with the wrong person. One or both of the spouses were living a lie: Pat, that she loved anyone but Dickson, and Henry that he could bear having a high-powered career woman as a wife. He could tolerate an affair though, or at least he thought he could, but he was no match for Dickson and Pat's plans.

*

Dickson's wife at the time was Ruth Adams Knight. Their divorce made both the *Palm Beach Post* and the *Miami Herald*.[291] Newspapers described Knight as the author of many children's books. She also eventually published twelve books for adults, won an O. Henry prize for a short story, and produced more than one successful radio series.[292] She was awarded the divorce on the grounds of "extreme cruelty and habitual intemperance." The terms sound so dramatic and libelous but getting a divorce then required grounds, and thus drama in the language of the proceedings at the very least. Divorce lawyers had to promote two sides of a "truth" to get their clients to agree. Pat asserted that Dickson's drinking began as the result of Knight's extravagance but his divorce from his first wife twenty-five years earlier also cited alcohol. Dickson complained that Ruth built a swimming pool at their country house, and bought Currier & Ives prints at $150 each.[293] At least he did not beat her as he did the boys while Pat was away in New York, or is that what "extreme cruelty" suggests?

The year Ruth married Dickson she published *Women Must Weep*, a novel with a despairing heroine who falls for "Dick," who then forces her to divorce her husband and marry him, just what Dickson had done to Pat—and very likely, Ruth. It was probably Ruth who ratted out Dickson to the FBI. Two of her friends were informants.[294]

*

While filming in Sudan, my ex-to-be and I visited a man with ten wives. He was delighted to see us: the wives were on strike, objecting to his courtship of an eleventh because he had not paid for the last. Cows were the currency, but their shortage hadn't suppressed his uxorial desires. His delight with us had to do with lunch. Nuer men don't cook, and the women's strike meant that he had to scrounge up his own food or go hungry, but our arrival was an occasion that had to be properly met with a full celebratory spread that he, as the patriarch, must attend. We did not find out these details until lunch was nearly over, when his wives refused to respond to the great praise he gave them for their cooking and burst out with their story of the strike instead.

Our encounter did not discourage my ex's dream of polygamy. Take-out is the solution, he said after we returned to New York, and introduced me to his new girlfriend, a Brazilian. She would not live in New York all the time, he protested. Half the year?

*

The US divorce rate reached an all-time high of 43 percent in 1946, the year Pat married Henry.[295] Was this the result of returning GIs rethinking very hasty marriages? Of women's recognition that they didn't want to return to the kitchen? Pro-marriage propaganda revved up in response, until the percentage of divorces plunged to nine percent in the fifties, the decade they divorced.[296] Divorced women were treated as pariahs then, with marriage counseling books accusing the wives as the cause for the failure.[297] Why didn't she change the menu, wash his clothing more often, keep the children quiet? Marriage was to be forever. Pat bucked the propaganda and put her writing career first, and that was quite acceptable to Dickson. The wife he'd just divorced had certainly put hers first, with all her publications and radio work. Besides, Dickson was older, a smooth talker, handsome, and a bit mysterious about his background, as befitting of someone with the persuasive talents of public relations-in-charge-of-censorship. When Pat first met him on her very first trip to the Pacific, she said he "wondered who that girl was that had her feet on his desk talking to a sergeant at 8:30 in the morning."[298] Only later did she learn about his first divorce and his sixteen-year-old son—and current wife. Under the palm trees, the warm tropical breeze, the six weeks of dark nights with alcohol-infused intimacy in Hawai'i, a place renowned for its romance, how could she resist? She became his third wife as soon as her divorce came through.

*

In the early eighties my husband made *Kidnap*, an award-winning short film, using footage from old family films and still photos to tell the story of his mother's kidnapping. He wanted to wring his own truth out of whatever visual evidence he could find: his father waving a white hankie goodbye to a departing car, Steve hugging the nanny Shawnee, the two boys flailing in the ocean, Pat beside a huge fish caught where—surely Florida—photos of a doomed twinkling Christmas tree. Steve speaks about the kidnapping as key to his emotional disorientation, the moment when wind slammed all the doors shut on the big Shelter Island summer house his parents bought for a pittance while they were married, the only property his mother let Henry keep after the divorce. A loud, final boom.

*

I divorce you, I divorce you, I divorce you, said my ex, standing on a Sudanese riverbank one afternoon. That's how the Arabs do it, he said, repeating the phrase another three times. It could be that easy. My first divorce six years earlier was nearly as simple. We were childless, and since that husband abandoned me, the papers were signed by mail. My second, with the aforementioned riverbank lecturer, ended with split custody. Not so fashionable these days. What it afforded the child was a struggle at every exchange, an extension of the grounds for divorce in the first place. My son would try to put our hands together whenever we met.

My ex did not exactly force me to become pregnant, but for nearly a year we had been living in cultures that revered children, and in near complete isolation from Europeans and Americans, people who most easily could advise me. He began a campaign for a child, saying he was 33, Christ's age when he died, and he didn't want to die without one. That kind of malarky should've tipped me off that his interests were purely selfish, but the intense dark of the countryside was populated by jackals, the occasional hyena and machine-gun toting rebels, the cement-like dirt we slept on was hard, and his caresses were not.

*

Pat and Dickson married in Forest Hills, with Maurice Pate, head of UNICEF, as best man.[299] The day before, Dickson's syndicated column ended with "A good dog is harder to find these days than a good wife."[300] Did he mean he hadn't looked very far? The boys were not invited to the ceremony but flew alone, aged four and five, to Colorado to stay with their grandmother during

Dickson Hartwell marries Patricia
Lochridge Bull, 1953

their honeymoon. When the boys returned two weeks later, they moved back in with the newlyweds, and spent weekends and vacations with their father Henry in a nearby apartment or on Shelter Island. This was the customary division at the time, but since Pat was seldom home, the boys saw her even less, and their father was busy at work. That left nannies or Dickson, when he too wasn't traveling.

Confronted by the film and Steve's narration, Pat refused to believe that the stepfather beat them until nearly the end of her life. Surely it was just the evil stepparent syndrome, she maintained, where children resent the new parent for replacing the old. But her niece, an occasional houseguest, remembered how he yelled at the boys.[301]

*

In the middle of Steve's 1995 interview of Pat, which he did as a favor for Nancy Sorel, who was researching her book *The Women Who Wrote The War,* he asks: "At one time you told me the reason they [the military] had asked you to come up there [Berlin] was in part to verify Hitler's death in order to prevent any resurgence of neo-Nazism after he died." She says: "Well, that's true." And she goes on to talk about her trip to South America—but says nothing about the photo.

*

My ex's ex was Marcel Duchamp's secretary, and he played chess with Duchamp, who would play anyone. I don't remember who won. Before her, he had a relationship with a glamorous UN translator of French and professional caster of spells. I was never sure whether he wasn't still under her influence. The one who came after me was a sex therapist. How did a poet fit in?

Five years ago, he died at home of cancer. He wouldn't have had medical insurance. When I lived with him, he had no social security card and paid no taxes and prided himself on such freedoms. Funds were always tight. He scavenged the trash for delectable tidbits, including old restaurant food, his most bounteous discovery being a hundred rounds of nearly-off Boursin. I never ate Boursin again.

*

Steve's father's Shelter Island house, where he spent all his childhood summers, can almost be seen from our tiny summer cottage that faces Greenport Harbor. His was a Dutch colonial with many bedrooms and had doors that were hung so well that they shut in almost any breeze, a slamming that defined his parents' divorce.

The doors of our shellfish shucking shack just across the water must be always coaxed.

Greenport cottage view, 2018

10

Abuse, Begetter of Lies

When Hitler was abused by his father as a child, his mother tried to put an end to it. "She [the mother] goes up to the attic, covers Adolf who is lying on the floor, but cannot deflect the father's final blow. Without a sound he absorbs it," according to Hitler's half sister and brother. Later Hitler told his secretary that eventually he simply stopped crying while his father beat him, and counted the blows as they came.[302]

Famed psychologist Alice Miller repeatedly suggested that Hitler's abusive regime can be traced to this treatment by his father. "Unconscious programming to be violent [begins] in every case with a brutal upbringing that demanded absolute obedience and expressed total contempt for the child." How did Hitler's father get away with such cruelty to an entire populace? "As recently as 1997, more than half of the parents in West Germany were in favor of corporal punishment as a means of bringing up children," Miller explains.[303] When somebody pushes an unconscious button that brings up the abusive side of a parent's childhood, the child always suffers.

Mary Trump, a clinical psychologist, analyzed her uncle's childhood in *Too Much and Never Enough: How My Family*

Created the World's Most Dangerous Man. According to her, Trump was ignored by his father or yelled at, criticized or punished from a very early age, and his mother, uninterested in him, abandoned him for a year. His father abused his older brother so dreadfully that he died at age 42 of alcoholism. All the while, their marriage tended toward abuse and emotional neglect.[304]

Not all serious harm comes from the belt.

*

Steve isn't surprised to hear that Dickson published "America's Bruised and Beaten Children" in a 1947 *Liberty*. Like many abusers, Dickson was probably beaten himself, and he most probably beat his first son Kent, before moving on to Steve and his brothers. After all, his future had been compromised by a child because he was expelled from the University of Pennsylvania as a freshman for getting a girl pregnant. Is the propensity to beat behavioral, learned, as it were, at the knee of the stepfather? But Steve can scarcely bear to hear of a flaw in his own sons, let alone punish them.

So why aren't you violent? I ask him.

Shawnee, he tells me. My dad must have hired her. She was from Oklahoma, where her children lived. I never thought about why she wasn't taking care of her own children. She made up for the fact that my father was always away working and my mom busy with her PR job or getting out of the house to see Dickson. Shawnee loved me. She wasn't there when Dickson first came on the scene. We had a white nanny in Florida, Barney.

Barney, he repeats.

You sound as if I've hypnotized you.

I'm feeling sorry for myself.

I'm the devil's advocate here: Dickson had his column to write and you two must've been trouble, even with a nanny. After all, you were very small children when they were married.

We had a broken home, as they called it in the fifties. We were sad. Nobody consoled us.

If they feel guilty, adults tend to think that the kids are the adult, or in the case of your father, sad about losing your mother in the divorce, and want the kids to care for him.

We amused Dad, even though he didn't want us. He tested his toys for his business on us. Dickson just wanted us to disappear. My mother denied the whole thing.

What would your mother have said to Nancy Sorel had you not been the one interviewing her?

*

I didn't have the experience of a broken home. Instead my parents were fond of a Disney recording of a mean bat singing: "You're nothing but a nothing, you're not a thing at all." We children knew our position in such a large family—nine kids— and we kept quiet about our powerlessness. When discipline failed, my mother would threaten that Dad would punish us as soon as he came home, and I felt such fear listening to the car pulling up, and of my father taking off his belt. Such punishment was not frequent, however, but we knew it happened to other children too. They spoke of it at school as if it were something expected and even boasted about it. *I got such a thrashing for that!* My father never forgot that power over us. When he was over ninety, my brother and sister and I broached the subject of assisted living. Being too weak physically to attack us, he said he'd sue us unto the grave if he ended up in a "home." And he sued.

*

Dickson liked to keep Steve and his brother hidden behind the door while he told Henry that they were unavailable, torturing both Henry and the boys for several long minutes, only to have them pop out just as Henry gave up and walked down the steps. Dickson also took away the boys' train set and sent it to his grandchildren in California. Why? The boys didn't deserve it. Protest was forbidden and complaint futile. Pat didn't believe their tale of woe, and he beat them harder if he heard they had tried to complain. His son Kent was terrified of him even as a young adult, according to Dickson's secretary who dated him.[305] Dickson's youngest son, born thirty years after Kent, was beaten at age ten for having accused him of cheating at croquet.[306]

*

There's a study that shows that if there is a reasonable chance of increasing parents' wealth with a stepparent joining the family, then there's little difference made between one's own children and stepchildren. But if the stepparent joins the family without money, there's the Cinderella effect, and the stepchildren are neglected or abused.[307] Dickson had thousands of dollars of medical bills when he married Pat.

By beat, you mean more than a spanking? I ask Steve.

More than a spanking, he says.

*

Henry didn't do very well in the divorce settlement. Along with the Shelter Island house, he paid her six percent on the money and property she brought into the marriage and had to provide ample child support. Dickson was hoping for alimony too.[308] He instinctively knew his money-making days were limited, though he resented his dependence on Henry.

You're 40 times more likely to be abused if you have a step-parent, according to a study in 1985, and between 40 to 100 times more likely to be murdered or maimed by them.[309] There's no deep emotional connection to the children, but the intense intimacy of parenting is the same. Did Dickson also neglect the two children he had with Pat? Are his mentions in his letters to her of escorting all four to the park with kites just proof to her that he's taking some care of them? Steve doesn't remember. "I should have hidden better the lack of love," says one stepfather, in an article about the ambivalence of raising someone else's child. This raises the question: Does a stepparent have a moral responsibility to lie about his feelings?[310]

*

Steve and I go deep into our storage space to look for Pat's Hitler photo, pulling down the paintings and drawings Steve inherited from his mother's naive art collection, battling old love letters, a box full of his yearbooks and TV star scripts (*I can sell this!*), Steve's patent for a single-launch low-gravity space station, an Inca ball and cup game, and a letter from Dickson that ends: "We love you mightily. We think you are a great person."

Steve stares at the handwriting, says maybe he underestimated him, maybe he wasn't such an ogre after all.

But I'd recently reread the letters my mother wrote during a similar period in my life and they too did not jibe with my experience. Surely a stepfather who had been awarded a bronze star in public relations as a censor knew what to say on paper.

*

Drinking alone at night after work, Dickson was stuck with at least supervising the care of Pat's boys and walking their two toy poodles, their adoption Pat's idea to assuage the boys' unhappiness after the divorce. Dickson started his career in 1933 by promoting dogs for the blind, would publish his only book, *Dogs Against Darkness*, in 1960, and often wrote about canine care and training in his columns, suggesting in one that it was best for young kids to be put in charge of training dogs "as young as six months."[311] Never mind that dog training should start earlier, and that the kids in question were still only seven and eight. When the boys failed in their attempts at discipline, Pat put the dogs on a train bound for DC, telling the boys they had an appointment to see a dog psychologist who worked for the Post Office.

Skipper and Woofy were never seen again.

*

Pat with Skipper and Woofy, 1953

In the early 1870s it came to national attention that one Mary Ellen Wilson, an eight-year-old orphan, suffered daily whippings at the hands of her foster parents. Children were then considered the property of the father—foster, natural, or step. The American Society for the Prevention of Cruelty to Animals had been founded nine years earlier. The orphan's attorneys argued that laws protecting animals from abuse should not be greater than laws protecting children.[312]

*

Shouldn't I have turned out worse than Hitler? asks Steve. At least Hitler's mother tried to protect him.

Think of it this way, I say, you protected your mother because your stepfather hit you and not her. But look at this. I point to a clipping from the *New York Times* I've found online. The *Times* had to publish a correction of Dickson's obituary because you and your brother were left out.[313]

The final blow.

11

Mothers

Before Covid set in, Steve was commuting to Yonkers as part of a medical start-up. When he stepped off the train one morning, he noticed a statue commemorating the Gold Star Mothers, those whose sons or daughters have died in war, but who organize to help the veterans who do return. Pat had told her sons that after seeing Germany's preparations for war during that biking trip with her brother, she helped found the Future Gold Star Mothers, which was the female counterpart of the newly formed Veterans of Future Wars.

As a lark in 1936, Princetonians organized the Veterans of Future Wars, their version of the VFW, after seeing a newsreel about the veterans of WWI who received bonuses a decade earlier than promised. Their founding principle ran: "Why not pay those bonuses in advance of a war, while dead-soldiers-to-be could enjoy them?" They even had a salute: hand outstretched but with "palm up and expectant" to receive a bonus. The Future Gold Star Mothers' manifesto put forward that a woman would receive her son's pension in advance, but if he came through the war unscathed, she would pay it back. The women also asked for money to visit cemeteries in Europe that might hold their future sons. Their demand was in response to 1930s Congressionally-funded trips for the Gold Star Mothers to the cemeteries and battlefields of WWI.[314]

What the students were really responding to was the increasing likelihood of America's involvement in another world war. While Hitler's propaganda machine was trying to disguise Germany's military designs on the Rhineland, Mussolini's Italy was in the process of conquering Ethiopia, and Japan had already fought with China. Trepidation was high—wasn't the last war billed as "the war to end all wars"? It didn't help that Congress had just concluded that the country had been dragged into the first World War by bankers seeking protection for their European investments, and by the US munitions industry.[315]

Eleanor Roosevelt got the joke but warned that others might not.[316] A Congressman from Arkansas believed "that these young women have been misled and unduly influenced" by the Princeton boys whom he labeled "communistic and un-American." In retaliation, the son of a governor of the territory of Alaska lobbied Congress with engraved invitations to Veterans of Future Wars gatherings, announcing "dancing in the streets between four and six."[317] Representative Maury Maverick, a disgruntled member of the real VFW and Democratic veteran who had earned a Silver Star during WWI, also understood its satiric anti-war message, and promised to introduce legislation in the House in their support.[318]

That the college men made fun of war was one thing—the Veterans of Future Wars' "commander," Lewis Gorin, had an ancestor who had been a general in the Revolutionary War—but the participation of women was another. Telling the women to go back to their knitting was common, and the real Gold Star Mothers were offended by their cynicism.[319] In response, Princeton changed the name of the women's auxiliary to the

Home Fire Division and remained true to their original premise of objecting to fiscal issues, those of irresponsible government handouts.[320] This managed to appeal to both sides: conservative students saw the group as an ally against FDR's spending, and pacifist liberals embraced the opportunity to rally against war and the military. After about a year of activity, the organization declared that their goal of awakening the country to "the absurdity of war" had been fulfilled, and folded, coincident with a number of the founders graduating.[321]

*

The Nazis loved mothers. "Take a pot, a dustpan, and a broom and marry a man," harangued Hermann Goering.[322] Fascists prefer that their women stay barefoot and pregnant in the kitchen. During the war, the Nazis gave mothers concessions on theater tickets and railways, mothers were favored in hospitals, and honor crosses handed out to those who bore many children. But once the war was over, German women were viewed as taking jobs away from returning soldiers, just as they were in America. During the war, American women flaunted Rosie the Riveter as the symbol of women's new role in beating back the fascists, but not when it was over, when capitalism required more consumers. Advertisements touting happy mothers abounded, looking very similar to Nazi propaganda. Both nations wanted women to return to a life of submission under the patriarchy. Most importantly, women were expected to purchase products for the home and teach the children to buy material goods. German mothers were as culpable as their husbands for the Nazi atrocities as those under capitalism are culpable for capitalism's oppressions, the destruction of the environment, and, in the case of mothers under Trump, the caging of children. Or is that fascism?

*

Women at Vassar, not Pat, seem to have been the ones who founded the Future Gold Star Mothers.[323] Perhaps Pat's claim was really that she founded the Wellesley chapter, although that distinction is lost to time. What can be documented is that her college was not so enthusiastic about the organization. An article in the *Wellesley College News* characterized the Princeton founders as "bewildered, thunderstruck young men whose imaginative carnival is getting out of hand."[324] In contrast, a week later, the Wellesley Home Fire Division participated in a huge peace strike involving at least a half million American college students who wanted to "laugh war out of existence."[325]

In an interview in 1990, Pat said: "I was very much into the peace movement."[326] She made a serious commitment by spending a week of the summer of 1936 in Geneva at the League of Nations' World Youth Congress as one of 700 delegates from 35 countries, discussing peace.[327] According to coverage by the *New York Times,* stripling politicians at the gathering faulted the "older generation" for being unable "to get rid of the pre-war conceptions of national self-sufficiency and power politics with the result that Peace is once more endangered."[328] What the 1930s had revealed to the public was the League's powerlessness in the face of serious political confrontation. By 1936, Hitler had marched 22,000 German troops into the Rhineland, in a direct contravention of the Treaty of Versailles. Like Pat, the British journalist Clare Hollingworth studied at the League of Nations a few years earlier, soon becoming the British regional organizing secretary within the British League of Nations.[329] "Geneva was like a seismograph . . . registering all the social and political upheavals of the world," wrote reporter Helen Kirkpatrick while covering the League as a freelance journalist in 1931.[330] It was in 1936 that Kirkpatrick witnessed the suicide of a Czech Jew in the League itself, after the distraught correspondent exclaimed that his country was going to be next.[331]

*

I find a 5"x7" photo in one of Steve's drawers of Pat standing beside a stack of bodies in Dachau. In a letter to her family, she says the sight "removed any last lingering pacifist doubts out of my mind."[332]

*

Director Taika Waititi's Jewish mother told *Variety* in 2020 why she encouraged him to show Hitler in his film *JoJo Rabbit* so idiosyncratically. "When Taika depicts him as the affable hero of a small boy's imagination, our idea of Hitler is skewed like a needle scratching across a record. This imaginary Hitler reminds us of an uncomfortable reality—that in the right climate, what we come to imagine can be deadly."[333] Another inspiration came from his reading that 66 percent of American millennials had never heard of or had no knowledge of the Auschwitz concentration camp.[334]

*

"Every mother wants her son to be protected in combat," Pat writes in "Vultures on the Home Front" for the August 1944 *Woman's Home Companion*.[335] "Taking advantage [of that] . . . several American companies have sold thousands of religious books with light steel covers at high prices through misrepresenting them as physical protection for the heart." She points out that "the ordinary rifle bullet becomes a virtual dumdum bullet upon striking an armored book." Mom is invoked again when Pat writes that mothers (and wives) sometimes paid $100 (the equivalent of $1,500 today) to those who promised to reveal the whereabouts of a soldier taken prisoner, information that was sent to the family for free as soon as it was known. Pat reports that a young woman, preying on these mothers' anxiety to see their sons home, went door to door in Buffalo, collecting money to defray the expenses of the returning soldiers and speed their return, until the FBI caught her.[336]

*

By 1957, three years into her job at UNICEF, Pat had borne two more sons to match her two sons with Henry, Dickson ever needing to even the score. By then they had moved to an East 92nd Street brownstone, with a live-in maid and a driver/handyman. Since Pat always had someone cooking for her, her first act upon establishing domestic duties in the new apartment was to order a case of canned string beans from Macy's. Was that akin to delivering cases of milk to children in Hungary? Perhaps she thought of her children as just another band of starving refugees. Steve says she was more likely to pull out a picture of African children than of her own, a professional hazard of those who serve humanity in general but may not love it in the particular.

*

My mother resigned from the job of mothering after her brain-damaged eighth child went into an institution at 21, the age, she said, at which all her children had to move out. Another of my siblings was schizophrenic, another had grand mal seizures. The brain-damaged son required four years of thirty minutes of therapy four times daily by everyone in the family until he learned to walk. He walked into his institution but was soon strapped to a wheelchair. That's when my mother began to drink seriously. She was not a happy alcoholic and liked to hold grudges. What was she angry about? She had many and mean abusive brothers, her mother was distant, eating a pork chop every night alone, her father, the dentist, forgot to remove her braces, leaving her with buckteeth, she had to marry the man who made her pregnant, not the soon-to-be-millionaire beau Peter Kiewit, she had to bear all these children, live in the wilds of southwestern Nebraska, and endure the success of those without handicaps who left, success she had to forgo because of that first unplanned pregnancy. Would another mother have turned that around? Her final words to me on her deathbed were: I wish you'd never been born. Granted, she meant that my birth, only eight months after her wedding, cut short her ambition to be an artist. She struggled to paint until she had her fifth child.

At least that's what I think she meant.

*

In 1968, Pat talked to Steve about what to do about the draft. When she was his age, she had no idea of the repercussions of staying out of war but had learned differently about pacifism at Dachau. It was a warning that his anti-war efforts should be carefully considered. At the same time, she certainly didn't want him going to Vietnam. She knew what war was like. Service, even in the 1970s, would not be at all similar to the UMT (universal military training) demonstration she saw while writing her article "Good and Different" in 1947, when the military treated teenagers to luxurious quarters, good food, entertainment, and guidance counselors in an experiment with mandatory service. That program was cut quicker than someone could say "Congress."[337] Classified 1A, Steve had to decide between going to Canada, enlisting or being conscripted, and developed such severe stomach pain while making the decision that Pat suggested a doctor who confirmed the diagnosis of an ulcer.

*

Working for UNICEF, Pat could assuage the guilt of not being around to raise her own children by saving so many others. The "someone has to do it" rationale. But didn't all the working mothers of that generation suffer such confusion? Since the turn of the century, pediatric authorities had urged stay-at-home mothers to keep strict child-rearing schedules and maintain a "seen and not heard" attitude, especially among the upper classes, who had nurses assigned to their children's care. Even the US government circulated a pamphlet in 1922 that warned against "excessive" affection by parents for their children.[338] Dr. Spock's revolutionizing book on child-rearing, advocating for closeness between mother and child, was published in 1946, two years before Pat had her first child, happily coinciding with a huge contingent of women abandoning their jobs for the rigors of childcare. But for women like Pat trying to make their mark in art or business or law or medicine, the cold wire monkey of psychologist Harry Harlow would have to be the better model. In Harlow's psychological experiments, rhesus monkeys preferred surrogates who were covered with a soft cloth to the bare wire mother surrogates that offered milk.[339] In short, the mother who brought home the bacon (the milk!) offered less comfort than the plush mother without.

*

Steve was applying for a passport at the age of sixteen when he discovered he was born on March 6, not 7. His mother hadn't noticed. And he was her firstborn.

*

Early in 1982, I sit abreast of my mother-in-law, my breasts dripping, the baby logrolling thighs. Who makes up the rest of the crush? Steve's cousin, asleep on the far side of my mother-in-law, and Steve in the driver's seat, talking about a film he hopes to make with a producer on the passenger side. I have married another filmmaker. The producer says *Whoa!* like that, in exclamation when Steve stops, ass-to-bumper-kissing, on the bridge into New York named after an unpronounceable Pole. The truck driver behind us crushes gears, threatening to tap us too, then guns his engine.

All four lanes halt.

Like at the top of a Ferris wheel, I say, trying to sound cheerful. We are on the Up. Cheer is what I've decided is the best tack to take with an in-law who has not only identified Hitler's ashes and broadcast for CBS but also worked for UNICEF. At least that line of work suggests that she has had some concern for children. Toward her son, she has warmed up to a distant, pleased-enough affection. She hasn't comprehended—her verb—grandchildren, but she is game. She touches her grandson's foot when he beats her leg in the ecstasy of milk-lust; she is sure he has her eyes. She is examining him now while I have him suspended by the underarms, head bobbing, drooling, irresistible. She has a second chance.

The drivers beside us crack their car doors. Try the radio, says the producer beside Steve, and then follows his own suggestion and tunes in—sports news—high pops from the outfield—temperature, cool enough to roll down the windows.

Where are those traffic helicopters when you need them? Steve says, tapping on the windshield near the crack we hope his mother will notice and offer to fix. Hope fills our car from windshield crack to baby-suck to the cocked ears of all, especially my mother-in-law, who casts out a comment regarding her son and his proposed project, surely to avoid admitting she finds babies dull and disorderly, including the one now kicking at her. She had her nannies, and back then saw the city's skyline from the top of skyscrapers during the cocktail hour. I suspect she now harbors the cocktail kind of hope.

I roll down the window and stick my head out. All that hope escapes. Someone adult many cars ahead is crying.

The baby cries too, drowning the other out, but we have all heard it. I roll the window up, the baby lunging for the opening.

An accident, says the producer in front. Must be bad.

Those others who cracked their doors have already shut them, to keep the AC in, if not the crying out.

If it were an execution in the 19th century, crowds would have gathered, I say.

I have a special knack for the dreadful.

My mother-in-law presses her fingers to the window and mentions liberating Dachau, so we know she has heard cries.

The caught fly that no one will kill flies *zzut, zzut*, behind the car visor and is now doing its hair with its legs, says the producer who brushes his hand at his own hair during in the peculiar silence we have after the mention of Dachau. In the car ahead of us swivels a plastic hula girl every time the boy in back shifts in his seat to get a better look at us. Wide-eyed, he must have heard the crying too, all their windows are down. His mother turns in her front seat and threatens him, in word or deed, to sit still and he does, for about three seconds.

Somebody better check, I say.

I have the hormones of life rushing through me, I can't help it.

Steve gets out, takes off his sunglasses and tosses them back into the car. This is no movie, says his cousin, blinking awake, vis-à-vis the producer in the front seat, who doesn't budge.

I roll down the window again. I'd go, I say, but—

The baby dances in my lap with hidden agenda, like more milk.

The producer waves Steve and the cousin off with an *I'll-take-care-of-them* gesture. Soon they are four cars ahead and then I can't see them anymore, weaving between the stopped traffic.

My, my, says my mother-in-law. She says that word of possession whenever anything gets out of her control. I actually like
her because she is so easy to assess: *my* not *your*, telegraphed
good and clear. I've given up trying to convince her that I am
more than a curious hanger-on, that the marriage idea came
from him, the gold to be dug being not readily apparent, and the
jewelry metaphor more diamond-in-the-rough.

The producer tries to talk more about films, a recital of titles
by someone my mother-in-law might enjoy. She warms to him,
but the crying outside is louder now, since I feel it isn't right to
roll up my window against it, and I want to hear Steve if he calls
out. Other cars have rolled theirs down too, perhaps anxious
and curious—did we really hear what we thought we heard?
One or two more follow Steve and his cousin with mincing-in-
between-the-car steps, but without cell phones because those
electronics exist in a more driving-dangerous future than this.
Only green metal boxes with pictures of receivers embossed on
their outsides allow stalled drivers access to 911 now.

This is not a stall, I say, out of the blue.

Steve is not there to tell me to stop being such a drama queen,
nor to give me the eye that says the same in front of his mother
but it's him taking so long that makes me blurt this out. Disaster
is catching, I know, the way women who are friends get pregnant
at the same time. I start talking about all the babies in our area
that have come out of the woodwork, as if wood is some weird
stork, then I stop.

Steve and his cousin's heads pop up over the horizon, carrying the blank faces of shock, especially Steve, who blanches
at every boo-boo the baby suffers. Such faces keep us quiet two
beats after they get back in but it is me, always me, the baby
pulling at my buttons for another milk session, who asks why he
is missing his belt.

Tourniquet, he says.

I had to run off the bridge to find a working phone, says his cousin. He opens his door again and tucks his head to vomit.

Lots of people there now, Steve says.

Okay, this is a bridge, not a tunnel, but a much-anthologized story by Alice Glaser comes to me: random cars gassed in a tunnel en route the beach every weekend as a means of population control. But at least I don't tell it, nursing the baby again.

A person sure can lose a lot of blood, Steve says. He grips the wheel as if it will fly up and hit him, and the traffic starts to creep forward.

The baby belches and everyone laughs, we laugh weirdly and the baby cries, startled.

It's a sweet child, says my mother-in-law, the first plus-plus statement she's made all weekend.

Mom, Steve says, clearing his throat, you won't live forever. He's rehearsed this line, it is supposed to be part of a private talk given when he returns her to her airplane, with regard to our hopes: her happiness, a loan, more letters. Now here this opening line sits.

The cars move more quickly. We pass the tow truck.

You have to be very careful, she says.

Her tact is something more to admire, I almost have the brains to admit, with the baby finally asleep, and an exhaustion no longer possible to contemplate.

*

Mothers formed human barricades as the "Wall of Moms" at the Portland Black Lives Matter demonstrations at the end of July 2020. "Fathers Against Fascism" appeared beside them, armed with leaf blowers to force the tear gas back on the police, and to prevent protesters from being taken away in unmarked cars.[340]

Trump armed his federal squads with their own leaf blowers.

*

In 1944 Pat published "The Mother Racket," a powerful expose of rightwing women's groups spreading the "the three d's of Hitlerism—disunity, distrust and defeatism." She traveled to five cities, Cincinnati, Chicago, Detroit, Flint and Philadelphia, and found six organizations "making political capital of the name mother." Mothers of Sons Forum, We, the Mothers, American Mothers, Loyal American Mothers, National Blue Star Mothers of America, and Mothers and Daughters of Pennsylvania rallied around the pro-fascist antisemitic America First Committee, at one time the largest anti-war organization in the US. Although some of the women professed to be Daughters of the American Revolution with framed membership certificates, they also believed that the DAR was a Communist front organization working with the Parent Teacher Association and the League of Women Voters. One of the leaders, a presidential hopeful with a seventy-five-page platform, said that it might be easier to shoot their opposition "than to fool with elections," and added "let's keep a clothesline handy in every little backyard to hang the traitors, or a gun." One of the organizers admitted that their members were "rather stupid."[341]

Pat mentions in an interview that while researching the article she was "hounded by detectives." She was threatened, and so was the magazine, but they stood by her.[342] "The Mother Racket" was received with much discussion: ten newspapers critiqued it. Eleanor Roosevelt's files show that the FBI also reviewed it and called Pat the "wood pussy" of journalism. I am familiar with the salacious overtones of "pussy," but the two words together also denote a class of small boat Steve used to race on Long Island Sound—and they also mean "skunk." Why would the FBI call Pat a skunk? Is it slang for someone deemed to be despicable or contemptible? It sounds as if she were worth being watched.

I've asked the FBI for her files. So far only Dickson's have appeared.

*

My mother, pregnant with me, and two of my aunts, equally pregnant, lived together one summer in a farmhouse in Nebraska with Grandma a few years after WWII. The three pregnant women bickered day and night—and helped each other with washing, cooking, and dressmaking. Grandma made sure that her two sons and her son-in-law had a big lunch when they came in from the field: chicken and noodles, coffee, and kolaches, Bohemian pastries that she kneaded at dawn. My mother said she was a terrible cook, her kolaches could be tacked to the wall, and she put anything she found in the fridge into her noodles. Did my mother say that out of envy, because as a newlywed she could only make grilled cheese sandwiches and fruit salad? Was her mother-in-law critical of her? The aunt that was Grandma's daughter played the piano with such ferocity that Grandma forbade her to continue, saying she'd hurt the baby inside if she kept pounding like that.

During harvest, Grandma made up a thermos of ice and lemonade and the wives vied with each other to walk through the wheat to deliver it, a scene I romanticize as being from Millet's *The Harvesters Resting,* updated to include the big machines, the golden late afternoon, the ripe pregnant woman offering a cold drink to the thirsty men.

*

At a reception in Sudan, I met the wife of an attaché who'd gone to Khartoum's orphanages to help, but the babies she minded kept dying in her arms. At that time, non-Sudanese were not allowed to adopt. Ten years later, eternally grateful for the support I'd had from Nuer women during my sojourn in the Sudan, I thought we might adopt one of the Sudanese orphans, but when I approached an agency in New York, all they offered were crack babies, and none from Africa.

*

My youngest son had just learned to crawl when Steve made him a roach costume for Halloween, and he scuttled around in winged black leatherette. Hilarious—everyone laughed—but now I think that's the stuff of subconscious trauma. Better he remember the next costume: Admiral, with gold braid.

*

When Pat celebrated her 75th birthday, she invited all four boys and their families to Hawai'i. We had a wonderful time. Although she was uninterested in holding my new boy, she did chuckle when he grabbed her hand, and when his brother successfully popped a balloon in the overhead fan. One unbearably hot afternoon while she and the others were elsewhere, I wrapped the baby tightly in the scarf that I used to carry him in, Sudanese-style, and took him down to the beach. After nursing him, I swaddled him in the scarf and left him at the door of an empty cabana that I kept an eye on as I swam. Every second underwater I was terrified he'd be carried away by a tsunami, or that someone would steal him. In the Cook Islands, a mere 2,800 miles away, babies are considered communal property and often end up sleeping in someone else's house—but we are here in America, I told to myself, where babies are trouble; I have nothing to worry about. Nonetheless, I gave up trying to snorkel and just paddled, facing the bundle on the beach, alert to his every wriggle. If some beautifully patterned fish swam around my legs, I had no idea.

*

My now 29-year-old son in New York City unexpectedly calls me midday. We plan our mother/son conversations, so such a call is very unusual. He says he doesn't know how to feel about the conflict between the police and the Black Lives Matter protesters. His roommate's boyfriend is a tattooed Hispanic gay cop who's been reassigned from community development to deal with the riots happening within two blocks of my son's apartment. They are all friends. I tell him the police are paid to keep the peace, it's their job. Sometimes they make mistakes, but they are trained not to. Sometimes they have agendas demonstrators don't know about, like taking down the press. The demonstrators are not organized for anything but loud protest, except for the agitators who have left caches of bricks and rocks hidden all through the city.

From the 11th floor our son can see the fires in the street. Our older son demonstrates enthusiastically elsewhere, having a half-Syrian girlfriend in touch with local politics. I'm not much of a demonstrator anymore, having broken my hip and wrist just walking around, let alone under a policeman's club. The next night I attend a vigil and honk for the twenty protesters in the small Long Island town we're sheltering in. Mostly masked, we're signaling compassion for others, mothering. We must mother.

*

And then there's this.

In 2023 the Indiana chapter of *Moms for Liberty* prominently featured a quote from Hitler on their newsletter "The Parent Brigade." Begun during the pandemic when the women objected to inoculation, masking and the closure of schools, the organization now boasts membership across the country. The Hitler quote, "He alone who owns the youth, gains the future," was taken from a 1935 speech that introduced Germany's Nuremberg Laws, which deprived Jews, gypsies, blacks, and anyone of color citizenship, and forbade intermarriage. One of the *Moms for Liberty* leaders apologized for the quote but received cheers at a national gathering for repeating it.[343]

Moms for Liberty is now concentrated on protesting against LGBTQ rights, race and ethnicity, and critical race theory. The organization has harassed teachers, school librarians, school board members and activists, and they're the primary force behind dismantling the Department of Education and banning books in school libraries. They have even managed to ban the book-length poem *The Hill We Climb* by Amanda Gorman who read it at Biden's inauguration.[344] In New Hampshire, *Moms for Liberty* offered a bounty to anyone who "caught" teachers introducing texts or lessons in violation of the state's new law restricting discussions of race in school classrooms.[345] Another *Moms for Liberty* newsletter suggested that the positive side of the Spanish Inquisition be given equal time with the persecution of Galileo.[346] Like the 1940's Mom organizations, the head of a *Moms for Liberty* group was caught fantasizing about shooting school librarians, saying "they would all be plowed down with a freaking gun."[347]

"Fan the flames" commands their website.

12

Invention

I never heard Henry Bull, my father-in-law, claim he invented
the Whee-Lo, but his proud sons have on occasion. He manufactured and distributed the toy, and made it into a nationwide
sensation in 1953, just before the hula hoop and Frisbee. A
curved double metal track that held a spinning plastic wheel,
the gyroscopic magnetic Whee-Lo is still available for purchase,
most frequently at airport gift shops. By flicking your wrist, you
propel the wheel and its spinning progress down the track and
back. Mesmerizing, it's a sort of fifties analog of the Game Boy.
First called the Magnetic Walking Wheel, it came packaged with
six colorful cardboard discs known as "Whee-lets" that created optical illusions as the wheel spun. According to *Fortune*,
Henry's company, Maggi Magnetics, sold two million units its
first year.[348] Like the hula hoop, which Arthur K. "Spud" Melin
and Richard Knerr claim to have invented in 1958, the Whee-lo
had been around for a while, although maybe not for the
uncounted centuries of the hoop.[349] One version of the Whee-Lo
was known as "Uncle Spinny Dervish" in the thirties.

Someone had given Henry a prototype, which he brought
home to test on his sons. Steve remembers it being about a quarter

of the size of the eventual model. His father had to improve its engineering because the wheel didn't have enough diameter and mass to create sufficient centrifugal energy to spin well. Terrible design, but interesting proof of concept. That someone was paid a licensing fee, and Maggi Magnetics manufactured it and patented improvements to the toy in 1972.

Two stories account for the genesis of Henry's interest in the magnetics business. During the Depression, he managed to get a job selling refrigerators for GE. He became frustrated because he had no way to affix the prices in the showroom until he discovered that magnets held the labels to the fridge fronts without leaving a mark. Voila! The fridge magnet. Dull and utilitarian-looking, he sold them nine to a box, displayed like chocolates, each with its own compartment.

The other story was memorialized by a Bill O'Malley cartoon that ran alongside a *House and Garden* article, "How to get rich in your own basement." It had a cartoon Henry standing in the then fashionable all-steel kitchen, puzzling over where to leave a note eye-level for his wife where she could see it. The article was written by Dickson Hartwell, and it was published in May 1950, three years before Pat divorced Henry to marry Dickson. Had Dickson written it to check out the competition? "When Bull discovered his wife was forever losing her kitchen pencil just when he needed it, he designed a magnetic pencil . . . It clings to the side of a refrigerator like a leech and refuses to get mislaid." (No Freudian overtones there.) Did Dickson even bother to interview Henry or did Pat just feed him the information? Despite the bitterness of his divorce, Henry saved the clipping for fifty years, with his name underlined. He was grateful for the exposure, damn the wife.[350]

*

Why was it called Maggi Magnetics? I ask Steve.

At eight I had a girlfriend named Magda.

No, he says later. That's what I told Magda. I think my father liked the alliteration.

*

Whee-lo, 1953

Astronauts took the Whee-Lo into space three times, on the six-teenth flight of NASA's Space Shuttle program, the fourth flight of the Space Shuttle "Discovery," and the third flight of the "Endeavor" in 1993.[351] They used it to demonstrate the conser-vation of momentum, angular momentum, magnetics, rotational and translational kinetic energy, and phase locking, but I suspect they were just as enamored of its mind-numbing challenges as the school children they were addressing during their on-flight experiments.

*

In 1984, Russians were interested in Steve's patent for a single launch low-gravity space station. The film business he'd worked in as an assistant director had slacked off, and he hadn't yet applied to NYU's Interactive Telecommunications Program; instead he was tinkering with inventions, like his father.

He brought the patent pending space station to Brighton's International Aeronautical Federation Conference, where Russians, looking more KGB than space scientist, asked for a meeting. He was so taken aback by the hangar-sized room they'd rented for interviews, especially the tiny shed they'd built in the very middle, complete with a dangling single light bulb, that he refused to talk. He wasn't going to be the next Manchurian candidate. Most likely the Soviets lacked the capital for setting up a decent conference display, but just a few years earlier, CIA operative Uri Geller, an expert in bending spoons with his mind, had given President Jimmy Carter a four-hour briefing on the Soviets and their efforts in the field of psychic manipulation.[352]

*

Steve's mother bought him an erector set, and not his brother, sole acknowledgement of her son's interests. She thought he should be a minister because he mediated so well, having had a lot of practice between the divorced parties. Where was she when Steve and a friend disassembled a high energy transformer from a TV tube to create an antenna a hundred yards long? Probably in Europe, said Steve. She wasn't around in the summer. Hoping for international reception, the two boys stretched a wire between the house and the detached garage where they kept their ham radio. At breakfast, a bolt of lightning struck the antenna and one ball of lightning went into their workshop and another into the house. Fortunately, nothing caught fire.

Steve studied anthropology in college instead of engineering, trying to please her instead of his father. A mistake, he acknowledges now.

*

Every night for six weeks! Really?

That was my response after the first night of Steve's space plant experiment, actually about an hour into the first night. Proof-of-concept for space farming in low earth orbit consisted of three layers of flats filled with plants under grow lights calibrated to mimic space time in lunar orbit. Forty-five minutes on, forty-five minutes off. That I was a farmer's daughter did not improve my appreciation for this experiment. The baby also did not appreciate this experiment. We slept in a loft above the lights, but no amount of curtaining could conceal the change. Just as the baby would start to relax, the lights switched on or off. The astronauts used blindfolds to avoid madness, but the baby wouldn't wear one, and I needed the baby to sleep. You, I said rather pointedly to my husband, can sleep through anything.

This particular experiment was cut short.

*

In the late nineties, Steve left the film business and graduated from NYU and we moved to Menlo Park where he worked in Paul Allen's think tank, Interval Research. It was nirvana for inventors: they sat around in teams (like comedy writers!) and thought up ideas for things you didn't know you even needed, like Steve's U-in-a-Movie, an arcade device that inserted your automatically-directed performance into an existing movie (you're a fake star!), and a music sensor that plays Jimi Hendrix's guitar at Seattle's Experience Museum (now the Museum of Pop Culture).

*

When I married Steve, I said if you're really an inventor, why fool around, why not harness lightning? I bought him Leyden jars. He suggested I hold the end of the kite string. When climate change arrived, I said why not save the world? So he patented Artificial Sea Ice, a system for containing icebergs, which should, in turn, slow their melting. One of his boyhood friends, Lawson Brigham, is one of the world's authorities on shipping and navigating sea ice. He was interested, and so was Steve's doppelganger, a European Steve Bull who headed expeditions to glaciers in Greenland. Funding remains a problem. Then suddenly everyone needed ventilators for the pandemic. Steve made a homemade ventilator with parts from the hardware store and one small Arduino kit. A wearable iron lung, the Venti is non-invasive and designed to keep patients out of the hospital. Awarded a FDA's Compassionate Use special permit, he has one patient so far, a polio survivor who is very grateful.

Steve and his Venti, a wearable
iron lung, 2025

There was also the Musical Chair a few years earlier, which could be played by pumping its seat, varying the tone like a trombone with oscillator pitches.

*

Was all this inventing to get his mother's attention? She seldom responded, and he often moved on, hoping to find something else that would catch her eye. I understood. After I raised a half million dollars for the PBS film project, instead of congratulating me, my mother asked why I was laying my laurels at her feet. And why do I keep writing so many books?

*

Author, Amy Hempel, Susan Minot c. 1995

Together Steve and I designed The Fat Game, and a board game to improve psychotherapy. Game agents were not enthusiastic about either. Governors' Island exhibited "Our Town Selfie," a cellphone project that combined my reworked Thurber script adjusted for virtual actors who "phoned in" their performances in real time and were then combined into a full performance, but the tech (then) was very slow. We worked on an electronic game called "It," a cat and-mouse hide-and-seek interactive outdoor cell phone game that won several prizes. For a number of years, Steve traveled to campuses across the country as an MC, organizing treasure hunts using cellphone clues I would figure out from college websites. One favorite involved invading the women's bathroom for a clue. He and Scot Gresham-Lancaster, a musician he'd met at Interval Research, developed Cellphonia, a tech server that combined voices from the cell phone into chaotic opera-like choruses, and they used part of my libretto from my opera WET for the prototype. That in turn inspired his work with the acolytes of David Tudor, and he electrified woks and other mundane objects, turning them into sound art at places like Brown and Caramoor. That one only required my pots. *The Daily News* backed the launch of his augmented reality Pokemon Go-like game, with some clues embedded in the newspaper, on September 11, 2001.

Such is the hit-or-miss life of inventors.

*

Henry had a game agent named Felicia with the deep raspy voice of a forties actress. She was the one who told us our Fat Game would never go, but she also had the distinction of having rejected Scrabble—we shouldn't have been discouraged. Remembering how she tossed it into a closet one weekend, and regretted it forever after, she was quick to point out however that two game manufacturers passed on it before Hasbro bought it.

*

Rearrange the Scrabble tiles of "mother-in-law" and you get "woman Hitler."

*

Henry's partner, a Mr. Roy Green, was an ex-GE engineer. A few years after Henry's divorce, Mr. Green made a deal to sell Maggi Magnetics while Henry was away on a sales trip. If Henry wouldn't sign, there would be a big lawsuit. The details of this humiliation were not clear. Obviously they didn't have a very sound partnership agreement. Were there lies involved? Although Henry said he supported himself for the next thirty-five years solely by playing the stock market, I imagine he must have had a big payout and collected a percentage on the ongoing sales, with his portion cut off when new buyers "improved" the toy and gained full control of the patent in the seventies.

*

The Whee-Lo appeared in the 2005 movie *Robots,* which idolizes inventors, and in a 2006 episode of *Family Guy.*[353]

*

Steve is a "blue sky man," a visionary. He understands all the pieces of whatever problem, reorients them to work better and generates enthusiasm for the change. Sometimes that results in an invention, but seldom does it result in money. You can invent all you want, but unless you find someone to promote your invention, you may as well not have filed for the patent at all.

Henry never said he invented the Whee-Lo, but he always took credit for it. After all, few would have picked it up if he hadn't promoted it.

*

"He invented that excuse." "The romance was just an invention to soothe her hurt feelings." "The stories he told about his military service were inventions." "A product of the imagination" defines "invention," especially as a false conception, a lie. A little arch, this use of "invention."

*

"The desire to invent legends and fairy tales . . . is (greater) than the love of truth," wrote Hugh Trevor-Roper, the first Allied intelligence officer to investigate Hitler's death. Forty-five percent of Americans polled in 1947 thought that Hitler was still alive, despite that year's publication of *The Last Days of Hitler*, about the results of Trevor-Roper's extensive analysis.[354] Trump has frequently praised Hitler, conveniently forgetting the nearly half million Americans who died in WWII to stop him, and the 17 million who died in the Holocaust that Hitler engineered.[355][356] Myths are not necessarily made-up stories, they can also be facts reworked. After over sixty court cases involving the legitimacy of the 2020 election were thrown out, one third of Americans still believed it was rigged.[357][358] Conservatives are now insisting that Trump's re-election proves that the 2020 results were false.[359]

*

A recent movie, "The Invention of Lying," is a comedy set in a world where no one has ever lied. Of course the one to "discover" lying is a screenwriter, Ricky Gervais, who ends the trailer with: "It is the greatest movie ever made."[360]

13

Evidence

Dorothy Thompson wrote a syndicated column called "On the Record." Dickson Hartwell's was "For the Record." The anthology he compiled with Andy Rooney for the Overseas Press Club was *Off the Record*. Records are what journalists provide, links to evidence.

*

Fifteen years ago, a friend of mine invited me to the Explorers' Club to hear a talk in a series that spotlighted women's accomplishments. Exploring is a field that is dominated by the male gender, at the Explorers' Club somewhat literally, given that its top floor displays a sperm whale's penis. The speaker that night was a woman who had spent a lot of time in odd places in Africa and the South Pacific. She was launching a book about women explorers, including herself. She had pearls and pedigree yet exuded the demeanor of someone who wanted reassurance that what she was doing was worthy. I was delighted to learn that she had spent time on Mangaia, one of the more remote islands in the Cooks where I had once been marooned for three weeks, and further elated to hear she'd visited South Sudan around the same time as I had. She provided few slides, however, but explorers are not always talented photographers.

Happy to accept my congratulations, the speaker backed off as soon as I began the six-degrees-of-separation questioning to which travelers to exotic locales are prone. Explorers of all eras, when crossing paths with others of their kind, fall over themselves to talk of types of poison darts or boast how they got past those damn waterfalls. At first I thought her avoidance of me was her way of asserting dominance, then I realized that perhaps she had made up these fabulous stories because they were about places so remote that no one would ever prove her wrong. I spoke with the chairwoman afterwards, trying to get the speaker's contact information. The chairwoman demurred, citing privacy issues. Of course. We happened to take the same bus home and during the ride she affirmed my hunch with a long hmmmm.

Real explorers must provide evidence, or at least corroboration. Since my ex is dead, I have no one to corroborate crossing the Nile with our equipment on our heads, fearing that crocodiles were just around the bend or slithering just under the surface of the water a few feet ahead. When God wants you, he will take you, said our guide. No evidence of this iconic moment—you'll have to take my word for it.

*

In *Love Goes to Press*, one of the reporters says to another: "You ought to pay that cook. He's been authoritative sources, reliable government circles, and last week, by god, you quoted him as a high-ranking Allied officer." Hank replies: "I did not. That was my jeep driver."[361]

*

My father—a farmer, a rancher, a lawyer, and for a two-year stretch, a district judge—was a big believer in the eyewitness. Hume was his philosopher, and his Jesuit education meant that he could argue his position. One late afternoon in winter, he and one of my brothers were driving from one snowy field to another when a "cigar-shaped flying vehicle" zoomed overhead. The Nebraska sky was blue all the way to the horizon, especially in winter, empty in all directions, no tree or cloud or hill to obscure anything. As soon as the object disappeared, my father stopped the car and looked at my brother, and after agreeing that they saw what they saw, they decided to take a break and drive to town for lunch. While they were discussing their experience with the waitress at the cafe, two strangers walked in and took seats right behind them. Strangers are seldom seen in that tiny town, and fewer stop to eat. The town's single cafe was not inviting, being really an extension of the bar and offering only whatever frozen sandwiches or soup that could withstand the microwave. While my father and brother sipped their soup—always on the lookout for metal can curlings, it was that kind of place—they listened to the strangers at the next table. Their talk was of the military doing experiments nearby, though they didn't say anything about the Air Force. Later, in the pickup, my father and brother decided that obviously the strangers were sent under orders to lunch there to allay the suspicions of witnesses. For years afterwards, my father was outraged that no one believed them. We saw what we saw, he'd say, quoting his philosopher, and dared you to contradict him.

*

Pat writes home that she visited Berlin April 29, 1945, a day before Hitler's suicide.[362] No American reporter had been inside the city since 1941—except Virginia Irwin who witnessed the Russian takeover two days before.[363] Had Pat discovered she'd been scooped, and hightailed it to Dachau? Or maybe she realized that like her unauthorized trip to Paris, she'd be in serious trouble if anyone found out. When four correspondents and a PRO returned from a four-day stay in Berlin on May 8, they were told the PRO would be court-martialed and the others discredited and sent home if their visit were known. They kept their trip secret until one of them revealed it in a book published in 1979.[364]

In her 1995 interview, Pat says her second visit took place a month after Goering surrendered, but I think, given the speed at which the Russians moved to secure Berlin, it must have been more of a matter of a week which correlates better with her letter home. "We were still buddy-buddy with the Russians at that point," she says. "I wasn't there at the time they burned the bodies. I was told they were and shown a not very large area, maybe ten feet or so, big enough to hold a funeral pyre." Steve asks her: "At one time you told me the reason they had asked you to come up there was in part to verify Hitler's death in order to prevent any resurgence of neo-Nazism after he died."

"Well, that's true," she says, and nothing more.[365]

*

The chanteuse was twenty years older than Steve, and the very word describing her occupation suggested *bedroom*. Steve and I were in France, producing the "Voices & Visions" PBS episode on Ezra Pound, documenting Pound's obsession with jongleurs and troubadours, and the south of France had the most convincing locations. Steve had been scouting castles, a hundred of them in three days the week before. I had just finished producing a shoot fifty miles away. The chanteuse had had a regular slot at the Westbank Cafe on the far west end of 42nd Street where Steve and a partner ran a cabaret, something to do between film shoots. Performers like Christine Lavin, with a guitar and a bird on her shoulder, sang or danced or "tried out material," a euphemism for performing skits they'd written themselves. At the time, I had my little boy to put to bed, and I insisted Steve not stay late, that his partner, a man whose other job was decorating Christmas trees in lobbies, close up. They eventually found the business too difficult to run, and it was sold. Steve must've mentioned he'd be in France to the chanteuse at her last show. *What a coincidence.* How did she track him down? This was the eighties, cell phones did not provide instant connection. But there she was, at our hotel door, and without her manager.

Steve had promoted her at his club so beautifully—perhaps he could help "manage" her here, she growled in her French accent, so softly that one had to lean close and have her repeat everything with the addition of a sad smile. "One" in this case was me, having arrived late on the scene, rejoining Steve for a few days before the shoot went elsewhere. My little son had died two months earlier and now I was three months pregnant with Steve's first child. The chanteuse said she'd made loads of money up to this point, she had the bookings and he had the experience—what could be better? The south of France, she purred. Without me, of course. Steve would be unemployed as soon as this shoot was finished, and film work was always intermittent. How seriously did he consider going off with her? He tells me now that I have a scar on my back that reminds him of her: evidence. But of what? I don't remember. Every time he catches a glimpse of it, he feels guilty about even considering the job.

It's located in a place I can't see, would never see, only he and a dermatologist can see it.

*

In 2009, Nick Bellantoni, an American researcher, was allowed an hour in Russia's State Archive to collect DNA from a blood-stained fabric on a couch that matched reference photos of Hitler's from 1945, and the skull fragment from a bullet exit wound displayed by the Russians in 2000 as the only positive physical proof that Hitler shot himself. Geneticists discovered that the skull, although found in a hole where Hitler's body had been buried, was that of a woman under 40. No reports indicate that Eva Braun shot herself. Did Hitler shoot her and then take cyanide? Was there a certain amount of distrust involved? [366]

*

In my role as producer of *Whitman*, the pilot of the PBS series, I was filmed standing beside the actor playing the poet, holding his wig while he practiced his lines. The segment was added to the script after Helen Vendler, one of the literary advisors, said that the average viewer might confuse the actor with the actual Walt. She insisted, at least for the pilot, that the evidence be made clearer. Notwithstanding the lack of trust in the sophistication of the average viewer—or acceding to his susceptibility to the fake—the scene was included in the final cut; thus the actor was protected from the paparazzi and fans mobbing him for autographs of their Penguin copy of *Leaves of Grass*.

*

The author as producer, 1980.

All reporters had "War Correspondent" on an emblem affixed to the left breast pocket and shoulder so they could blend in while reporting in the field but stand out from active-duty troops. Although treated as captains, a rank that allowed them to mess with officers and facilitated POW exchanges if taken prisoner, they wore uniforms without symbols of rank, to indicate they would neither give nor take salutes.[367] "I never knew any correspondent to wear their green press tags because we thought that was a sure way to get killed," Pat told Steve in her 1995 interview.

Steve had never seen his mother's uniform before Jay sent him a photo of it hanging in her closet. Evidence of her corporeal self, of her being physically present in that war.

*

At what point does the facts of a life turn into legend and thus become unbelievable? Relatives of Freeman Bernstein thought he was a total blowhard, but the vaudevillian-turned-con-artist did indeed cheat Hitler out of thirty-five tons of embargoed Canadian nickel—among dozens of other cons, according to his journalist great-nephew Walter Shapiro—in *Hustling Hitler*, published by Blue Rider press, an imprint of Penguin.[368]

And what did the Bloch family think of the receipt they found that read: "Certificate for the safekeeping of two postcards (one of them painted by the hand of Adolf Hitler) confiscated in the house of Dr Eduard Bloch"? Their ancestor was Jewish, and according to Meriel Schindler, author of *The Lost Café Schindler: One Family, Two Wars, and the Search for Truth*, Bloch was a doctor much beloved by Hitler and his family.[369] Other stories of revelation are less benign. Sylvia Foti discovered much confusing evidence while writing the biography of her grandfather Jonas Norieka, a Lithuanian famous for fighting the Communists. The Google headline says it all: "My grandfather wasn't a Nazi-fighting war hero — he was a brutal collaborator."[370]

Periods of great turmoil like war or immigration can obliterate physical evidence and suppress the emotional. Many an Edwardian pioneer shucked his identity emigrating West, all evidence of his previous life disappearing on the boat he disembarked. My mother always insisted that her great-great-great-grandmother was an Irish princess who ran off with a commoner to America. But doesn't every Irish girl who comes over tell her children that she was once a princess? I asked Paul Muldoon, then poetry editor of the *New Yorker*. He said I should learn something about Irish history. I read the book he'd recommended (the title lost to memory now) and contacted a cousin who was very involved in the family's lineage. He had heard the princess story and knew exactly where she might fit in the tree. On a trip to Ireland a few years later, I asked the tourist board if they'd heard of the Sely Castle, the one my mother said was her ancestor's. I had googled every spelling I could imagine and had come up with nothing. The woman behind the computer quickly produced a printout. Bishop Sely built the castle in the 15th century but lost it when he ran away with a married woman. It became known as Kilklief, after the church beside it, and who knows how it came into the Irish princess family. We rented a car, and that afternoon I was standing on the banks of the Irish Sea, its towers behind me. All I had was my mother's boast as evidence of my claim. When I proudly told the castle's neighbors of my discovery, they laughed. "You Americans are always claiming kin," they said, shaking their heads.

*

Kilklief castle

Pat knew those weren't Hitler's ashes—Steve tells me she admitted as much—but she saw the necessity of pretending that they were, if evidence that Hitler was dead would save lives. Maybe she showed us the photo burning the Nazi souvenirs taken in Berchtesgaden, sure we wouldn't know that it wasn't shot in Berlin.

*

Pat burning Nazi paraphernalia, 1945

Someone may note, I realize now, that I don't appear in the credits of Voices & Visions. The executive director and I had a disagreement while finishing the Whitman film, and he replaced me. Angry, I threw out everything concerning the series: two file boxes full of paper, the treatments for thirteen programs, our contract, every grant proposal and script. The only evidence I have of those three years of work are legal papers filed when I sued the production company for unemployment, and won.

*

By the time Steve was eight, Dickson's consumption of alcohol had dramatically increased. He would brag about the AA meetings he attended, swearing he'd quit. Steve wanted evidence. He marked the bottles. At his age, it was his only retaliation, and Dickson slapped him around in a fury. Without cuts or bruises, there was no evidence of mistreatment. Steve never reconciled his mother's acceptance of Dickson's punishments with the rationale that he "must have needed it." Storytelling is what every family engages in, to the detriment and benefit of its members.

*

My first memoir, *Black Glasses Like Clark Kent,* investigated whether the US military had executed black American GIs in postwar Japan while my uncle guarded Sugamo prison in Tokyo. I interviewed five witnesses who confirmed at least one execution, but all the official paperwork regarding any hangings had vanished or been destroyed. My uncle and other witnesses remembered the gallows being built at the center of the prison. I could find no order for its construction, though photos show it elaborately built; my uncle and others noted that it came decorated with black bunting. Those witnesses remembered at least one midnight execution, the shadow of the hanged body at dawn. They too were outraged that the records were gone. "An American soldier was killed by our own people? You would think that actually seeing someone being hanged would verify that it happened," exclaimed one old veteran, incensed by the lack of documentation.

*

O did not publish a piece I was commissioned to write on torture survivors because it did not fit the magazine's mandate of uplift. The organizer of Bellevue's torture survivor program was extremely positive, but none of its graduates—mostly Tibetan at that time—had become CEOs or public school teachers. All they had done was their best: they had survived. Their bodies appeared intact, with any evidence of torture covered by clothing, and they responded to my questions about their new jobs and social life well enough. But their spirits were crushed: you could see it in their eyes. Imagine their ordeal to make it as far as the Bellevue program: the years of asylum-seeking (I'm leaving out the torture that credentialed them), that long first plane ride blotting out the past with the anonymity of cloud, landing in JFK and someone from the state department collecting their luggage—all the refugees had in the world—then receiving only eight months of public assistance while seeking a job, some of them without knowing a word of English. They had done that, been there, but all the light in their eyes had fled, that darkness only visible evidence of their tortured past.

That sounds melodramatic.

*

Many of the Nuer who survived the Sudanese civil war have resettled in Nebraska, of all places. It offered cheap rent, flat country, and equatorial summer heat, never mind the snow. The Nuer had little material evidence of their African heritage, but like many refugees, they seldom wanted to be reminded of all they left behind. I hadn't imagined that when I organized a presentation at the university on the similarities between Nuerland and Nebraska. I thought they'd welcome the recognition. Of course, I saw it from my point-of-view: it was remarkable that I had spent nearly a year trekking far into the hinterlands of the largest country in Africa, to film and translate the songs of one of Sudan's most remote people, and that they should move to within a hundred miles of where I was born. After the slide show—with parallels of climate and geography and big fish, only a little facetious—I read my translations of their oral poetry from *Cleaned the Crocodile's Teeth,* and asked for someone in the audience to perform one in the original. About seventy-five people were in attendance, including a large contingent of Nuer from Omaha for whom I had arranged transportation. Not one volunteered. All the Nuers I met in Sudan knew hours of songs and would break into one at the first mention of performance. I had to cajole my audience, I begged. They protested: no one remembered songs anymore. A culture whose major art form was oral poetry? Even in the refugee camps, people had to be singing, at the very least, mothers to crying children. Finally a young man volunteered and sang an ox praise song. He brought down the house.

It was during the reception that I saw the haunted eyes. Nuer women, dressed in homemade modest satin sheaths and colorful office wear, clustered around the brownies and cheesecake, Midwestern crudités. None of them spoke, not to me, not to each other. It was only after I insisted that I meet the wife of my co-organizer, when I looked into her eyes, and then into the eyes of the other women, that I saw what they shared with the torture survivors. Years later, I heard that one Nebraskan refugee had been raped something like 400 times even before she arrived in the United States".[371] Male refugees lose status in a new country and endure the difficulties of seeking employment, and so do women, but women have the extra burden of protecting themselves from disappointed men. Married women can't turn to their children for solace because the children often become alien to them, speaking English so much more fluently than their mothers, and usually teenage slang on top of that. The women are alone, in double exile. Of course, this is not true for all Nuer, nor all female refugees, but this particular set, so forlorn at this celebration of their culture, seemed to make it true.

*

"Shocking or surprising images can cause pupils to enlarge, however, the researchers discovered this reaction was highly exaggerated in people who have experienced a traumatic event," according to a recent UK study.[372] Surely Dachau survivors had those eyes, and, although I've never met any of the soldiers who liberated Dachau, I imagine that they too had them. Did Pat? I never thought to look. When I met her, forty years had passed, and as one ages, the eyelids begin to droop anyway, as if to keep from seeing too much more of the world. She did have a glint.

*

"Oh, those concentration camps couldn't have been that terrible," one veteran remembers civilians saying to him after the war.[373] Responses like this belittled his trauma, while soldiers equating their experience with the survivors' seemed trivializing to those who hadn't witnessed the liberation. To make the soldiers' psychic isolation worse, few civilians wanted to even hear about seeing such a shocking situation. *The war is over, let's get on with it.*

Or the trauma couldn't be put into words. The evidence had to speak for itself.

14

Propaganda or Promotion

Dickson and Pat had been married for less than a year when he suggested that she apply for his job at UNICEF without revealing her sex or their relationship. There would be little to give her away: she wrote her journalism under her maiden name. "Oh, they will never hire a woman, an American woman," she told him. Dickson sent a memo to Secretary General Dag Hammarskjöld, "giving [her] background, but not giving [her] name." Duplicitous, but she got the job.[374] "Wife Succeeds Husband at UN" reads the *New York Times* headline on September 14, 1954.[375] She said it brought her back to her original interest in international relations, because she was really convinced "that if you could get people to sit around the table—then UNICEF had thirty nations on board—and talk about peace and what you should do for the children, then eventually it could lead to bigger things."[376]

As Director of Information at UNICEF, Pat held a key position in an organization that was born out of the need for propaganda. After a terrible world war, why not use children to promote the unity of nations, break down isolationist attitudes, and reduce the fear generated by the Cold War? President Herbert Hoover had deemed her boss, UNICEF's founder Maurice Pate, "the most efficient and dedicated human angel I have ever known." Pate even looked like a sort of angel, with white hair haloing his head—and perhaps he had to play the role.[377] With much struggle, he had recently wrested permanent status for UNICEF at the UN, although Pat's friend Eleanor Roosevelt had urged its disbanding because the children of Europe were no longer suffering. When a Pakistani UN delegate accused Eleanor of not being "willing to come through for the equally needy children of the developing world," a great hush descended on the gathering. Eleanor blanched and backed down.[378] Since UNICEF was organized without direct UN funding, it relied primarily on the energies of such an angel as Pate—and a robust public relations effort from Pat—to generate revenue.

In 1949 a little girl in Czechoslovakia sent UNICEF a picture of grateful children dancing in a circle that was circulated in-house and used in local fundraising.[379] "Why not ask Raoul Dufy, who was living in a Paris suburb, to create and donate an original design to UNICEF?" asked Helenka Pantaleoni, founder of the US Committee for UNICEF. Then "a determined young woman" dispatched from UNICEF's Paris office "made many visits over a period of months [no dates] to the artist's country studio."[380]

This is the closest that UNICEF comes to acknowledging that Pat collected the art for UNICEF's famous greeting cards, published and promoted them, creating the most successful fundraising effort of its kind. While she was at the advertising agency Byoir, she had been involved in developing a line of cards for Hallmark, using the art of Winston Churchill and Grandma Moses. She had also worked with the Wildenstein Gallery, which handled most of the important artists of the time, including Matisse, Dufy, and Chagall.[381,382] In the 1990 interview Pat says: "Dufy was our first artist. I was able to establish certain criteria—that all artists would be invited, [although] no one would be paid." She describes making a pitch to Matisse:

> I went to see [Henri] Matisse when he was dying and asked him to do a work. He could no longer paint . . . And he took a [card] which he had left over, and with his scissors and papers, he created just in an hour that I was with him a kind of torch which he then [chuckles] pasted on the back of his daughter's wedding invitation and gave to me, properly signed.[383]

But UNICEF announced the Dufy card in 1952,[384] two years before Pat took the job, and the Matisse card was issued in 1953.[385] Then I discover in one of Jay's scribbled notes from his interview with June Downey that Pat was a consultant to UNICEF at the time.[386] At the beginning, Pat had nearly full authority over the project. "Except for the director of UNICEF, I did not have people standing over my shoulder looking," she said in her 1990 interview. "And I didn't make many mistakes, only one. A very famous Mexican artist [Rufino Tamayo] was really a flop, and I manufactured too many cards." She also said that she personally bought the work at whatever the artist wanted for it, rather than returning it. She felt they had to get some money out of it.[387]

*

Steve inherited four paintings by the Indian painter Jamini Roy, all of them very similar to the one on the 1956 UNICEF card, surely evidence that she was the one who did the collecting.[388]

*

Steve's good friend Dr. Nilay Shah is Jain, a religious group from India that does not allow the killing of any living thing. Not only are they vegetarian, but they will not eat vegetables that, when harvested, kill the plant. This includes beets and carrots. Nilay is not quite so observant but his penchant for ordering rice with chickpeas and bread triggers a story from Steve about his mother. UNICEF was spraying India with DDT to kill mosquitoes and prevent malaria, but the Jains weren't allowing it. She ordered the crews to treat only the walls and told the Jains that the mosquitoes were committing suicide, dying voluntarily, when they landed on the treated areas. The Jains relented.

*

In a newspaper interview in the 1970s, Pat reaffirms that she was "the instigator of the UNICEF Christmas and Greeting Card which has grown beyond all expectation."[389]

Instigator, another interesting word, like inventor.

*

UNICEF films were shown after the cartoon but before the movie feature, and afterwards a collection was taken up for children suffering in the rest of the world. I remember the little tin cans with UNICEF branding, how they clanked after we started filling them with our pennies, passing them to each other in the dark of the theater. No one could resist shaking them and that's what I think made contributing so irresistible: you heard exactly how much you cared, a very clever promotion.

*

Fabrication suggests weaving, of something made that wasn't there before, of processing raw materials into a finished product that can be promoted and sold to a consumer. Made up out of whole cloth. Lying? Complete fabrication.

*

After his years at UNICEF, Dickson returned to the ranks of *Mad Men*, not advertising per se, but its brother, public relations. His stellar rise had begun at twenty-six, working for a prominent New York firm, Harold F. Strong Corp.,[390] and after a few years, he helped found Hartwell, Jonson, and Kibbee. His extravagant profile of Hannagan in *Colliers* in 1947 might have had something to do with Robinson/Hannagan hiring him as executive vice president in 1954.[391] [392] A *TIME* magazine article credited Steve Hannagan for having "established the principle that truth is fundamental to good public relations."[393] Refusing to take on political accounts, Hannagan stated: "Politics is a compromise and I am not a compromise man." His motto was "Do the honest thing," not so different from his most important clients' slogan, Coca-Cola's "It's the real thing." After Hannagan's death, William E. Robinson became head of Coca-Cola, and sold the firm to Hill & Knowlton in 1955, taking Dickson along.[394] Hill & Knowlton was two years into its campaign to convince the public that tobacco wasn't dangerous, a fifty-year effort that they knew was wrong from the start. Their innovative contribution to PR practice was to sow doubt through medical research committees paid by the industry itself, a technique in frequent use today.[395]

*

In 1985, Steve worked as assistant director to Lindsay Anderson on the Wham! shoot in China, coordinating five film crews and directing a few scenes. Wham! was the first rock n' roll group to visit the country, a big PR coup for them, and a test of what freedoms could be had in Communist China. About a week into the job, I was walking the dog and the baby and saw the headline "Wham! Musician Goes Berserk, Sends Jetliner into Nose Dive."[396] All I discerned from the newspaper was that the plane didn't contain Wham!'s two pop stars, George Michael and Andrew Ridgeley. Fax machines were the best form of communication then, calls were too expensive and difficult to place—but anyway, where could I reach him? They were on tour. It was a full day before I heard that Steve was alive and pushing Anderson around in a wheelchair because he'd fallen off the Great Wall.

Or he could have been faking an injury, says Steve.

Steve Bull pushing Lindsay Anderson wielding his cane, 1985

"I have no interest in Wham!," Anderson wrote in his diary at the time. An old lefty with many film awards, he bristled with the requirements of a long form music video. He did, however, have an interest in Communist China, but that interest was layered. "Revolution is the opium of the intellectuals" is the graffiti filmed in *O Lucky Man!*, part two of his dark surreal trilogy critiquing freedom in the British class system, capitalism, and institutional bureaucracy. The Communists too were ambivalent about the tour and its PR. When more than 10,000 fans enthusiastically stood up and danced during a Sunday night performance, police forced them back into their seats with clubs.

The shoot was difficult: the band was exhausted, having just come off a successful tour of Japan and Malaysia, and treated China as a vacation, management quarreled with the director, and who knew what the many roving cameramen had captured—there were no dailies. The only thing everyone agreed on was that the banquet food sucked. Their plane made those headlines when their trumpeter saw demons on the wing and tried to stab himself with a penknife. By the time security subdued him, the plane was racing back to Beijing, the Chinese certain they were being hijacked. All those who spoke English, suddenly did not. The last Steve saw of the trumpeter he was playing taps from his gurney.

Not the right kind of PR.

Both the English production team and their stars identified as "music missionaries," and the Chinese Communists used Wham! as propaganda. China was in a culturally isolated moment not unlike North Korea today, with little expertise in the contemporary scene. They wanted to invite a rock group that didn't challenge authority. In that, Wham! was an excellent choice: everyone on tour was drug and alcohol free, and the biggest thrill was the threat of George Michael exposing too much chest hair. On Wham!'s side, the Brits could brag that they were the first to capture the enormous Chinese market. The Chinese thought they could control the youth through this new propaganda vehicle (and possible addiction) but only a few years later, the youth exploded at Tiananmen Square. The lesson is: it's very hard to control propaganda—or associations of any kind.

*

Using public relations to manipulate information always exploits the (often unknown) distance between hard facts and opinion. It is a creative art, and recently it has become less artful—or the public much more gullible. While in office, Trump announced that "fake news" was "one of the greatest of all terms I've come up with."[397] His claim of originality is baseless. The term "lügenpresse," meaning "lying press," came into use prior to 1830. Used as a tactic to discredit the free press by hostile Catholics during the 1848 Revolution, it also countered enemy war propaganda in WWI. Marxists used the term after that war, expanding it to "bourgeois lying press." During WWII, the Nazi propaganda minister Goebbels greatly increased its use, generating an unrelenting bombardment of fake news against all Jewish, Communists, and foreign presses. Given that the Germans were the first to applaud alternative facts, it's appropriate that *Der Spiegel* has the magazine world's largest fact-checking department.[398]

Pretending to have invented "fake news" was just one of Trump's approximately 30,573 lies he'd made during his first four years in office,[399] and the efforts to hold him accountable regarding the 2020 election turned into something his supporters rallied around.[400] In October 2024, CNN reported that he told forty lies in just two speeches in Pennsylvania prior to his re-election."[401]

Don't all politicians lie? "Donald Trump is different," writes Carole McGranahan in "An anthropology of lying: Trump and the political sociality of moral outrage." "He is the most "accomplished and effective liar" to have ever participated in American politics; moreover, his lying has reshaped public discourse so that "the frequency, degree, and impact of lying in politics are now unprecedented."[402] Even the truth about the identity of his PR firm was murky during his second campaign, when Trump switched PR firms, funneling money to his attorney as his "political consultant." *Newsweek* reported that the director of Federal Campaign Finance Reform complained that "It's concerning to see [Trump's] presidential campaign reporting thousands of dollars in payments to a newly formed, obscure company with a bare-bones description of the services that company is purportedly providing to the campaign." His previous PR firm, Launchpad Strategies LLC, provided no information about its owners or services.[403]

*

"Something has to be done to get millions of people to think the thought you want them to think and then to get them to act on that thought," according to Carl Byoir. In 1933, Hitler hired the Jewish Byoir to portray Nazi Germany in a positive light at $6,000 a month ($120,000 today). Byoir worked for over a year on the campaign, trying to increase German tourism.[404] Perhaps Pat's bicycle trip with her brother in 1936 and Martha Gellhorn's earlier jaunt were the result of that effort. Byoir, Pat's employer right after the War, was Hill & Knowlton's chief rival in billings when it was finally swallowed up in 1986. Hill & Knowlton, for many years the largest PR and lobbying firm in the world, was known to be "a company without a moral rudder."[405]

*

I had no idea Dickson was so high up, says Steve.

I've just told him that his stepfather was vice president of Robinson/Hannagan, at the time the third largest PR firm in the country. It was a prime target for Hill & Knowlton, which had just started a buying spree to consolidate PR firms in America. Robinson/Hannagan sold for $1.5M in today's dollars to Hill & Knowlton, where Dickson retained his VP title, although there was more than one vice president.[406]

Still, that's a lot of pressure, I say.

*

Both Pat and Dickson were involved in "The Railroad Trucker's Brawl," a lawsuit that helped redefine the role of public relations in politics.[407] The PR executive for the Pennsylvania Motor Truck Association pointed out in a letter to the editor of the *Pittsburgh Post Gazette* that the agency Carl Byoir is "the lucky one[s] who receive the million bucks or more a year from the Eastern Railroad President's Conference" and went on to observe that Byoir "plant[ed]" newspaper and magazine articles" for their clients.[408] Dickson had written such an article for Pat, then in charge of Byoir's magazine accounts. He rebuts the executive by providing a list of sources, says there's no room to cite details, but does not deny the mechanism of its placement.[409] It was the early fifties, when the Interstate was being built and railroads wanted a monopoly on the heaviest loads. The prosecutor found a memo in which Byoir was directed to "soft pedal and sidetrack stories that were detrimental to the railroads." Pat testified that she provided only statistics and clips for these articles and did not write them, although she was nominated for a prize for one article.[410] Pat also lobbied Congress, met with the Maryland Highway Commissioner who was writing the guidelines for the Interstate, and hired her roommate, a freelance researcher for *Colliers* and *Readers Digest*, to snoop around the players, but not say for whom.[411] In the end, the judge found the trucking industry within their rights to complain, and told the railroads to cease and desist their campaign. Although it would take nine years, Byoir was cleared of conspiracy charges and violating the Sherman Anti-Trust Act and the Clayton Act.[412] The upshot of the ruling was that the PR industry had to become much more circumspect about how they exerted their influence. These days the experts quoted in articles are apt to be on the payroll of the clients themselves but cloaked in a relationship with a foundation or non-profit.

*

The American press, perhaps due to Carl Byoir's influence, contributed to Hitler's PR. The *New York Times*' first article in 1922 stated that "Hitler's anti-Semitism was not so violent or genuine as it sounded."[413] It published features on his Eagle's Nest retreat in 1937, 1939, and 1941, portraying it as simple and beautiful, and noted how much he liked his chocolates.[414] The 1937 piece came out a month after Hitler bombed Guernica; the 1939 piece just before signing the Nazi-Soviet pact, and the piece in 1941 ran while cities in Europe burned and Jews were herded into ghettos. *Better Homes and Gardens* published an equally adulatory piece of his place in 1938, after the annexation of Czechoslovakia.[415]

*

Walt Whitman was a pioneer in promotion—for himself. Even before he self-published his first book, *Leaves of Grass*, with its famous narcissistic beginning ("I celebrate myself, and sing myself"), he wrote his own reviews. These reviews—"An American Poet at last!"—were reprinted in a 64-page promotional handbook that he gave away for free.[416] "Every sentence," runs one entry, "and every passage tells of an interior not always seen, and exudes an impalpable something which sticks to him that reads." Whitman was sneaky: he included some bad reviews to create an atmosphere of controversy. "It is impossible to imagine how any man's fancy could have conceived such a mass of stupid filth, unless he were possessed of the soul of a sentimental donkey that had died of disappointed love," opines one Rufus W. Griswold.[417] Not even his contemporary P. T. Barnum used unfavorable material in his hype. Whitman pioneered another tactic by hustling himself not as an author, and the work not as literature, but something entirely new.[418] This reframed any criticism and redirected readers to think of his work as distinctive, obeying totally new standards. Whitman also included parody, to suggest that readers who recognized it were in the know, and articles claiming that the poet had given up poetry for bus driving, to emphasize his corporeal self.[419] He refuted the notion of the time—and the future—that promotion should be concise and simple, appealing instead to a sophisticated reading audience who didn't mind long paragraphs.

Much later, Whitman denied that he had anything to do with the publication of the pamphlet.[420]

Whitman also knew his physical appearance was quite important for book sales, and availed himself of the brand new medium of photography, his first author photo emanating "sexy" with "an air of mild defiance."[421] He subsequently became by far the most photographed writer in the 19th century, and made sure everyone knew it: "No man has been photographed more than I have."[422] He further boasted that the butterfly perched on his finger in one of his later photographs was empirical proof that all creatures were attracted to him. The cardboard insect is now in the collection of the Library of Congress. After the *New York Tribune* excerpted a letter of praise from Ralph Waldo Emerson without Emerson's permission, Whitman took "I greet you at the beginning of a great career" from the letter, and had it printed on the spine of his second edition. Whitman also boasted that thousands of copies of this book had been snapped up—"readily sold"—but at that point in his career, he would have been lucky to get rid of a dozen.[423] In 1872, Whitman wrote an essay praising his popularity in Europe, which he commanded a friend to sign and publish in Kansas and then managed to get it reprinted in two Eastern newspapers. When the Comstock anti-obscenity laws banned his book in 1881, he changed publishers and sold thousands of copies—six thousand, in fact—in the resulting controversy.[424]

His self-promotion was successful beyond anybody's wildest dream. Before he died, schools asked to name buildings after him, and universities requested poems for official occasions. Camden, New Jersey, where he died, opened flower shops, movie theaters, heating companies, pharmacies, and a luxurious hotel using his name. His signature still appears on cigar boxes (though he didn't smoke), whiskey and two craft beers (though he didn't drink). There's been a "Miss Walt Whitman" beauty pageant, Whitman applesauce, ice cream, espresso, fruit cocktail, chili sauce, coffee, bubblegum, grocery stores, fighter planes, perfume, life insurance, canned vegetables, a china pattern called *Leaves of Grass*, the Walt Whitman bridge over the Delaware, a shopping mall in Long Island, a Virginia winery, not to mention camps, parks, truck stops, corporate centers, AIDS clinics, and think tanks. Lisa Simpson reads his work to comfort a beached whale, and one *Breaking Bad* character gives another a copy of *Leaves of Grass*. He's been quoted in a Levi commercial and one for Volvo. A hundred feet of New York harbor features a Whitman quote on a railing. When shown the advertisement for Whitman cigars at the end of his life, he exclaimed "That is fame!"[425]

When Whitman's supporters raised money for a beach house or at least a replacement for his ramshackle cottage in Camden, he spent it all on an ostentatious castle-like grave monument to himself, to be certain that his physical self was remembered as well as his work. "The public is a thick-skinned beast and you have to keep whacking away at its hide to let it know you're there," Whitman wrote. His promotional efforts did not go unnoticed even in his time, and by 1929 a critic had written "Whitman as His Own Press-Agent." [426]

*

PR is always first on a government's agenda when fighting a war. Even before the US joined WWII, FDR did his bit for promotion through his fireside chats, urging the nation to donate war material to the Allies: "Suppose my neighbor's house is on fire and I have a length of garden hose . . ."[427] Once the US agreed to fight, snappy uniforms and military parades were needed to sell moral validity and encourage young men to sign up. The "Uncle Sam Wants You" poster, the military's most effective recruiting device, dates from WWI.

After the fighting begins, the public is terrified and needs censorship.

*

Ten years after I produced the pilot on Whitman for the PBS series, Steve and I directed *Margaret Sanger: A Public Nuisance,* a documentary that focuses on Sanger's manipulation of the press to change the terms around birth control, an example of using public relations for positive results. Sanger coined the term "birth control," and used every available means to promote her cause, and was not above self-promotion. Her

Still from Margaret Sanger: A Public Nuisance

biographer Ellen Chesler could never authenticate Sanger's tale about how she came to dedicate herself to birth control. She said she witnessed the death of a woman from a botched abortion and then "threw my nursing bag in the corner and announced . . . I would never take another case until I had made it possible for working women in America to have the knowledge to control birth."[428] Sanger learned her theatrics from Emma Goldman, America's first birth control advocate, whose lectures were so incendiary that she always brought a book to speaking engagements so she'd have something to read in jail.[429] Once, when Goldman was forbidden to speak in public, she sat on the stage with a handkerchief stuffed into her mouth, an idea later used by Sanger to get the press on her side.[430] After Goldman distributed pamphlets called "Why and How Small Families are Desirable," and "The Child's Right Not to be Born," Sanger published "What Every Girl Should Know" and staked her claim as the nation's foremost birth control promoter, avoiding Goldman ever after. Although Sanger's publication contained no information about birth control, Anthony Comstock, anti-vice activist and US Postal Inspector, deemed it obscene because it included the words "syphilis" and "gonorrhea." In response, Sanger started her own newsletter, "The Woman Rebel," and this time promised to publish everything she could find on the subject of birth control. Instead of preparing for her defense, she published "Family Limitation," offering all the necessary information for twenty-five cents. Eventually published in thirteen languages, it sold ten million copies.[431] Rather than stand trial in 1914, she fled the country, gaining more publicity and European backing. A year later, with Comstock dead, her husband in jail for distributing "Family Limitation," and her young daughter having died of neglect, Sanger returned from her exile to launch a cross-country speaking tour, talking to everyone from the Junior League "to the women's auxiliary of the Ku Klux Klan."[432] Journalists across the country reported favorably, and when she appeared in court, the charges were dropped, partly because of sympathy due to the death of her child. Eight months passed, during which she used $50 she received from a woman in California to open a clinic in Brooklyn, and was arrested nine days later. Charged this time with distributing contraceptives—and being a public nuisance—she was found guilty. The judge held that women did not have "the right to copulate with a feeling of security that there will be no resulting conception."[433] Apparently judges today feel the same way with the revocation of Roe vs. Wade—and the rise, once again, of the Comstock laws to prohibit the mailing of abortion pills.

Being jailed did not deter Sanger. While she was in prison, she educated the other female inmates about birth control, and made sure the press knew about it. By the time she was released, she had rocketed to national celebrity with enormous fundraising capabilities. Two years later, doctors were allowed to prescribe birth control. In 1917, she founded yet another outlet for publicity and support: the *Birth Control Review.*

Radical poet Lola Ridge edited Sanger's *Birth Control Review* for several issues. An immigrant from New Zealand, Ridge was an anarchist like her friend Emma Goldman who also often reframed the details of her life to suit the public. I published her biography in 2016 and discovered that only at Ridge's death in 1941 did her husband find out that she was ten years older than he'd been told, and she never revealed that she was a bigamist, most of the time claiming she was Australian, and always put forward that she came from a privileged background. She was raised, in fact, as the daughter of an alcoholic gold miner, but she needed a proper history to attract patrons, to get the support to write her poems about labor, riots, lynchings, Wall Street, immigrants, and political executions. As an anarchist, what she valued more than truth was her freedom—which included no work other than the literary, and like Isadora Duncan, she did not make adjustments. This lifestyle resulted in extreme poverty, but she was conveniently anorexic. My favorite quote of hers is "Nice is the one adjective in the world that is laughable applied to any single thing I have ever written." That line sold books.

*

Lola Ridge, 1935

Nice is not the word associated with anything Trump has done or his rise to power, but he hasn't needed it. He—or his PR consultants—have revolutionized public relations. As president, he himself inserted highly controversial and often untrue material into the echo chambers of tweets to be picked up by the media, rather than the media targeting the public with information from the White House. Promotion turned on its head, a new world of participatory propaganda.

15

Mothers-in-law

What is the difference between outlaws and in-laws? Outlaws are wanted.

*

For legal purposes, the term "in-law" was coined in the 14th century, to define prohibited relationships in the family. For such relationships to have to be legally circumscribed, they must be tempting. Consider in-law jokes: they are so numerous and so often violent they reek of the forbidden, in particular, the unacknowledged attraction between the husband and his wife's mother and vice versa. Indeed, in Taiwan sometimes a prospective daughter-in-law is adopted into the family at birth, often making the groom much nearer in age to the mother than his wife-to-be, creating sometimes intolerable tension.[434] In some families, the relationship between mothers-in-law and sons-in-law boils down to the mother-in-law's polite *Love my daughter, love me. Am I not still attractive?* Sons-in-law can be blinded by the fawning attention.

*

I picked my mother-in-law up at the airport last night.
   Yeah, those airport lounges are so dark!

*

My first husband, a pre-med student and frequently out-of-work ironworker, was bedazzled by my mother, in particular when she flew to Seattle to convince me to leave him, fearing (rightly) for my virginity. At dinner in a dark and expensive restaurant, she told the two of us that she would postpone a scheduled operation for her life-threatening condition until I returned home. She was very beautiful, and they flirted between ultimatums. I knew then that my happiness wasn't what was important to my mother. Or was she trying to prevent me from making her mistake of babies too early? She went home alone, and we had leftover steak to tide us over another week. It would take me another year to discover how important my happiness was to him. And, yes, my mother had the operation.

*

Do you know the punishment for bigamy?
   Two mothers-in-law.

*

How well did Pat get along with her first mother-in-law? Metta lived in Boulder where she kept accounts for the university. As I have mentioned, Steve and his brother, were put on a plane alone to visit her just after the divorce, then Metta summered in Shelter Island for several years as caregiver. Pat considered asking Metta for her help while Dickson was ailing ten years later, but nothing came of it.[435] I met her a few years before she died at the age of 97. She kept her own apartment and served us apple pie. When she contracted a urinary tract infection that required hospitalization, Henry decided against intervention. Steve and his brother were her only grandchildren.

*

Behind every successful man stands a devoted wife and a surprised mother-in-law.

*

I was never double-in-lawed. Henry's second wife, Janet, died years before I married Steve. She was Pat's mother's boarder in 1953, taken in after Pat's father died. For money or for company? Family finances are not clear. Pat's mother foisted Janet onto the newly divorced Henry who was then so disinterested in his children. What's a mother-in-law to do, when her daughter doesn't work out, if not to scramble for a more reliable mother for her grandchildren? A Canadian who eventually ran the National Film Board in New York, Janet Scellen was "a severely pleasant girl with rimless glasses and a high color on her cheekbones," according to National Film Board history. She is credited in *Documentary Film* as one of the three people responsible for its existence, and worked with founder John Grierson from the beginning.[436] A photo of Janet in a *Glamour* magazine article announcing her appointment to the New York office in 1946 shows her with a big professional smile.[437] Another career girl—how could Henry resist? But Janet was in no hurry to give hers up. They did not marry until 1962, after she retired and became the boys' full-time disciplinarian. Neither boy remembers any modicum of affection, but Henry's mother-in-law got her wish.

*

The awe and dread with which the untutored savage contemplates his mother-in-law are amongst the most familiar facts of anthropology. — Sir James George Frazer

*

In extreme cases, cultures do not allow the mother-in-law to talk to her son-in-law at all. Avoidance is not the worst approach, if a mother-in-law takes it as a sign of respect rather than of bad feelings. Australian aborigines have a special language they use within earshot of mothers-in-law, using an unusual voice quality and pitch that sometimes uses its own pronouns.[438] Perhaps something similar is used everywhere, just a jot less linguistically formal.

*

Two men were in a pub. One says to his mate, My mother-in-law is an angel. His friend replies, You're lucky. Mine is still alive.

*

The tradition in my family is to test the prospective husband by putting him on a horse to help round up the cattle in the fall. Steve fared well, because by that time the horses had been replaced with ATVs, but the previous husband, going on about how cattle were treated in Sudan, did not. My father put him on a horse whose saddle was not quite cinched tight, and my ex rode off into the sunset slowly slipping sideways.

*

My wife accused me of hating her family and relatives.

No, I don't hate your relatives, I replied. In fact, I like your mother-in-law a lot better than I like mine.

*

After Pat kidnapped the boys from Henry and held them in Florida until he granted her a divorce, she didn't see him again for another thirty years, not until our wedding. The woman Henry was seeing at the time declined her invitation, making a reunion theoretically possible. Steve, imagining his mother and father falling in love again, reported a recurring dream of joining their hands, just as my own son actually tried so hard to do with mine. They both wanted their divorced parents back together, if only for a moment.

Steve's parents were cordial.

*

Last night a police officer knocked on the door and said, Sir, it looks like your mother-in-law has been hit by a bus.
I know, but she has a great personality.

*

My first wedding, with the ironworker, was celebrated barefoot, in the groom's grandmother's backyard, but the marriage didn't last long enough for me to be invited over to the in-laws for dinner. The ceremony was just as rushed. Between medical school at McGill and a construction job in the northwest, my beau had stopped at my family's place in the middle of the country, only to refuse to leave until I married him. I had known him long enough, four years, and after all, it was the late sixties, I decided it would be radical to actually marry him and not just live with him the way everyone else was doing to annoy their parents. But being married made adultery even more radical and within a year, he walked off with someone else, precluding even the obligatory holiday visit.

My second mother-in-law admitted that she tied her son and his sister to a tree whenever she had to clean the house. "That was the best I could do," she said. She informed my soon-to-be-ex that I'd "turn to fat," in a not so *sotto voce* minutes after I arrived at their trailer. Since I'd spent the bulk of that relationship in Sudan and on an island in the Pacific involved in anthropological filmmaking, I maintained an anthropological distance.

*

I can't stand my mother-in-law, says the cannibal. The other says: Why don't you just eat the vegetables?

*

I'd always imagined a mother-in-law living down the street, rolling out pie dough, providing little extras from a pension kept in her change purse. The possibility of an in-law actually living with us sounded downright polygamous to me, after my Sudanese experiences in large compounds of extended families where jealousy and envy ruled. But what about the benefits of a sitter and cook, I thought, and maybe solace when the husband was difficult, although this last sounded pretty tricky. Mothers tend to side with their sons, although a mother who has endured a patriarch's behavior might be sympathetic and have strategies for dealing with learned behavior. Since Pat lived in Hawai'i and we lived in New York City, I was spared such intimacy, though when we visited her, it was for weeks at a time. She took a lover after Dickson died, and since she had not shaken her propensity to choose difficult men, we usually stayed holed up in a garage bedroom to avoid him, as he too was jealous of all but his own children and grandchildren. Described as "jester to the queen dowager," he would hover over the Thanksgiving turkey, before both his and her families, whetting the knife with cutting remarks about hers.[439] She ignored those remarks as she had Dickson's. We fled to the beach, and my husband fixed her lamps in the evenings, his astonishing ability to repair anything further honed as a way to attract some evidence of her acceptance, and forget her betrayals.

*

Did you hear the one about the cannibal who got married, and at the wedding reception, toasted his mother-in-law?

*

The plant Sansevieria trifasciata is known as "mother-in-law's tongue," a/k/a the snake plant, a/k/a the viper's bowstring. Evergreen. Tough. Drought resistant. The leaves are very sharp. Nigerians use it in rituals to remove the evil eye.

A common houseplant everywhere.

*

Mother-in-law's tongue

A pharmacist tells a customer: In order to buy arsenic you need a legal prescription. A picture of your mother-in-law just isn't enough.

*

For less than forty hours Franziska (Fanny) Braun was Hitler's mother-in-law, although she often visited their enclave while Eva was posing as his secretary. Hitler was never told that the Brauns were 1/32 Jewish, according to Nazi race laws, a fact discovered by Adolf Eichmann.[440] Once a ski champion, Fanny lived to age 96, many decades after her daughter's death, and Fritz, her husband, to 84. Fritz had been quite displeased when his 17-year-old daughter began seeing 40-year-old Hitler. A Catholic, he wrote a letter telling him to leave her alone, but Eva tore it up. Fritz eventually saw the advantages of associating with Hitler and gave up teaching to become an army officer.[441] Reels of movie footage of their visits with Hitler taken by Eva, an amateur filmmaker, show an affectionate family, prone to wading through streams, sunbathing, frolicking with the dogs at the beach, sunbathing, nude babies, and occasional costumes. During a round of toasts, Fanny wears a hat with a heart attached at the front.[442]

Hermann Fegelein, her other son-in-law, was married at Eagle's Nest surrounded by the family, and acted as Himmler's liaison officer. Did Fanny flinch when Hitler had him shot for desertion?[443]

*

I bought my mother-in-law a chair for Christmas, but she wouldn't plug it in.

*

Most of the in-law jokes are from the husband's perspective, although often problems between in-laws stem from the relationship between the wife and the mother-in-law. A wife will pick up on subtly disparaging remarks that the husband may miss altogether, which explains why a wife becomes angry with her husband for not taking her side. What lengths does a wife have to go to prove her point? Does she have to kill the mother-in-law, at least metaphorically, to avoid being a victim, or even worse, a shadow mother? Does she have to divorce the husband to spite his mother? Only a husband would find the situation comic.

*

Executive: "Sir, can I have a day off next week to visit my mother-in-law?"

Boss: "Certainly not!"

Executive: "Thank you so much, sir! I knew you would understand."

*

The Nuer son-in-law is never to be naked before his mother-in-law (which must have been somewhat difficult; when I visited, few people had clothing), he must not eat with her, and he must not talk to her directly. As soon as a child is born, however, the son-in-law is known only as the father of [insert name of the child], and the prohibition of conversation with the mother-in-law is lifted.

In other words, she can't complain until after the fact.

*

Why do they bury mothers-in-law 18 feet down, when everyone else is buried 6 feet down?

Because, deep down, they really are very nice people.

*

Are you good enough for my child? This is the question that underlies many a dig from a mother-in-law, but I didn't have to worry about that. Pat confided in me that my husband was lucky. He had a hard time focusing and I didn't, and she recognized that I appreciated what he, as a smart wide-ranging but scattered thinker, had to offer.

*

What's the difference between a mother-in-law and a vulture? The vulture waits until you are dead before it eats your heart out.

*

I'd learned a lot of "self-silencing" around my mother, but I didn't want to sacrifice knowing Pat just because I might be hurt. A daughter-in-law needs information about the family she's joining, where the skeletons are buried amid the bombshells. Consider how much I could learn from studying her: she knew how to handle General Patton as well as Lieutenant Colonel Hartwell; she knew how to steer UNICEF, having managed to convince Maurice Pate that although young and not academically art-credentialed, she should be the one to select the artwork for their world-famous cards. She did not force her opinions on me, although once she did buy my husband, a small man, a plaid wool suit in Scotland. He did not wear it for long. Her visits to New York tended to be brief and formal: dinner at her hotel, an afternoon at a museum. She inspected the first beach house we bought, one without running water in a rundown part of Long Island where the quarter acre plot was so overgrown that, on closing, we found a 1950s finned Cadillac and two boats that we'd never seen—and she did not disparage it.

*

After one particularly amazing magic trick, someone in the audience screamed, Wow, how did you do that?
  I would tell you, answered the magician, but then I'd have to kill you.

After a moment's pause the same voice yelled: Could you tell my mother-in-law?

*

No in-law of mine ever provided childcare. For that matter, neither did my mother, so that conflict was never kindled. Until you feel a kinship with someone, the theory goes, it's hard to hate him or her. And until your in-laws feel like parents, it's harder to fight with them the way you fight with your own parents.

I find a sentence in a letter that Pat wrote to Henry before our wedding: "She will make an excellent wife." Although she doesn't say why, she does notice that I love him very much.[444]

*

Pat, my mother and father at our wedding, 1981

There are no mother-in-law jokes. They are all true.

*

Since we're now quarantined to avoid Covid, we visit our storage facility. For fun—and for another go at finding my mother-in-law's Hitler photo. I mean, how much fun can we have in a 10 x 15 storage space? We haven't yet found the "important place" that Steve says he's stored it in. Along with a Queen Ann armchair without a pillow, a complete hammer collection and my sons' childhood books, the storage facility houses mostly the remnants of Pat's naïve art collection. Unpacking them in case Steve has slipped the photo inside, I notice gestural similarities between works. A naive painting of a man stiffly playing an accordion, paintings of stiff-looking houses—houses without perspective—itinerant painter's portraits of stiff miscellaneous Early Americans, the stiff paintings of elephants and kohl-rimmed maidens by Jamini Roy. I wouldn't have been surprised to find a sarcophagus in the lot. The stuff of the dead, or at least the unemotional.

16

Witch Hunts

Senator Joseph McCarthy took the truth and twisted it. His mandate of rooting out Communists wherever he could find or invent them reached deep into many aspects of Pat's life, both personal and professional. Was McCarthy's long reach partly about class? In his country-wide search for Communists, he was really only interested in those who had something to lose but were not quite powerful enough to defend themselves, especially those who "have had the finest homes, the finest college educations, and the finest jobs in Government we can give."[445] Not just anybody. At least at first.

*

As a relatively new organization devoted to internationalism, the UN was immediately suspect, and UNICEF, even newer, was an easy target. An organization devoted to giving away milk to children? Obviously communist. Ludwick Rajchman, a Pole and chairman of UNICEF, was not only from a Communist country but refused to back the US demand that UNICEF deny aid to the Chinese Communist children. He lost his job and his visa. In 1953, Dickson's press aide Ruth Elizabeth Crawford was fired for having signed on as a Communist for only a year, over twenty years earlier.[446] [447] The article in a local paper reads: "UN Fires Woman Press Aide. Self Admitted Red."[448] Dickson himself had work read into the Congressional record that same year, defending UNICEF's importance to world unity. He had just finished a 12,000-mile trip to see what UNICEF had accomplished. The speech begins by deriding those who felt that the US should get out of the UN because it had communist leanings and ends with: "People are drinking this brew and it's making them dizzy."[449]

*

Dickson's wife at the time, Ruth Adams Knight, was important enough in the media that she was third to name names to the "Subversive Infiltration of Radio, TV, and The Entertainment Industry" Senate committee.[450] Her previous husband, Raymond Knight, had a star on the Hollywood Walk for the "Cuckoo Hour," a wildly popular radio satire in the thirties and forties, and she was deeply involved in radio politics.[451] Organizing radio freelancers for better wages on the East Coast, she had become enraged by a seeming coup of younger writers in California who had been more vigorous in their attempts to unionize. "When we said the group was Communist what we really meant was that as opposed to the very dignified group in the East, they were noisy and unruly; and their meeting was conducted in the manner that a Communist meeting is popularly supposed to be conducted," she told Congress. Despite the flimsiness of her testimony, no doubt it ended a number of careers. She complained of the "constant derision of capitalism . . . of the average citizen . . . [there was] no such thing in their scripts as a decent banker or lawyer." She provides an example: a script about partisans in Yugoslavia being compared to American Revolutionary War heroes. Eventually she admits that the real problem was the leftist group getting all the best work, one example being the producer/director Hi Brown, who survived being blacklisted and eventually produced over 30,000 radio shows, including "Inner Sanctum," "Dick Tracy," and the "The Thin Man."[452]

*

Steve's first employer in the film business was Hi Brown's son, Barry. Working in a shipyard, Steve thought someone was playing a joke when he received a call to interview for a film job. A screenwriter on Shelter Island had seen potential in his college film about boat building in the Bahamas and contacted Brown. In the middle of the interview, an editor rushed in and said the 16/35mm editing machine had broken, and no one in all of Manhattan could fix it. Steve fixed it, and got the job.

Barry Brown never asked him about his communist sympathies.

*

What did Dickson think of his wife Ruth's testimony? He had moved out but they were still married. A year later, she published *Day after Tomorrow,* a novel about the communist infiltration of American high schools.

*

When Janet Scellen, Steve's stepmother, was made head of the National Film Board's New York office, it was 1946, the year after her boss John Grierson was forced to resign as one of the million Canadians—filmmakers, writers and civil servants—investigated by the Security Panel, the Canadian equivalent to the House Committee on Un-American Activities. Under Grierson's direction, the NFB had become the world's most successful wartime propagandist, having produced the best films with the best circulation of any country. Coining the term "documentary," Grierson wrote that "the once haunted concept of propaganda may have a democratic interpretation, and that its democratic interpretation makes propaganda and education one."[453] Charismatic and arrogant, progressive and visionary, and above all, productive, Grierson made many enemies, and the combination of his left-wing politics and his threat to commercially produced film was difficult to swallow. He was at the height of his power when, two days before the end of WWII, a clerk defected from Canada's Soviet embassy with evidence of a North American spy ring, the first incident in the Cold War. It named a National Film Board secretary (not Janet) a spy, implicating Grierson.[454]

Janet's colleague, Oscar-winning animator Norman MacLaren, traveled to Russia ten years earlier to affirm his commitment to Communism, but he kept his job. A MacLaren watercolor of a sprite at a fountain hung in Steve's father's house for decades, a gift to Janet when she retired at her marriage to Henry. Among her papers is a letter from MacLaren, embellished with whimsical curlicues and hand-drawn illustrations, requesting a shipment of film stock to Mongolia. But he wasn't filming. It was 1950, and after traveling to China to teach animation for UNESCO, he was trapped in a small village for five months in the middle of the communist takeover.[455]

No one knows what happened to the watercolor.

*

Steve says the photo of Hitler's purported ashes is not something I made up. We both saw it in Hawai'i, and he remembers receiving the photo along with other papers just before Pat's death. It's in a file folder with blank sheets that Hitler signed, says Steve, in case Hitler needed to dictate from the grave.

What? I say.

She never said how she acquired those.

A year later I uncover a letter to her editor Bill Birnie that offers him "some of the last documents signed by Hitler, commendations for medals" that she collected from Eagle's Nest.[456]

*

Family lore has it that Pat's mother, furious about the divorce from Henry Bull, used her position as a member of the Daughters of the American Revolution (DAR) to try to turn over Pat to McCarthy for having met with Chagall. The artist was, after all, Russian, albeit living in Paris and decidedly not a Communist, having become disillusioned thirty years earlier. As a devoted member of the DAR, Pat's mother opposed the UN and UNICEF for their calls for international unity, as well as the Peace Corps, rock 'n' roll, water fluoridation and integration. As a career woman, Pat was a suspected subversive to start with. Women in the postwar period were supposed to stay at home and consume in order to restore capitalism. Those who worked outside the home already bore a communist taint. And she had traveled to Europe—to both sides of the Berlin Wall!

Pat's divorce from Henry occurred in 1953, the same year Pat's mother took seven-year-old Steve in bow tie and suit to a DAR dinner meeting in New York City, and the same year that the DAR passed a resolution condemning UNICEF cards, a move later endorsed by the American Legion. The DAR's main complaint was with the UNICEF card's nondenominational imagery but since some of the images came from the Soviet bloc countries, the cards were also anti-Christian, godless and certainly Communist. UNICEF had deliberately chosen images to reflect its ecumenical position, with the raison d'etre that there was no such thing as an enemy child. "A Communist-inspired plan to destroy all religious beliefs" was the DAR verdict.[457] Pat endured pressure from the Eastern European bloc as well as from the

DAR and her mother. "Governments would begin to push artists on us. Some of them 'notable Communists.' [I] would have to perhaps say, 'Well, [he] doesn't really kind of fit our criteria.'"[458] It was only when First Lady Jacqueline Kennedy revealed that she bought UNICEF greeting cards that sales picked up.[459]

*

Walter Winchell was a powerful crony of McCarthy's. He acted as McCarthy's star shill, and dined regularly with McCarthy's right-hand henchman, Roy Cohn.[460] During WWII, Winchell broadcast against the Nazis but became concerned about Russian infiltration at the end of the hostilities and turned virulently anti-Communist. When he named a name, it was as lethal to a career as testimony before Congress. Winchell went easy on Pat. She first showed up in his column in July 1944 as having exposed "no-goods" in her article for *Woman's Home Companion* about bullet proof Bibles. She appeared a second time as the first "white woman" in Guam since its recapture, and as Elmer Davis' "Girl Friday" at the Office of War Information.[461] Her third appearance was Winchell's mention of her engagement to Lt. Hank Bull,[462] and her fourth and last was of Steve's birth in 1948, which was also announced on national radio.[463]

*

Nineteen forty-eight was the year that Dickson chose to take on Winchell. Was Steve's birth that year the impetus for Dickson to indulge in his self-destructive impulses? He must have felt that Pat becoming a mother made her even more unattainable. Or was going one-on-one with Winchell, the most powerful man in media, simply irresistible to him as a professional? Five years later Dickson would be deemed a "top-flight author" along with Upton Sinclair and James Michener in a launch notice of the syndicated column "For The Record," and elsewhere called "one of America's top columnists" carrying fifty newspapers, but in 1948, Winchell was definitely tops, broadcasting to twenty million people a week, and his column read by 50 million.[464,465,466]

In Dickson's *Colliers* article, "Walter Winchell: An American Phenomenon," he admits that Winchell is "a man of singular talents and tremendous influence," then goes on to point out egregious mistakes in his column and his tremendous egotism as bad for the practice of journalism. Winchell, he says, is someone who defines boredom as "other people's conversation." Dickson publishes Winchell's salary and announces that "his ignorance of finance is unlimited," and that many of his cherished accomplishments "are trivial." He states that Winchell "never has to face the vexing problem of having to choose good from bad."[467]

According to Dickson, after reviewing the final draft, Winchell responded by saying "I would rather have a piece like this than a sugary one like 'The Man Nobody Hates' which I know is not true."[468] But Winchell was not at all happy when it came out, and became so relentless in his public complaints about the piece that others noticed: "Nor are we, like Winchell, so stung by criticism, that we must write a column in defense as he did in answer to *Collier*'s story by Dickson Hartwell," writes the editor of the *Mansfield Advertiser*.[469]

Other journalists thought Dickson was crazy. "You're a fool to write about Winchell. No matter how fairly you write, if you criticize him, he'll attack you," comments a reporter in Dickson's "How *Walter Winchell* Came To Be Written,"[470] an essay in *A Guide To Successful Magazine Writing* in which Dickson provides the rationale for such a suicidal project. Although he protests that he is no "typewriter Galahad seeking to slay the Winchell dragon," he coauthored this explication with a Donald Robinson, so perhaps he needed help with said rationalization. The article's inclusion in the book, however, is also a sign that the attack was widely admired by other writers. He ends the piece with bravado, saying that the only gamble a reporter can't make is "the risk of being dull." Perhaps that was Winchell's credo too.

Winchell didn't sue for libel—the piece was well researched.

*

A few years after Steve's grandmother took him to a DAR party, his mother offered him the family Ku Klux Klan robe to wear for Halloween. She pulled it out of storage, holding it over him, its point crumpled. Would their Jamaican maid iron it for him in the morning? She and Dickson were drunk but Steve, who had been schooled about the Klan and slavery by the maid's husband, an angry ex-paratrooper, said he'd rather be a clown.

Steve learning weaving from his
grandmother, 1955

The Klan was one of McCarthy's biggest supporters.

*

Pat wasn't racist. She gave a speech at Wellesley in 1950 admonishing the Wellesley girls to consider the plight of contemporary Black people in the South. The setting is of white women dressed in hoop skirts, giving tours of their gardens. They pass "a shack that is the courtroom of an ignorant, malevolent, Negro-hating justice of the peace."

> They never step inside to see what happens to black prisoners; they are not concerned with the grave responsibility that rests upon the whites in a white-dominated society; they do not seem to care that the hapless black must inevitably be found guilty because the judge makes his living by assessing fines that go in part to him . . . They do not even seem to understand that without equality of justice our legal system becomes a tyranny.[471]

*

Ancestor Henry Ware lived in Belle Grove, one of the biggest plantations on the Mississippi, with seventy-five rooms.[472] Pat claimed he was descended from Gebhard von Blucher, the Prussian who turned back Napoleon at Waterloo. Her mother's middle name was Blocher. Although a planter and all that entailed, Henry Ware publicly advocated that the Southern states should end the Civil War through a "peace convocation." After the war ended, he ran for election as a delegate to the convention to bring Texas back into the Union. His platform was that secession was wrong, and he argued that freedmen deserved fair treatment and education, and advocated for their right to vote.

His rival attacked him as a traitor to the white race. The election was quite close: Ware was only sixteen votes short of winning.[473]

*

What happened to that KKK costume? No one admits knowing. Like the DAR, the KKK were anti-immigrant racists and antisemitic white supremacists, perfect for McCarthy, and flourished even in the corner of Nebraska that I'm from, where you can still see the old schoolhouse that was turned into a meeting hall for the Klan, organized against the immigrant Bohemian Catholics, like, for example, my family.

*

Steve's middle name is Medaris, after his mother's ancestor Domingo Medearis who died in Virginia in 1680. In 1619, the Portuguese were the first to sell slaves in Virginia, taken from their colony Angola, but records indicate that Medearis imported his help through indentureship. In the 1600s, indentured servants far outnumbered slave labor in the American colonies. Medearis would have received land as "headrights" for financing the trip of the indentured, some fifty acres per transported person. Eventually he accumulated so much land that it became unmanageable, and he gave up a large portion. His grandson lived across the Rappahannock river from George Washington—who definitely had slaves—and married into Washington's family.[474]

*

Harvey Matusow, a paid FBI informant who named hundreds of people for McCarthy, went to jail only after he told the truth and retracted his testimony. Among those affected by his accusations were members of the State Department, CBS, the Boy Scouts, the Girl Scouts, the YWCA and the UN.[475] Matusow said there were

500 communist teachers in the New York City school system, and made headlines by saying things like "The Sunday section of the *New York Times* alone has 126 dues-paying Communists. On the editorial and research staff of *Time* and *Life* magazines are seventy six hard-core Reds. The New York Bureau of the Associated Press has twenty-five."[476] In 1952 he destroyed Pete Seeger's group, the Weavers, by insinuating that they had communist leanings.[477] He flipped three times, making him an anti-anti-Communist. "I'm not saying that I'm a credible person," he said in a much later *Rolling Stone* interview.[478] He argued that the problem was not the people he crushed and ruined but the country that produced him and pushed him to power. Serving four years in jail, he saw himself as a sort of Daniel Ellsberg of his time.[479] Although people paid thousands of dollars a week not to be named by him, he insisted that he used the sale of a patent on a new version of the Whee-lo to pay his lawyers. Was he the inventor Henry negotiated with to start the Whee-lo business? The patent was filed in 1940 and renewed in 1963 and many times thereafter, but nowhere is Matusow mentioned. Perhaps he meant a variant of the Yo-yo—or else he lied.

*

Even Mr. UNICEF, Danny Kaye, Pat's charge while she was Director of Information, had a brush with McCarthy. After Walt Disney and Ronald Reagan named names (including Kaye's) to the House Committee on Un-American Activities in 1947, Kaye flew to Washington to protest the government's targeting of the film industry. He was accompanied by Humphrey Bogart, Lauren Bacall, John Huston, Judy Garland and others. They sat in on the hearings, smoking sardonically, representing themselves as the "Committee for the First Amendment." Later, when several in their company turned out to be Communists, Bogart shouted at Danny Kaye, "You fuckers sold me out."[480]

*

Three times during the first Trump presidency, the *New Yorker* ran an article about the similarities between McCarthy and Trump.[481] [482] [483] "The Model for Donald Trump's Media Relations Is Joseph McCarthy," written nine months after his presidency began, points out that McCarthy had a cheerleader in Walter Winchell, control of the Hearst papers, that he forbade some reporters from attending his press conferences, encouraged the harassment of journalists, and constantly lied. "The likeness is uncanny," agrees Louis Menand, author of the second article. McCarthy was a man with "no ethical or ideological compass, and most of his colleagues regarded him as a troublemaker, a loudmouth, and a fellow entirely lacking in senatorial politesse." The point of the third *New Yorker* article was that since Truman had already unseated all the spies, McCarthy's efforts were only intended to destroy the First Amendment.

*

Surely it was Ruth, Dickson's angry wife, who turned him in to the FBI. As I have mentioned, two of the complainants were friends of hers, the only two with negative views of Dickson. The FBI opened the case just six days after Ruth counter-filed for divorce. Two years earlier, she was naming names for McCarthy and would have known exactly whose ear to whisper into. The informant is identified in the much-redacted report as T-1 "of unknown reliability," and referred to in the neutral "he." Whenever the investigation lags, he/she telephones Hoover's office and makes further allegations, with intimate details about Dickson's entire history, from the farm in Connecticut to his service in Hawai'i—but the first gripe is always about the affair with Pat. For example, T-1 complains that $1,500 of a $5,000 mortgage taken out on their Connecticut property was spent on Pat in Florida. Ruth's FBI interview takes place late in the investigation, perhaps to allay suspicion that she is the informant, but even there, the FBI report that her statement is "vicious and slanderous."[484] T-1 depicts his/her rival, Mrs. Patricia Lochridge Bull, as a "hard-boiled ambitious person" of whom he/she has "no question of her disloyalty," but then withdraws that statement when pressed for evidence.[485] This telephone interview is conducted on the same day as Dickson and Pat's marriage. Two weeks after the FBI starts investigating, Ruth launches her own, convincing her friends to sneak around the hotel where Dickson and Pat are romancing, and sends a package addressed to Pat that she has to sign for. This results in a bit of comic testimony about the real Mrs. Hartwell shadowing Mrs. Hartwell-to-be.

The only other obvious candidate for snitch is Walter Winchell. Although he had easy access to J. Edgar Hoover, who received all the reports on Dickson, by then Winchell would have licked his wounds over Dickson's castigating article five years earlier, and he wouldn't have had T-1's knowledge in such detail. As a prominent radio producer and informant, Ruth probably had access to Winchell, although there are no letters between them—but Winchell kept few letters at all, and Ruth none. Three months after the FBI investigation is well underway, his column evinces a hint of glee.

> Investigators are working on Dickson Hartwell, an author for the mags. He is now on a world tour for UNICEF, collecting magazine material for the UN. The government probers feel taxpayers would enjoy knowing who hired a man with his record (for episodes that never leaked out in print) to go on that joy-ride."[486]

T-1 telephones the FBI on the same day that Winchell's column appears, with new information, and when nothing much happens, telephones four days later with additional accusations gleaned from conversations with his stepbrother and colleagues. Once again, when they are interviewed, Dickson is absolved.

The hundred-page report on Dickson is a good example of the seriousness of such an accusation. Agents in Portland, Philadelphia, Miami, Los Angeles, New York, New Haven, Washington DC, Phoenix, Baltimore, San Antonio, San Francisco, and Richmond, Virginia work from May to December of 1953, interviewing not only relatives, friends, housekeepers, employers, neighbors and associates but those bellboys and switchboard operators. Because Mrs. Bull has given Dickson magazine assignments, the FBI has the perfect excuse to talk to her. She gives Dickson a sterling review. They also check everyone's credit records. A mole "acquainted with some phases of communist party activities in the New York area" does not know Dickson.[487] The FBI is thorough and follows every lead. After all, Dickson has just returned from that 12,000 mile fourteen-country world tour and no one wants America's stand on international relations compromised by a Communist—there's a Cold War on. Indeed, many put forward that Dickson drank too much and that once he was arrested for disturbing the peace in New York City, and it's proven that he's been having an affair with Pat, whom he marries in the middle of all this, but in the end no one agrees to testify: not even Dickson's half-brother, who accuses him of having "pro-Red" sympathies after finishing college (he was kicked out), and not Ruth's two friends, sneaking around the hotel, hoping to catch a glimpse of Pat—and not even Ruth. The final interview is with St. Clair McKelway, a *New Yorker* editor and a lieutenant colonel when Dickson was a major in Hawai'i, and who also knew Pat as a war correspondent, and among the many writers he'd hired was Philip Hamburger. He states that Dickson is an honest, sincere, conscientious person and that he never questioned his loyalty, that he had never heard him make any comments "which could be considered hostile to the best interests of the United States," and that, yes, he would recommend him for a position of trust.[488]

If T-1 is indeed Ruth, "of unknown reliability," her testimony without sound evidence or witnesses would be suspect, especially since she's just divorced him. No wonder she wouldn't testify. She was just fishing, hoping to pin something on him, but wanted someone else to incriminate him. Perhaps the year abroad she took during their separation was more to avoid repercussions from those radio professionals she'd trashed the year before rather than Dickson?

For Dickson, it was a close one. He knew he was being investigated, maybe not right away, but surely by the time Pat was interviewed. He lost his press aide, but kept his job until he resigned for Pat. The FBI investigation of Pat found her trustworthy as well, and little else.

*

Pat's long-ago colleague at CBS, Edward R. Murrow, was the powerhouse who finally took down McCarthy. On his March 24, 1954 TV newscast "See It Now," he forcefully made his case. McCarthy had been closing in on him too, but having covered WWII very thoroughly, Murrow knew the territory considerably better than McCarthy. "I require no lectures from the junior senator from Wisconsin as to the dangers or terrors of Communism." The incident was beautifully dramatized in the film *Good Night and Good Luck*, produced by George Clooney. The film earned six Academy Award nominations. Unlike his film *Monuments Men*, with its confused priorities and last-minute re-edit, this time Clooney produced a winner. He emphasized journalistic responsibility as a voice of dissent, in opposition to the current vogue for "both sides," an approach that does not prioritize truth supported by evidence but instead the journalism's interest in a more provocative double story.

*

As far as I know, Pat was never a member of the Communist Party, and never betrayed or hurt anyone accused by McCarthy. She was a member of the Author's League, an organization the FBI deemed infiltrated but not dominated. Dickson's hearings epitomized how easily such evidence can be twisted. Or maybe not. A few people actually were Communists, that was true, but whether they were actually a threat in a country that purportedly allows the co-existence of contradictory beliefs is another question entirely. But the way that McCarthy's accusations came so close to so many parts of Pat's life set the tenor of the times: it was dangerous to tell the truth.

17

Addiction

The drunk journalist is a well-worn stereotype. The specter of the alcoholic reporter conjures up bottles hidden in bottom desk drawers. War correspondents in particular are seen as drowning their PTSD in round after round of newly-captured liquor or the last bottle in some bar full of bullet holes. One of the more important discoveries journalists made in the European bars during World War II was that large orders from the Champagne region usually preceded major Nazi offensives.[489]

*

Pat did like a martini at six, that I witnessed. An alcoholic? Not like my mother, who would drive through a snowstorm in her eighties to get to the package store. Although Pat lost frequently to correspondents in poker, she could hold her own when it came to drinking. "A wooden leg," said one early admirer.[490] A May 20, 1941 CBS News Bureau photo shows her as a 25-year-old radio news correspondent with a tipsy grin, wearing a hat (with a veil!), pearls, a suit with a lace collar, and white gloves after a three-week working vacation in Bermuda. Asked how she enjoyed her stay, Pat said "Three bottles of scotch every day."[491] Unimaginable.

Pat's Bermuda interview, 1941

In June, the *Times Dispatch* reports that while in Bermuda, Pat danced with the exiled Romanian King Carol Lupescu. What did he say? "It's very hot," replied Pat.[492] What was she drinking? By September the Texas press reports that she's visiting Bermuda for *Woman's Home Companion*, covering "changes transforming the pleasure resort to an American defense base."[493] Another syndicated article that September showed Pat returning from Bermuda with the report that the soldiers stationed there were forced to drink rum because the beer was too expensive.[494]

*

Alcoholism was the disease du jour of a certain generation of writers. Half of the Nobel Prize winners from the US were alcoholics: Sinclair Lewis, Eugene O'Neill, and William Faulkner, and these three were about the same age as Dickson. Dylan Thomas died of drink in 1953.

*

"I think many women achieved what they were able to do as reporters because the guys were too interested in sticking around the bar and having a drink," Pat revealed in her 1995 interview. "One of the reasons I was successful at CBS was that my boss was an alcoholic and didn't like getting up early with his hangovers."

*

Pat's mother responded to her husband's alcoholism as a classic codependent, by trying to control everything and everyone in her life. She lost control and even contact with her husband when he moved to Washington without her, and she seldom joined him. She was successful in controlling her daughter by getting Pat to marry Henry, less successful in keeping Pat married to him, then successful again, on the rebound, in marrying Henry off to Janet, her boarder.

Steve still remembers the sound of the liquor cabinet being opened by his stepfather.

*

Having had an alcoholic father, Pat must have had few illusions about drinking but might have had the inevitable dream of managing Dickson better than her mother had her father. Thus she would save not only her husband but unconsciously her father, who was well-beloved. "Hope, dear, that you're being a good guy and behaving yourself and saving all existing stocks of whiskey to celebrate my eventual return," she writes to him just before she flies home from the war.[495] In another letter, she tells him she's had dinner with a family friend, Texan Major General Blakeley, and ends with "Take care of yourself, baby,"[496] in a reversal of roles. As countless AA members can attest, rescue by others seldom works, no matter what the cause; it's the alcoholic who has to change, and that requires the alcoholic to accept the truth of his addiction.

*

Steve keeps taking over a story about his mother I'm trying to tell at a party. I'm the one who researched it, it's my story, no longer his. I ask whether his father talked over Janet and no one heard her and that's why no one remembers anything about her.

He agrees that no one remembers her.

Now it's the morning after the party and he hasn't had his coffee yet. I'm trying to understand mansplaining, I say. You learned it from your father?

Of course he agrees with me.

But I know better than to press my advantage. Did you ever manage a relationship with Janet after you were grown?

He chews down his granola, he takes a sip of his coffee. Hot! he says. He looks at his napkin. I remember the time I taught her to smoke marijuana.

I laugh, then he says, It was when she was dying of cancer. She coughed a lot, taking a puff.

Did she just ask you if you had some? Were you a pothead back then?

I looked like a pothead, he says, like now.

Since the pandemic, his hair has grown into a seventies mane. It's attractive, or is it attractive because that's how I remember him when we first met in the eighties? I've told him I like it.

He looks down at his napkin and when his face faces mine again, it twists, and after a long pause, he says, she was my champion.

I'm surprised, very surprised. And he is too, he says this is the first time he's figured that out. He made a film in the Bahamas before his last year of college, and she must have stood up for him because his father didn't insist that he spend all summer at a job. She'd seen a few nascent filmmakers in her years at the National Film Board.

Did you ever hear her defend you?

No, he says. I never realized before that she did. She must have.

He puts his dishes in the sink. I didn't see her very much while she was dying.

Didn't you hate her?

My mother was always gone when I was shipped off to her house. Janet was the one who had to discipline us.

The wicked stepmother.

Her sister-in-law, Louise, came in the summers and tried to explain what was going on. She spent a lot of time pulling grass out between the driveway paving.

Did you love Louise?

He doesn't say.

I'd met Louise—just a sister-in-law, not even a sister, with a German accent, who kept house for Henry for a few years, and took no nonsense from him, I'm sure. I remember the tiny script of her letters, a forced cheerfulness of someone with few choices who worked in retail in Queens and went into assisted living in Arizona with a friend rather early. She didn't smoke pot or drink, she was the one who told Steve the truth about the kidnapping. Well after the letters stopped, busy with our children, we understood she had died.

*

Alfred Kazin wrote that drinking was a symptom of the writer's "loneliness, creative aspirations, and frenzies."[497] Writing requires isolation, the writer alone with his words, his world, a natural introvert. Drinking bolsters self-confidence to continue writing, eases the loneliness after those words are released to the public, and relaxes the writer after a long day of concentration.

With writing, you can't say your colleague dropped the ball, you take on all the pressure. Not to mention deadlines for the three daily syndicated columns that appeared under Dickson's name in all those many newspapers.

*

After a harrowing career as a war correspondent, Andy Rooney, Dickson's co-editor for *Off the Record*, spent thirty-three years on *60 Minutes,* and was not an alcoholic. Like Pat, he was among the first to visit the concentration camps, and like Pat, found the experience drove the pacifism out of him—but not to drink.

Pat, Andy and Dickson were all members of the Overseas Press Club. Founded in 1939 with Franklin Roosevelt as an honorary member, very quickly its luncheon discussions became a live radio staple. By 1947, the year Andy joined, it had five hundred members and had published a book called *Deadline Delayed,* precursor to *Off the Record,* also about journalists' hijinks. Still very active today, the club's ostensible purpose is to train journalists in staying safe while reporting, to promote best practices in the trade—and to drink together. Dickson also joined in 1947, two years after Pat who, by 1952, had appeared thirty-nine times in the newsletter, having headed or co-chaired many committees while having a full-time job, two children under the age of four, and a long affair conducted not far from the clubhouse.[498] Pat was the workhorse co-chair with Edward R. Murrow in 1953, and raised over $364,000 (over $4 million today) for a permanent home for the club.[499] President Eisenhower opened the new location and presented her, not Murrow, with a thank you plaque.[500] By then Pat had been vice president of the club for two years and had joined the board of governors. Murrow's contribution had been titular. The club gave him an award at the 1951 Waldorf Astoria gala that Pat helped organize, where

Overseas Press Club banquet a year after its founding

her old boss Elmer Davis also received an award, and her friend Eleanor Roosevelt was one of four speakers. Both Dickson and Pat are noted on the gala invitation as part of the dinner committee. They were also both members of the Society of Magazine Writers.[501] Just around then they were planning their respective divorces—no doubt over drinks.

*

Henry and his friends drank too. It was the preferred vice of the era. His friends' girlfriends took care of the two boys while the men fixed the drinks, although once Steve remembers a bald guy helped them catch a rabbit in a box baited with a carrot. After the rabbit clawed Steve's brother, Steve hid the box under the house, which had a crawl space of five feet. He thought he could use the rabbit in a trick and went upstairs to find a big hat. On the way, he let the door to the inside slam shut. One of those girl-friends—or it even could've been a man— screamed, *Headache!*

When Steve's mother had been there, the doors in this house slammed in the middle of the night during quarrels. What was that? he or his brother would say in the morning, and their mother would say, Just the wind.

It's just the wind, Steve shouted to his father when he complained about the slamming. By the time he made it back downstairs, his father was already tipsy, setting out a game of backgammon on the porch. Admission to the magic show is ten cents, Steve said, ducking into his hiding place under the porch, and if you bring another kid with you, you can still get in for the same price.

There was the crunch of his father taking a seat on the wicker.

Steve placed the hat on top of the rabbit and the hat just about fit, if the rabbit moved its feet closer together. He carried the rabbit and the hat out from under the house onto the front lawn. His brother was hanging around, showing off his claw marks to one of the ladies. Watch the hat for a minute, he told him.

That's too boring, said his brother.

Steve stood on one foot, then the other. I'll be right back.

The poker he needed was either propped up in the coat closet in the boys' bedroom where they used it to clean out a mouse hole, or holding up one of the curtains, or maybe beside the fireplace. No. Bingo, under the blue couch in the living room. Ladies and Gentlemen, he shouted, waving it, the show's on the lawn.

Not so loud, said the girlfriend of the bald guy, holding her head, then the bald guy was the first to come out.

After collecting the money, his brother took a seat in the second row, eating peanuts somebody had brought out to go with the Manhattans. By the time his father produced the ice bucket and another chair, the bald guy had pulled a playing card from his sleeve. Cheater, cheered the audience, and they clapped anyway. Let's get the show on the road, said his father.

Steve whirled the fireplace poker around the hat and said Hocus Pocus, and lifted the hat. The rabbit was gone.

He thought for a minute it was magic.

You didn't want the rabbit anyway, said his brother. What did he do except eat?

You let it go.

His brother did a card trick that pretty much worked.

Okay, folks, freshen up your drinks, said his father. We've got a cocktail party to go to.

The audience stood and stretched. The bald man tousled Steve's hair. Better luck next time, pardner.

*

Magic tricks are perfect for an audience of drinkers. Their cognitive abilities are dampened, they can't tell the truth from one moment to the next or discern the difference while watching the magicians' hands move quickly in front of them. They become gullible, and apt to stretch their stories for their own audience: the rabbit's not in the stew.

*

Dickson wasn't drinking because he suffered PTSD. He was too young for World War I, and his bronze star for the second was won at the office. But he understood Pat's drive to improve his story, blaming his first wife's avarice on his problem. Public relations is always about the story.

His previous divorces, and his subsequent divorce from Pat, and surely the destruction of his prominent career was caused by alcoholism. As I noted before, Pat maintained that Dickson began to drink too much because he was under so much strain, paying for Ruth Adams Knight's New York apartment and their farm in Connecticut. But Knight was no helpless housewife spending all her pin money shopping for Currier & Ives prints. The same year she published *Women Must Weep*, ostensibly about her marriage to Dickson, she also published *Lady Editor*, which celebrated women's writing and editing—an early feminist media history—and later eleven other novels, and years more of radio scripts. She could've paid for the prints with her own money.

*

In early 1962, Dickson's physician told him that if he didn't stop drinking, he'd die. Those long martini-soaked *Mad Men* lunches couldn't have helped. The only cure the doctor knew of—aside from AA—was a change of location to lessen the stress. Dickson had tried AA and scorned it. He and Pat conferred about moving but made no decision. She went off to Czechoslovakia where she was collecting art for UNICEF, and he cabled her mid-March, telling her he had sold the Cranach to a dealer and was buying a newspaper in Arizona with the money.[502] She wouldn't be back for a month. In the meantime, he would sell their stocks and their apartment, arrange a mortgage on the new house. He was on tranquilizers, as well as drinking. This worried even the children. One of the boys was still wetting the bed at age ten.[503]

He writes "sorry you are getting the jitters about Arizona," then he mentions, during all his frantic activity, that it seems as if she hasn't been getting all of his letters.[504]

18

Truth in Art

Cranach's "Cupid Complaining to Venus," one of Hitler's favorite paintings, hung in Pat's 92nd Street townhouse until it was sold to the firm of E. A. Silberman in 1963 to finance their move to Arizona. Dickson wrote: "rarely have I seen a man so in love with a thing as is Mr. Silberman with that picture . . . he was caressing it." He also said that "he doesn't want us to talk with anyone about the picture or even to show photos of it."[505] Obviously Silberman knew his deal was fraught with problems—and big money. Dickson suggested that Pat do the research for its provenance from Czechoslovakia, knowing full well the grueling work obligations she had with UNICEF abroad. Was he trying to derail her, or get her to come home sooner to help him sort things out? He was so determined to sell the painting, he accepted only $33,000 from Silberman almost immediately. As a bonus, or perhaps feeling guilty, Silberman threw in a surrealist painting by Segovia, son of the classical guitarist, worth about $1,000, and turned around to sell the Cranach less than a year later to the National Gallery in London for 134,000 pounds. (Today's equivalent would be about four million pounds, or

$5,400,000).[506] The National Gallery deemed it to be "very near to [Cranach's] rare best."[507]

In 2019, another Cranach painting of the same period was estimated to be worth $12 million.[508]

Out of the dozen versions of "Cupid Complaining to Venus," the painting Pat selected was most likely the first.[509] Painted between 1526-27, it was in Hitler's personal collection, but removed from Munich sometime during the war to protect it from air raids.[510] The afternoon after being traumatized by Dachau, Lee Miller made her way to Munich and photographed Hitler's apartment, describing the paintings left behind as mediocre.[511]

*

"Cupid Complaining to Venus" shows a lithe young woman looking seductively toward the viewer, dressed, as it were, in an aristocratic wide-brimmed hat of the 1500s and a necklace—and nothing else. The background is forest, castle, river: the accoutrement of a wealthy woman. Belief in *weibermacht,* the power of women over men, was popular in Germany at the time, and that's what her frank gaze of seduction suggests. She's clothed only in mythology, art's grand pretext for nudity. Contemporary in her beauty, she's thin, no Reubens, Hitler's dream of Aryan women without the confusing musculature that his health regimes produced. Steve attests to the painting's power, saying he found it titillating as a young boy. Bees circle Cupid's head, and he holds up a hive while beseeching her: *Is the pleasure of lust worth the pain?* The caption is from Theocritus, written in Latin directly onto the painting. Like, Mom, do you really need this honey? It's as if the painting hanging for over twenty years in Pat's home was always scolding her for having decided on Dickson, the lusty alcoholic, rather than Henry the tame. Or else

Cupid Complaining to Venus, 1526–1527

it's about Steve, trying to get his mother—the sultry seducer—to notice him. She's reaching into the tree of knowledge, about to eat the apple. He's warning her but she's not listening. All the painting is missing is the wily promoter, the serpent. Except it is there: Cranach's signature of a black-winged serpent holding a ruby ring in its jaws and wearing a crown, painted on a rock face beside Venus' raised foot.

*

In 2008, Charlotte Higgins, the *Guardian's* arts correspondent, theorized that "Hartwell was given the painting by the local

United States commander as a thank-you for writing a positive piece about the local military administration."[512] Like the other WWII correspondents, Pat was all about writing positive pieces during the war; that was her main mission with *Woman's Home Companion,* and her article "I Governed Berchtesgaden" was no exception. After having her photo taken with the (fake) Vermeer, had she said thank you very much, and tucked the Cranach under her arm and just walked out, the way she walked away with so many of Goering's medals pinned to her blouse? She had been dead for eight years before her son Jay contacted the National Gallery about the painting's provenance. Although the National Gallery purchased "Cupid Complaining to Venus" in 1963, Jay's revelation in 2004 of his mother's sketchy acquisition was big in the news cycle for two years, with articles in the *New York Times, Reuters, Washington Post, Globe and Mail, Guardian, L.A. Times, BBC,* and newspapers in Spain, Italy, Holland, Poland, France and Germany.[513]

I ask Jay why he outed her after her death.

I thought the museum should know its whereabouts from 1945-1962 and from that they could then determine what steps should be taken. Had no idea that public museums were required to report new information on "suspect" works in order to facilitate returns…One thing that we learned in the process—based on the photograph of Hitler's apartment and the year taken—is that this piece probably was NOT looted.[514]

Elsewhere he says he wanted to make sure the painting wasn't the property of Jewish casualties of the war. Most recently he told me that he and his wife had been planning a trip to London and wanted to see the painting. Since it wasn't on display, he had to make a case for bringing it out and thus revealed how his mother was involved.[515]

*

Many documents and inventories that allow scholars to confirm past ownership and the movement of Nazi-era artworks have become available in only the last ten years and posted online. In 2015, Helen Mirren starred in *The Woman in Gold*, a film about a decades-long fight to reclaim a Klimt portrait of a family member. She later testified to Congress in support of the Holocaust Expropriated Recovery Act (or HEAR Act), legislation that lengthens the statute of limitations for stolen artwork to a uniform six years from the date the art is identified and located, and evidence of ownership has been presented. President Obama signed it into law in 2016. At the end of 2017, the Holocaust Claims Processing Office under the New York State Banking Department announced that it had facilitated the restitution of over $176 million in claims.[516] But that is loose change in the art world.

Museums are now required to place a placard alongside the works that were "confiscated, seized, forcibly stolen, or changed hands due to any involuntary means in Europe between 1933 and 1945." MoMA has 620 works listed on the Nazi-Era Provenance Portal, the Guggenheim has 289, and the Met fifty-three. Have you seen any labels? Many of the artworks are no longer exhibited. The Carnegie Institute immediately hid a painting suspected to have been taken from the Schloss family collection, and only much later discovered it to be a copy.[517] [518] [519]

In April 2020, the National Gallery returned a Picasso drawing to the Mendelssohns, Jewish bankers whose family included the composer. This was only the third work that the National Gallery deaccessioned for reasons of provenance. Like so many other museums, they are not terribly excited about seeking out the true owners and returning their inventory or labeling them, but at least they seem to be assiduous about posting the results of their investigations online.[520]

*

E. A. Silberman's offices were once located on East 57th Street with all the other blue chip art galleries. Luminaries such as Eleanor Roosevelt visited, she in 1956 to see contemporary British art.[521] On the internet, Pat's Cranach, along with several paintings by Hieronymus Bosch, are set out as important examples of what was shown before its closing in the 1980s.[522] Two years after its founding by two Jewish art dealers in 1938, E. A. Silberman Galleries sold an unsigned and undated Rembrandt to a Hollywood actor for only $45,000, asserting that it came from "a princely Polish collection," and that further provenance was unavailable due to the firm's records having vanished during World War II (untrue). The painting ended up in Harvard's collection and was eventually proved to be fake.[523] Aside from "Cupid Complaining to Venus," two more Cranachs were found to have been looted by the Nazis, one in 2000 and the other in 2016. They have been awarded to the museums that hold them instead of the Jewish descendants of their owners.[524] E. A. Silberman Galleries is still listed on Oberlin's Nazi Era Provenance Internet Portal, having sold a confiscated 14th century Italian crucifix in 1942 to Oberlin's Art Museum, and another stolen 14th century artwork in 1947 to the Grand Rapids Art Museum.[525] "It is unlikely any other pieces in the museum's collection were stolen," protests its director. One does wonder. E. A. Silberman Galleries bought a stolen Schiele portrait in 1947, which it then sold to a Boston woman who later bequeathed it to the Museum of Fine Arts. In the late nineties, the rightful heirs sued for the painting, but the museum won the right to keep it. "What museum conducts eighteen months of research into a provenance that allegedly clears its title and then hides the evidence?" asks the blogger who reported on the scandal.[526] Typical of the entry notes on the paintings sold by E.A. Silberman is what is listed with Yale University's "Amorous Hunt," a 15th century tempera on panel by Master of Charles of Durazzo (possibly Francesco di Michele), which says that the Rabinowitz family purchased it from Silberman sometime "before 1945-1959," and nothing before that. It has been put in storage.[527]

After inspecting a catalog at The Frick showing that the Cranach's last official owner, Emil Goldschmidt, had auctioned it to an unknown buyer in 1909, Dickson first tried to sell the painting to the Metropolitan Museum of Art, but was refused. A 2020 article about the Met's acquisition of a 17th century painting in 1984 illustrates their acquisition principles at the time. Although the painting may have belonged to a persecuted Jewish refugee, the provenance was cited as "a property of a gentleman." Art dealer Guy Stair Sainty says about these transactions: "You bought something in Christie's or Sotheby's and you didn't even think about it. Unless you had a suspicion then, you had no reason to check, but nowadays we don't buy a painting without looking."[528] The Met must have turned down Dickson's offer in 1962 for reasons other than lack of provenance.

*

Am I deflecting Pat's guilt by commenting on the equally nefarious practices of art galleries and museums? What was Pat going to do with the painting, years after she had taken it—give it back to the Army? Provenance, especially of these stolen artworks, is extremely difficult to pin down even now, with the internet. E. A. Silberman told the National Gallery in London that the painting "had been passed down by family descendants" of the

1909 owner at the Berlin auction, meaning the Hartwells. What she should have done is sold it and given the proceeds to a Jewish relief agency, without knowing who it belonged to. The benefit of the doubt. A hard and very unlikely choice.

*

Before WWII, Georges Wildenstein, a descendant of Jewish cattle-dealers whose father founded Wildenstein & Co., one of the most successful and influential art-dealerships of the 20th century, had a partnership with an equally influential dealer, Paul Rosenberg, for exclusives with Matisse and others. Both claimed they lost a good deal of inventory during the war. In 1940 more than 2,000 artworks held by Rosenberg were declared "ownerless cultural goods" and seized by the Nazis. Rosenberg's son Alexander, a lieutenant for the Allies assigned to Italy, dynamited train tracks late in the war to discover the overturned Nazi boxcars were full of artwork taken from his father's home. The incident was made into *The Train*, a 1964 film starring Burt Lancaster. In 1997, the Rosenberg heirs instituted the first lawsuit against an American museum concerning ownership of art looted during WWII, suing the Seattle Art Museum to recover Matisse's "Odalisque."[529]

Wildenstein's partner, Paul Rosenberg, owed his life to the Portuguese Consul-General in Bordeaux. Aristides de Sousa Mendes gave him visas to Portugal in his role as ambassador to France, defying the direct orders of his government. Mendes worked night and day to issue thirty thousand of these documents to other refugees as quickly as possible. In retribution, Mendes lost his post in 1940, and was never again employed, dying in a pauper's grave in 1985.

In 2011, I was commissioned to compose a poem in Mendes' honor for the Yeshiva University Museum on the occasion of an exhibit of his great grandson's art, written to honor his ancestor's bravery.[530]

Circular 14

Sousa Mendes signed his fate over and over,
blackened it in a week on 30,000 visas.

Had he gone mad? Dictator Salazar said so.
Sanity is the twin of madness.

Mendes took to his bed for two days,
his hair turned white, deciding to do it.

His deliberate hand speaks on the visas:
how determined, how simple, as if

there was no Circular 14, condemning him.
Collecting the stranded all along the border

in a sedan custom-built for his fifteen sons,
he drove to a post without a telephone

so the guards wouldn't know
of his "insanity," and signed.

Even on the bridge, he signed.
Even on newspapers. For decades,

his name could not be uttered in public,
the doors of his home were burnt for firewood.

His twin was a war minister in a monster time
and didn't offer his brother a rag.

Mendes was buried in monk's robes,
a pauper with fourteen sons in exile.

After the war, Salazar claimed he'd saved them all:
the Habsburgs, Robert Montgomery,

the entire Belgian cabinet,
and so many Jews. Salazar lied.

In contrast to the fate of Paul Rosenberg's inventory, Wildenstein was sued by a Jewish family for putting their illuminated manuscripts up for sale the same year as the Rosenberg family began their legal battle. This time, the claim of looting was brushed aside as made too long after the fact. Three years later, the gallery was again accused of profiting from business with the Nazis. This time Wildenstein sued for defamation—and lost.[531]

*

In a recent email, Steve's brother Jay says that when he talked to Pat's college friend, Edith Hamburger Iglauer Daly, she told him that she and Pat's mother were aghast that Pat had brought the painting home. Edith said that his mother hung the work behind a door in the apartment so it would not be seen by visitors.[532]

Steve says it was never hidden. I've seen a photo of the living room of the period that shows it prominently displayed.[533] Jay was seven years old when it was sold.

*

Painting by Cranach far right c. 1960

I once had ambivalent feelings about the poor rich people who had hundreds, sometimes thousands of paintings confiscated by the Nazis. What about all the poor people who had nothing to give the Nazis except their lives? I then read *The Orpheus Clock* by Simon Goodman, whose father spent decades trying to reclaim the Gutmann family heirlooms, some nine hundred paintings, a huge collection of silver that was particularly coveted by the Nazis, and the Orpheus clock of the title. The book reeks of privilege. For their birthday one year, the two Gutmann children received half-size electric 1928 Bugattis, and their parents hired an entire circus. On another birthday they invited an Olympic medalist equestrian team and their horses to entertain the guests.[534] Their cousins in Berlin lived in an eighty-room palace owned by their great uncle Herbert, a banker. "At the home of Herbert Gutmann you find the entire diplomatic corps, part of the Foreign Office, most Reichminister and the leading lights of high finance." Not to mention several kings, namely King Faisal of Iraq, King Fuad of Egypt, King Amanullah of Afghanistan, and the King of Sweden.[535]

Such a privileged life leads directly to a dangerous belief in exceptionalism, in particular, the patriarch thinking he was invincible to the Nazis, or that the Nazis could be controlled. Indeed, the Nazis gave Gutmann and his wife time to pack fourteen bags and they were allowed to bring along their fur coats when they were forced out of their home, but their limousine was not driven to safety in Italy, the stated destination where their friend Count Galeazzo Ciano, Mussolini's son-in-law and Italy's foreign minister (later shot for treason) waited, but to the gates of Theresienstadt. Still, they had their own room, while fifty other inmates shared rooms of a similar size, and enjoyed privileges that no one else had.[536] But when the patriarch refused to sign documents transferring the silver to the Reich (the Nazis were oddly fussy about these documents), Gutmann was beaten. He was determined, however, not so much to hang on to the silver, but believed, rightly, that as soon as the Nazis had it, he and his wife would be tossed aside. Another car came to the camp and the couple, still impeccably dressed, exited with far fewer suitcases, to the great envy of the other inmates. However, Gutmann was taken to a place called Little Fortress, where no one lived for long, and his wife went on to Auschwitz.[537]

Still, the Nazis paid him for the art. Sort of. I discover that after the artworks were devalued to a comical level, the subsequent "payment" made to the owners of all these confiscated artworks was held in escrow in Nazi-controlled bank accounts, and the money withdrawn by the Nazis just before their surrender. Only involuntary sales were eligible for later restitution, and the Guttmans' were "sold."[538] To prove anything at all, the author's father needed death certificates, and of course mass crematoriums did not issue such things. To prove that his parents were dead, the author's father had to track down an Auschwitz survivor who had miraculously both witnessed the death of his father in Little Fortress, and could testify to the death of his mother in Auschwitz.[539] A few months later, the son stood in front of his ancestral home, stripped of paintings, furniture, china, silver, carpets, cars, and filled with the children of Dutch Nazi sympathizers whose parents were in prison.[540] In order to reclaim the property, the Dutch required him to pay the back taxes and unpaid mortgages, and the property had to be sold shortly afterwards. The Dutch government had also impounded the nine hundred family artworks that the Monuments Men and others had retrieved from the many Nazi hideouts, and the son had to buy back every object. By the time he had jumped all the hoops in the postwar chaos of suspicious government caretakers, he had had to sell whatever he found in a depressed market in order to pay the lawyers.[541] What was left the family squabbled over. Only very recently has the grandson retrieved a few paintings held by museums. In 2018, a Cranach of theirs—also known to have been in Hitler's private collection—was recovered as a result of someone reading *The Orpheus Clock*.[542]

19

Stories

Steve asks, why don't I start with "We had just made love, and I was blowing smoke rings over the bed when you asked me whatever?"

Because you don't smoke.

I mean, really, he says, why are we always talking about the book every time we take a walk?

We pass twenty flower gardens. It's Victoria, B.C. where gardening is a sport, not a pastime. I gained permanent resident status in Canada six months before Covid and we bought a houseboat here to escape the virus, and Trump. Couldn't have been more timely. You talk best when you're moving, I say.

I can move in bed. He gives a brief demonstration.

We're old. Nobody wants to know that. Pillow talk is better. Everybody assumes old people spend a lot of time in bed.

He laughs. We're well past our 10,000 steps today. Okay. He says he remembers his mother weeping when UNICEF medical supplies meant for Lebanese hospitals were stripped from a boat in Beirut's harbor and found in the thieves' market. Nothing could be done.

I tell him I've found his mother's secretary's contact information. June D. Downey. She's at least 95. There's no obituary online. Wish I were in New York now, because she lives or lived in Peter Cooper Village.

Get your therapist to check on her. He works nearby, doesn't he?

Isn't that against a therapist's code of ethics, to pierce their bubble?

You can ask.

The next day, I zoom, and I'm surprised that he is eager, but it takes three weeks of reminders. Detective work is not so much part of his job. Finally he reports that she's been removed from the nameplate. Apparently you don't give a forwarding address if you have become so incapacitated that you go into a rest home, you disappear as if you were in a witness protection program. You start over, like Dickson.

*

In 1962, with the money from the sale of the Cranach, Dickson bought the *Arizonian,* once the first newspaper in the Arizona territory. Its first editor died in the battle of Gettysburg, the second suffered a political skirmish that claimed the newspaper, the third was murdered in Las Vegas, the fourth missed two issues wandering in the desert.[543] "Read Nearly Everywhere" was its motto, and the newspaper had a circulation of 5,000 when they bought it, according to Dickson.[544] A kind of journalist's rebuttal to the travelogs and photography of the famed *Arizona Highways*, its layout was flashy: a photo covered the whole front page, and inside were long opinion pieces about local politicians like Barry Goldwater, interspersed with in-depth interviews of Mrs. Frank Lloyd Wright or the governor's wife, or Paolo Solari, alongside notices of local events like the debutante balls. At last Pat was a publisher like her father, and Dickson had his own newspaper, the dream, she said, of every journalist.[545] At least that's what they gave their New York friends as the reason for their departure. Not because Dickson had to start over.

*

The Arizonian, 1963

Paradise Valley was (and is) the wealthiest town in Arizona, with a population of about ten thousand. Along with Erma Bombeck, Charles Boyer, Erskine Caldwell, Hugh Downs, Dick Van Dyke, Sandra Day O'Connor, and William Rehnquist, it was also home to Ned Warren (aka Nathan Waxman), the kingpin of Arizona land fraud and model for *The Producers*, having bilked $39,000 out of supporters for the Broadway play *The Happiest Days*,[546] and Herb Applegate, an associate (as they called them) of the Mafia, who owned the Arizona franchise Hobo Joe's, which was essentially a cash pipeline for the mob, which involved such notables as Robert Goldwater, Barry's brother.[547]

In the early sixties Arizona, especially nearby Phoenix, was a hotbed of mobsters, rampant land fraud, exploitation of illegal immigrants, and judicial and other official corruption. The state had few rules or institutional checks, and the migration of Midwestern gangsters and their relocation in the witness protection program left the Mafia poised to exploit the situation. All of this made journalism very important. Reporter Don Bolles was hired by the *Arizona Republic* in 1965 and won a Pulitzer nomination that year for exposing bribery and kickbacks in the Arizona state government.[548] He was murdered eleven years later, having produced two series on crime in the area. Angered by the extreme intimidation, forty journalists from all over the country swarmed the area to complete his work. They published the "Arizona Project" in newspapers nationwide, a 23-part series of exposés of the Arizona underworld. After the stories broke, Barbara Walters asked Barry Goldwater if he had been on the take during the sixties. It had been eight years since his 1964 run for president. "Hell, back then, everyone was," he replied. [549]

*

For me, the most fascinating souvenir of Arizona was a gold LP of Goldwater's speeches from my father's stint as a Republican delegate to the national convention. Not that we played it. We weren't allowed to, for fear the "gold" would rub off and disappear. The idea of the Republican ideals wearing out if they were put into practice now seems particularly apt. Back then, Goldwater was considered wildly rightwing, but now he's a pussycat, having supported abortion rights and the legalization of marijuana—and he was the one who urged Richard Nixon to resign. Thirty years later, my father became so incensed by national politics that he changed parties and ran for State Senator as a Democrat at the age of ninety-three. He carried three districts without campaigning, the Czech name appealing to a solid voting block of Bohemian Nebraskans.

*

Svoboda means freedom in Czech, Russian and Ukrainian. Svoboda was painted on the side of the Berlin Wall and shouted by revelers. More accurately, Svoboda means freed serf, a good name to advertise one's status: everyone likes to repudiate the idea of slavery, especially if it's theirs. Freeman was a popular Black name after the Emancipation Proclamation. Slavery—the word *slave* comes from the Slavs—has oppressed Eastern Europe from the 9th century to today, with ongoing human trafficking of both men and women, especially in Russia and Ukraine.[550]

Of Bohemian ancestry, I've kept the name through three husbands, except for a short period while I worked in a bank under an assumed name in Montreal to dodge immigration officials. Isn't a married name assumed too? "A Lucy Stoner" is how a friend used to introduce me. Lucy Stone was a suffragette enraged by the practice of sublimating everything, even one's name, to a husband. The rationale for the practice of using your husband's name is to bind you more closely to the family who takes you on, grafts you to that tree full of in-laws and great-in-laws. Other cultures have different ways of securing the lineage—cows, in the case of the Nuer. When I mentioned my father was a cattle rancher, Sudanese suitors suggested he put them on a plane as bridewealth.

In an Orwellian twist, Svoboda is also the name of arguably Europe's most influential far-right movement, and its Nazi taint has been touted as an excuse for the invasions by the Russians. Between 2011-2017, the Svoboda party held torchlit assaults modeled on the stormtroopers in the late 1920s and 1930s against gays, Jews, elderly ethnic Russians, and other "impure" citizens—like the Charlottesville marchers in 2017. But now they behave more like the "American Tea Party or right-wing Republicans," according to a US-based expert, Alexander J. Motyl.[551] The party's chief motivation is patriotism, and anger at Russian provocations and the attack on Ukraine. Although influential in a country that has for many decades needed a strong nationalist attitude to protect it from Russian invasion, Svoboda is not large, and the antisemitic strain is hardly widespread—after all, Ukraine elected a Jewish president. Now it's been absorbed into the Azov battalion, the group that held Mariupol for so long.[552] Show trials of those taken prisoner began in 2022 to highlight the Russian narrative of "denazification" propaganda.[553] A reorganized unit participated in the Battle of Bakhmut and declared it won for Ukraine.[554] Unfortunately, that story turned out not to be true.

*

Every Wednesday in the fall of 1962 Steve helped prepare the *Arizonian* for the mail, which meant printing and applying labels and fastening the newspaper shut. He worked with Michael, a lanky, gap-toothed, over-tanned Scotch Irish Arizonian almost twice his age: a thirty-year-old drop-out. One early spring evening, while they stamped and sorted, Michael told Steve he might want to join his club.

Steve admired Michael in a young-punk way and was flattered that he thought him worthy of membership of anything. Being new to Scottsdale High, Steve had few friends, and little to do after school except fold newspapers. What do I have to do to be a member?

Michael leaned close. You have a car, don't you?

Steve did, if he asked his stepdad. Sure, he said.

You like the desert?

Steve snagged his thumb on a staple. Yeah, he said, staring at the cut.

You have to take somebody out into the desert and kill him.

I see, said Steve. He tried to be cool. He was cool, icy in fact, after hearing Michael say such a thing. Maybe he was to think that he was Michael's next somebody? Would he pin him to the ground and drag him off into the cactus? Or was he pulling his leg?

Who do you mean "somebody"?

You just have to bring back proof. A picture is best. You have a camera? You're a rich kid, your parents run the place, you have a camera. Go kill somebody and you can join the club.

Steve couldn't quite nod. Is the club very big?

Michael smiled, and pulled out another set of papers. He didn't say another thing, and neither did Steve. Was the story made up to intimidate Steve, or was it true?

Steve wasn't sure whether that's why the FBI turned up on their doorstep a few weeks later, but there were two of them, dressed identically, like *Men in Black*, with the sunglasses.

*

His parents didn't fire Michael. They either didn't believe Steve's story or thought he was exaggerating. Or else cheap labor was hard to get. Steve was bumped to debt collector, riding his bike from business to business to cajole creditors into payment. People either didn't come to the door or they opened an empty cash register. Run the ad, they'd tell him. Or else don't, and I'll never pay.

It was easy with a kid.

*

Just a few months after the Hartwells took over, the *Arizonian* received national recognition for an extremely ambitious four-part series on education, investigating "teaching machines, program learning and television in the schools." It featured paid essays by a doctor, a member of the school board, public affairs at Arizona State, the headmasters of private schools, and a double-page spread by the superintendent answering questions like "The intelligent child vs. the creative child. What can an educator do about it?"[555] Dickson won three major journalism awards in subsequent years, one of four reporters (including others from *Look* and the *New York Times*) to be recognized for excellence in writing about business, economics and finance, and "outstanding merit" from the University of Missouri's School of Journalism for reporting in the nation's weeklies.[556] The *Arizonian* had its own foray into crime reporting, and Dickson won the top award from the Arizona Press Club for investigative reporting about the owner of a racquet club about to be extradited to New York on forty-two grand theft charges.[557]

Maybe the extradition was why the FBI showed up.

*

I know something about crime in Nebraska. I was my father's secretary the summer before I went to college.

Steve laughs. Your dad was just the county attorney.

And the coroner. I saw pictures. Mostly dead couples who argued over house plans. Not Mafia. The closest underworld character was a guy named Mugsy that Dad prosecuted.

Uh-huh, says Steve, making coffee.

It was the late sixties, the interstate had just been built. You know those small safes shopkeepers used to have to keep their cash in? Dad said Mugsy was a bear of a man and he'd go in and steal them, just walk them out of the shop and out to his truck. He then threw them over the interstate interchanges and ran down to collect all the bills that came fluttering out. That's the level of sophistication in the Nebraskan crime of my youth.

Easy money, says Steve. Bricks were thrown through our windows more than once. Political bricks or from disgruntled advertisers or Mafia? He doesn't know.

*

All went well for the Hartwells at the beginning, prizes piled up, the paper was enthusiastically received, advertising increased, though Pat mentions in a column that Parke-Beret had just auctioned a Cranach for more than $100,000. Perhaps she was annoyed with Dickson for selling it so cheaply?558 Steve started his freshman year in high school and had his job working at the newspaper, the younger boys adapted. Then Dickson had a heart attack and, while convalescing, resumed drinking, obviating the reason for the move in the first place, and quickly draining their finances.559 "Greatly saddened to hear of your situation," writes Pat's good friend Edith. She knew Pat well. They had met at Wellesley, attended Columbia School of Journalism together as well as working at the OWI, and Edith also reported from Europe. In 1961, working for the *New Yorker*, Edith traveled to the Arctic on Pat's suggestion to investigate the Inuit, stayed in Canada and became a Canadian legend.560 She suggested that Pat take the kids and move to Washington.561

Pat writes to Maurice Pate, her old boss at UNICEF, for help. Not only had he acted as their best man, but he was known for his paternalistic approach to management, and gave his staff "considerable discretion in the exercise of their responsibilities."562 She admitted to Pate the paper they'd bought was failing, she had only a few months of money left—and she'd filed for divorce, even though Dickson was still sick. "Naturally my greatest hope is to return to UNICEF at headquarters or in this field."[563]

Pat in Arizona, 1962

*

Steve says he raged all through high school, he raged at breakfast, he raged at lunch, he raged at dinner. Why couldn't they be honest? I tell him adolescents rage, they hate their parents even if their parents are saints. Jesus Christ probably raged. It's a way to make the inevitable separation from the parents less painful. Let them lie. If the story is they're awful, who needs them?

It wasn't like that, he says.

*

I scrutinize the notes Jay has just given me on interviews he did twenty years ago for the book he didn't write about his mother. June Downey, her UNICEF secretary, says that Pat asked for a year's leave of absence to go off to Arizona, and I find the letter in a download. It's dated April 20, 1962, where Pat uses gynecological problems as her excuse. She mailed the letter to Pate in Brazzaville, where he was distributing UNICEF goods in the Congo. She couldn't wait for his answer, she was flying to LA to settle her mother-in-law in a rest home and flying on to Arizona, she didn't want to resign but Dickson hoped to leave immediately.[564] June says that something dreadful happened at the Coffee House Club, an elite social club that still meets on West 44th Street that Pat and Dickson frequented on weekends.[565] Some additional professional disgrace must have led to such haste, and surely some metabolic shift that the doctor foresaw that led to the heart attack five months later. No one mentions Pat or Dickson in the UNICEF history, although she was third in command for six critical years, and Dickson worked in her position two years earlier, for a total of eight Hartwell years.

Perhaps Maurice knew more about marriage and alcohol than Pat.

*

He responded to Pat's letter quickly, but he didn't open his arms. "I shall postpone any thoughts of coming East until the fall," she replies in her very formal answer.[566] She takes on all the jobs: "mother, father, editor, publisher, laundress, reporter, cook and nurse," as she tells her friend Edith. Pat's patience with Dickson's drinking is formidable: "His doctor says he is making progress, but it's hard for me to see as I get tireder and tireder and more and more worried."[567]

*

When Pat hesitates to sell the newspaper, it is because "the doctor warns that with his [Dickson's] heart, he can't take too much of a beating."[568] She writes in a letter to June Downey: "I am in fear that Mr. Hartwell will come to some awful end. He looks very badly, is still hopeful that I can be persuaded to stop the divorce action, but unable to either stop drinking or go into the hospital where it can be stopped for him."[569] He is not exactly calm about the divorce: he buys two guns and starts cashing large checks. The lawyer freezes the assets, but no restraining order is put in place. His settlement is $1,000 and the car.[570] She tells the kids that he's gone to Mexico, and he moves into a nearby apartment, where he edits an occasional article for the newspaper.[571]

*

After I returned from Sudan, my ex told me he'd been working with the CIA throughout the trip. Was he lying just to further confuse me about his motives and strange behavior? Maybe, but Sudan was on the cusp of another war; the CIA's interest in his travels made sense. I was devastated. Knowing a spy was unsettling enough, but sleeping with one unbeknownst for four years? I was in the midst of trying to write my first novel Cannibal, draft number twenty-eight, and had come to recognize that I had no idea what the Nuer were thinking, and now I had to come to grips with the fact that I didn't know my ex's motives either. My third person point of view was a clueless arrogance. I rewrote the book in extreme first person, recounting only what I understood or guessed to be true. Me, pointing at that.

*

It takes a great deal of charm to win back a mate after she has kicked you out of the house and divided the property and stood up in court and enumerated your faults in public until the contract between you is null. Since Dickson was always going away, the children weren't alerted to anything other than their subconscious certainty that whatever the problem was, it was serious.[572] He must've sent letters; I've seen none. Pat was lonely, she admits this to June Downey.[573] She was still relatively new to town, her old friends were two thousand miles away. Her brother Lloyd flew in to console her, her sisters sat smug with their successful husbands.[574] Her children? She thought her boys would be scarred for life if they knew what was going on.

Of course they were scarred for life.

*

I love my husband so much, the woman sobs, but our divorce will be final in a few days! This is at Al-Anon, which I attend now and then virtually, having had an alcoholic mother. You can hear the woman's struggle in her voice, her love for a man who refuses to get help for his addiction. Her mouth twists, she takes off her glasses, she puts them back on, her voice breaks, she reveals the two children want their father too. They don't know what's going on, but they know.

*

Dickson moved back in with Pat unmarried for several years, pretending otherwise, attending the symphony, herding the boys, writing the occasional article for the newspaper and handling communication/PR/speeches for Valley National Bank as a full-time employee reporting to the president Walter Bimson.

"My dad was not a bragger," writes Jay, "but when one of his speeches (written for someone else, like Valley National Bank's Walter Bimson), ended up in the monthly "Vital Speeches of the Day," the national publisher of the "important addresses of the recognized leaders of public opinion," Dickson pointed it out.[575]

Pat claimed that she wrote these speeches.[576]

20

Artifice and Erasure

"My father having lost out as owner and editor of the *Austin Statesman* after World War I, I lost out as editor-publisher of *The Arizonian* in Scottsdale for some of the same reasons, lack of capitalization and more interested in content than in selling advertising," says Pat in an interview.[577] She omits the problem of alcohol, and she still had four hungry boys to support. But she did not take in typing or other people's children or act as receptionist, the main careers open to divorced women of that era. Instead, she allied herself with art.

In one of her inaugural columns in the *Arizonian*, Pat had written: "if Scottsdale builds for beauty, its prosperity will last."[578] The *Phoenix New Times* credits her with founding the Scottsdale Arts Commission in the 1960s, transforming the city from a mere "cow town."[579] She oversaw the building of the five million dollar Scottsdale Arts Center and began the first of its many festivals. By 1998, the city was the "arts capital of the Southwest, home to more than 125 professional art galleries and studios, one of the highest per-capita rates anywhere in the nation."[580]

*

Jonathan Marshall had owned the *Scottsdale Daily Progress* for only a year when he took over the weekly *Arizonian* in 1964, keeping Pat as editor and Dickson an occasional contributor. Rivalry aside, good journalists were hard to find in those parts. A year after its purchase, Dickson reiterated the aims of the paper to Marshall in an eight page letter, expressing his opinion that the paper should promote "community living not related simply to its size; standards of education not tied to a tax rate, and applied standards of business ethics which make cheats, frauds and sharpsters uncomfortable."[581] They might not have wholly agreed since Marshall makes no mention of the newspaper in his exhaustive biography *Dateline History*. He sold the *Arizonian* two years later to Mae Sue Talley. Having studied journalism in college, Talley imagined she could manage the paper just fine without Pat, and cabled her in 1968 that she was fired, reasons unstated. Later Talley bought the Frank Lloyd Wright-designed Biltmore Hotel and Castle Hot Springs, a ranch resort founded in 1895, both of which burned to the ground shortly thereafter, much like the *Arizonian*, which folded after only a year of her editorship, once Talley discovered she couldn't run it herself.[582] Given that Talley's credited on several sites as the owner and publisher of the *Arizonian*, with no mention of the Hartwells' six years of struggle prior to her gutting it, it seems she was most skilled at erasure.

*

Ru Marshall and I have been friends for only a few months, ever since they invited me to read from my biography of Lola Ridge, *Anything That Burns You,* at a gallery. There I discovered that Lenore Marshall, who gave my biographical subject Lola Ridge money to fix her teeth (and much more), was Ru's grandmother.

We meet for a drink at whatever bar is open on New Year's Day. You picked this place, Ru says, looking past our booth at the faux ferns surely dating from the early 1980s.

I just picked the corner. You walked in.

Ru laughs. The drinks arrive and we toast: To Carlos!

I only have another two hundred pages left, says Ru. Castaneda has invaded my soul. They clutch their pearls. Identity, gender or otherwise, is a subject on which Ru is an expert. For a decade they've been working on the biography of Carlos Castaneda, who, as a cult leader, was an expert on identity manipulation.

Biographers choose their subjects to reflect their souls, and often their upbringing. What did your father do? I ask.

Journalism, Ru says.

I take a sip. The gin and tonic is as weak as the lighting. My husband's mother, the Hitler one, I tell him, went into newspapers after the war.

Ru's heard about my book proposal. What are you writing next? is nearly the first question writers ask each other as soon as they publish a book.

My father's newspaper, says Ru, was in Arizona. Not exactly the *Times*.

Arizona, I say. Really?

I grew up in Arizona. Scottsdale.

Is your father named Jonathan?

Ru nods.

This is downright Castenadan destiny, I laugh. Where are the crows?

What Ru does not tell me is that during Jonathan Marshall's twenty-four years as publisher, he was twice nominated for a Pulitzer. He, like Pat, had acquired a self-taught appreciation for the arts and collecting, he by publishing *ARTS* magazine, but he also had the city planning expertise that the Hartwells had dabbled in. It must have been galling that it took until the *Arizonian* was dead and gone for the *Scottsdale Progress* to win awards the *Arizonian* collected immediately. [583]

*

Over dinner, Steve and I are talking about the Scottsdale Town Enrichment Program (S.T.E.P.), the brilliance of three hundred people voluntarily getting together, week after week, for over six years, to remake Scottsdale's identity, and about how Dickson was a member while Pat wrote and published their 1969 report, which ran some 110 pages.[584] I had read the report the night before, and was wondering at its complexity, its seamlessness, when Steve says he worked for the Scottsdale city planner around then.

It was right after college. Mom arranged it, he says. I was going to ASU's architecture school in the fall, and it made sense for me. From her point of view, there were all kinds of rifts about what direction the town should take, and she thought I could keep an eye on all of it.

What could you do, other than watch?

Native Americans had drained the valley a thousand years earlier and I wrote memos about how, he says. I'd just gotten a degree in anthropology from Occidental. I also dug ditches and took photos. I believed in the planner's dream. He wasn't much older than me, a real idealist, a landscape architect. He'd written a column in the *Scottsdale Progress* after one of their floods, and suggested they turn the desert into a showpiece with a greenbelt. It took him twenty years, and plenty of people were against it. What was his name?

I google. Bill Walton? Not the basketball Bill Walton but this one.

We watch a video of an interview—he's still alive! Still proud!

I make a note to find his phone.

I spent the next semester designing floating homes, Steve says. He looks around at the one-room houseboat we've moved to, anchored in Fisherman's Wharf in Victoria. Something like this, he says, which is actually also a replica of my design for the artificial Arctic Sea ice.

Whoa! You're living your dream.

We listen to the houseboat rub the pier. Then his grin gets bigger and he throws up his hands. I know where it is.

The ice?

The Hitler photo! It's in the flat file drawers in New York.

Thirty years ago, we found three purple storage metal drawers on the street, and gave one set to Wolf Kahn, the painter who lived on the top floor. The kids' drawings, wrapping paper, nudes from my time at art school, flat paper items no one has looked at for all those years—it's possible, I say.

*

At the behest of the S.T.E.P. Committee, Pat wrote and published a catalog for all the art held by the city of Scottsdale in 1975—Diego Rivera, Earl G. Hammock, David Chethlahe Paladin, Albrecht Durer, Louise Nevelson, Alberto Giacometti, Hiroshige, Alexander Calder, paintings by local artists as well as other European and American paintings of note, and the donated Andres Segovia that was partial payment for the Cranach.[585] This catalog solidified Scottsdale's commitment to the arts, and to Pat, who became Scottsdale's Arts Commissioner—but not the director. She was given nine months to view other arts buildings across the country, select an architect, and oversee the building of the Scottsdale Arts Center. In a letter to a friend, she complains that the selected architect, Bennie Gonzales, wanted "a Greek temple."[586] Nonetheless, the resulting Arts Center is spectacular, Gonzales' most impressive work, and it opened on time, in 1968. Pat then went to Nancy Hanks, chairman of the brand-new NEA, having known her when Hanks was with the Rockefeller Fund (and Dickson knew her deputy), to obtain funding for a Louise Nevelson sculpture to adorn the courtyard.[587] Pat called reporters when Nevelson came to meet with city officials and they wrote about the artist wearing a paisley-printed full-length chinchilla coat and inch-long eyelashes, waving a cigarillo.[588] Nevelson had been their second choice. Pat wanted Alexander Calder, but he insisted on green carpeting, and according to Pat, Gonzalez wouldn't hear of it.[589] Pat is not, however, in the photo of the grand reception for the Nevelson sculpture. She must have decided taking credit was somehow impolitic.[590] This reticence must be why she is not remembered, or was erasure of a woman's accomplishments required by the times?

In the first two flailing years of the Scottsdale Arts Center, it hired three directors, all men—but not Pat.[591]

*

When asked to be on the Nebraska Arts Council, my mother demurred. She told me it was because she said she feared she might be seen taking advantage of her position to help me. You could always recuse yourself, I said. The reality was that she couldn't reconcile my fledgling career in writing with her own failed ambitions as an artist due to her obligations as a mother. That I managed despite my own children didn't matter.

My sons enjoying each other, 1992

My mother did serve on the Nebraska Interstate 80 Bicentennial Sculpture Project, helping to select abstract sculptures for rest stops across the state. Similar to Pat's push for Bennie Gonzales's services as an architect—"the thing was," Pat said, "to get them to accept modern architecture"—Mom had to convince locals that curving steel beams were as beautiful as horse-and-riders.[592] One objecting Nebraskan announced that the entire sculpture project was probably "the greatest hoax that has ever been perpetrated on the state of Nebraska."[593] Letters poured into the *Omaha World-Herald*, the state's biggest newspaper, more letters than those regarding the impeachment of Nixon. "Vandals would look at them [the sculptures] and figure that all possible damage had already been done," reads one.[594] The controversy received national coverage. The *Village Voice* ran a headline asking, "Can sculpture stand up beside toilets?"[595]

On October 31, 1975, Mom appeared on the *Today Show* with artist Linda Howard to defend the committee's aesthetics.[596] I recently watched a copy of the interview. Mom is frightened, her voice unusually high when she says: "They're beautiful things once you look at them." Just as she launches into the controversy, Howard cuts her off to say that by the end of her residency, locals came up to her to say that they saw arresting patterns in the irrigation systems.

*

Pat wore a wig all the time in the seventies. We teased her, says Steve. See that picture?

A newspaper clipping shows her wearing a headband in an attempt to conceal the fake hair attached to it. Another shows her at the cocktail party she held for Hubert Humphrey, then running for president. Look at the headline, I say, "Democrats to unleash stylish young people for the Humphreys' visit."[597] Wigs were all the rage then. A lot of women wore them. People were trying on new, wilder identities. I even had a hairpiece for the prom made from the waist-length hair I cut off right before high school. It's probably in storage somewhere even today.

God forbid.

Maybe she wore a wig because she had chemo. She had a hysterectomy in 1968 that might have been the result of a cancer scare, something to do with her bladder.

I never thought about that, says Steve.

Nobody remembers when she had the first bout, she was so good at subterfuge.

*

Fired from the paper in 1968, Pat went to Europe the next summer, this time accompanied by Dickson and her two younger sons.[598] She had catalogued Scottsdale's municipal art, put on a few shows of local artists, and now she wanted to present naive art, the genre she was most familiar with, since it was most often the one chosen by UNICEF. She visited her old haunts, and said she even resumed her prior duty of identifying art for UNICEF.[599] Maybe Maurice Pate did come through. Where else would she find the money to tour? Dickson was leary of the whole venture, and almost backed out of the collecting trip, but eventually relented. "I can't bear the thought of not letting you do what you really want to do. For you the best of all possible worlds; for me this satisfaction of making them possible."[600]

"It was Mrs. Hartwell's job to find naive artists in every participating UN country," reads the *Arizona Republic* article written a few days before Pat offered The Hartwell Collection to buyers in Scottsdale. Seventy-seven naive works were for sale. She had learned at UNICEF that naive images were easier to price and sell than more sophisticated works by famous artists— as the headline intimated: "Naive Art Can Command Quite Sophisticated Prices." [601]

Naive art also had sophisticated champions. André Breton felt it was closer to the subconscious and therefore liberating; Jean Dubuffet had a more prejudiced take, positing that it was primitive because it was often made by the uneducated poor. Naive art is particularly susceptible to fraud since it's amateur in the sense that the practitioners aren't trained, the art comes without provenance so validation is often made on purely aesthetic grounds, and the artists are often unknown and without an artistic identity. Fraud becomes a concern. Native, rather than naive art, in Arizona is an obvious parallel. Pat knew that some of the Native American art in Arizona had to be fake: there was too much of it.

*

In addition to her Arts Commissioner job, Pat was teaching international relations and history of the Far East at Phoenix College, one of the oldest community colleges in the country, which, over a period of two decades, graduated actor Nick Nolte, artist Eric Fischl, two governors and two Miss Americas.[602] Two articles were written about her upcoming teaching, meant to drum up students, a tack seldom seen in academia, one of them a feature in the *Arizona Republic*.[603] She reeled off various facts and figures about China to establish her credentials, although she had only a B.A. in political science, demonstrating the chutzpah that made her mayor of Berchtesgaden on the same merit. She compared the "corruptive" qualities of the Chinese tongs to that of frontier sheriffs and then weighed in on the war in Vietnam with a UNICEF solution: "Give them know-how. That's more problem solving than men, money, and materials." She doesn't mention that she is also concurrently taking a class in Chinese history at Arizona State University.

The two articles are often inaccurate. The first one opens with Pat claiming that her grandfather was governor of Texas (he was comptroller of the university), and that she moved into the White House with the Roosevelts when she couldn't find an apartment in Washington (a story reiterated to her sons). The second article ends with her saying she almost gave birth while covering the coronation of Queen Elizabeth. She meant the first US visit of the King and Queen in 1955, when Jay arrived unexpectedly. Two articles in a row like this meant that they probably weren't errors in transcription.

There is, however, a distinct possibility that Pat did stay at least a night in the White House. Her friend Edith Iglauer, a reporter for the *New Yorker* like her husband, also claimed to have stayed there, but neither of their names are on any official list. At the Franklin Delano Roosevelt Presidential Library and Museum handwritten informal slips exist, sent to the Usher by the President or Mrs.

Roosevelt, notifying him that, for example, "a cousin of mine will be staying the night" but without identifying the visitor.[604]

*

When Pat wasn't named director of the new Scottsdale Arts Center, she became bitter.[605] She had done all that work to foster art in Scottsdale and to promote and build the Center. Starting in the late sixties, she began to split more of her time between Arizona and Hawai'i, the second with fond memories from the war, and where she still had friends. By 1972 she was making four or five roundtrips a year to Oahu from Scottsdale. "The ocean keeps getting wider and more expensive to cross," she writes.[606] Nothing if you were used to rounding the globe with thirty stops annually for UNICEF, but uncommonly frequent for most mortals. Besides teaching that year, she installed the Nevelson sculpture, put on two naive art shows, wrote a regular art reviewing column in Hawai'i, moderated a talk on school testing for Kailua's PTA as vice president, and sat on the Communications Committee for Arizona's board of Planned Parenthood.[607]

*

My mother was high up in Nebraska's Right-to-Life organization. She did not approve of, nor see the Margaret Sanger film Steve and I co-directed, *Margaret Sanger: A Public Nuisance,* even though the Getty named it one of the two best bio-docs of the decade. Her identity was very bound up in *mother of nine children*, and she had her beliefs via the Catholic church.

*

Pat was leaving her two youngest sons, aged fifteen and seventeen, alone in Hawai'i for weeks at a time. When asked about this unusual freedom, both say that not much untoward happened, no wild parties or girls. It was Dickson who boasted that his youngest was a girl chaser, but this was all projection, according to the youngest, who ducks a shy head.

*

Steve says his mother was a coyote. Inscrutable. Tricky. While interviewing her in 1995, he asks her point blank: "Did the Russians supply any photographs of Hitler's funeral pyre?" and she answers: "No, they did not." He asks her again: "Did they give you photos of him dead?" She says that if they had them, they didn't offer them to her for publication.

That was fourteen years after she showed us the photo of her pointing at his ashes.

*

My mother always liked young men, ergo, she liked Steve. She also liked the previous ex but told me after our divorce that she would have had the good sense to move on after a few weeks of his hijinks. Whenever I achieved something later, she would turn it into Steve's accomplishment. The grants won for the PBS series were somehow a result of his being in the Directors Guild, not that I was the producer. Even my novels could have only been written with his help.

She is dead now and only subconsciously relevant, and I have produced twenty-four books and many videos trying to get her attention, and for that I am grateful. Prolific is the word most often used to describe my output after all these years, and it always sounds as if I've had too much to say, or whatever I've written is redundant. Now that I'm older, I understand Pat's situation better. Few like to hear about the accomplishments of a woman. The subject is quickly changed.

*

Ru Marshall and I surmise that he and his siblings cavorted with Steve and his family in Scottsdale, though the ages aren't quite parallel. Pat's recipe for baked avocado appears in a collection Ru's mother published for the community. I imagine a rocky relationship, however: at first Marshall's a savior, buying their newspaper and retaining their services, even allowing Pat to write on occasion for his *Scottsdale Progress*, then comes a spate of sniping Dickson editorials, and then Marshall's sale of the paper. In the end it was Jonathan Marshall who finally pushed Pat out of Arizona, arguing that her living half the year in Hawai'i made it inappropriate for her to remain Scottsdale's Fine Arts Commissioner—though many Arizonians live elsewhere for months at a time.[608] An article in another magazine made disapproving mention of the Hartwells working for S.T.E.P., evidence of a concerted effort to get rid of them.[609] Pat had just attracted 25,000 people to the Scottsdale Arts Festival, but the state's largest newspaper's headline says it all: "Woman coordinates Scottsdale's City-owned Collection"—she isn't even named. "To this city, art is as important as police or fire protection," she is quoted (still nameless) deep into the piece.[610] Scottsdale and Paradise Valley are relatively small towns, and everyone had been on civic boards together, which made the Marshalls' campaign against Pat very personal.[611]

Professional, she could beat.

21

Fake

Soon after Pat settled for good in Hawai'i, she sought to put
down art forgeries. Big hotels with their overpriced galleries
were a kind of tourist trap into which wives dragged their husbands who would never visit at home, and she suspected that
their inventory contained fake Dalis and other artists' forgeries, similar to the practice of those who had advertised in the
Arizonian, and in her experiences with naive and native art.[612]
Her suspicions were correct. It was claimed in the sixties that
Dalí could sign as many as 1,800 print-ready sheets an hour. He
boasted that "Each morning after breakfast I like to start the day
by earning twenty thousand dollars."[613] People began to come
to Pat with stories of young military men who invested their life
savings for their parents in prints that could not be resold.[614]
Even today experts estimate that one-half of all limited edition
prints in the art market—especially by Pablo Picasso, Joan Miró,
Marc Chagall and Alexander Calder—bear false signatures, and
are actually fake reproductions.[615]

But before taking that on, Pat wrote an arts column for the
Honolulu Advertiser and Dickson wrote about books. Soon
they combined their talents and put out a monthly review of the

art scene called the *Cultural Climate,* featuring headlines like "Neither artists nor politicians qualified to set public taste" and others that delineated the rivalry between crafts and art, and the impact of art on the aging population. People took notice. Pat became the second director of the Hawai'ian Arts Council, after the first, a young man from San Francisco, lasted only seven months. To hold together an arts council for four years in the hotbed of cultural controversy that is Hawai'i is no mean feat. As executive director, she organized every island, including "ethnic representatives," which meant appointing an executive committee of seven, and seventeen directors of major cultural organizations, including literature and the Hawai'ian Congress of Parents and Teachers.

Her initial foray into lobbying was to keep the state's one percent for the Arts law intact. In 1967, Hawai'i had been the first state to pass such legislation. Ten years later, she was publicly thanked for saving it by the president of the Honolulu Symphony.[616] Lawmakers had been trying to auction off pieces in the state's collection, and she organized a phone tree to testify to the collection's importance. Many artists and supporters spoke. The lawmakers backed down, and she even convinced them to add money for landscaping and restoration.[617] Twenty years later, she wrote and edited the very attractive *Retrospective: 1967-1987* on the impact of the state's art in public places.[618] She also put together the first economic survey in Hawai'i to prove that culture makes money. It was directed at the same lawmakers who saw the whole endeavor as frivolous. She did her own interviews and asked tourists on Maui and Oahu if, prior to a cultural event, they'd gone to the hairdresser or a restaurant or hired a babysitter, and how much gas they used to get to the venue.[619] She also suggested that the symphony play at the opening of the legislature as a kind of thank you, and they have done so now for decades. A 2019 study showed that the arts contributed more than $2.5 million to the state's economy—in just one year.[620]

She began approaching the problem of the Hawai'ian art market by once again lobbying the state legislature to require sales tax be paid on art sales. Jay, then a summer intern at the *Honolulu Star-Bulletin,* took on the job of notifying the public of the art forgeries, supported by his mother's research. After the publication of several of his articles, Pat approached the Better Business Bureau and consulted with the Council's pro bono lawyer about her next step. Because the prints went into national circulation and thus involved the post office, the fakes were also a federal problem. But prosecutions, she was advised, were rare and difficult. She did a lot of investigation across the country herself (pre-Internet), and determined that "New York . . . insists, among other things, because people can forge signatures, that artists must put a thumbprint on the back of their work, which cannot be faked."[621] "Help for Those Who Buy Prints," an 1978 article in the *Honolulu Advertiser,* described the legislation that she was so instrumental in eventually passing.[622] Now if you stroll into one of the many contemporary art galleries lining the big Hawai'ian hotels and decide on a whim to buy a print, they should be authentic (although perhaps still overpriced), thanks to Pat.

*

NFTs were once touted as providing perfect provenance, having a clear and direct history of who bought and sold a given asset. These "non-fungible tokens," to de-acronym NFTs, are assets like a piece of art, digital content, or video that have been tokenized via a blockchain. Tokens are unique ID codes created from metadata with an encryption function. These tokens are then stored on a blockchain, while the assets themselves are stored elsewhere. But it turns out that anyone can mint a NFT token, even if they don't own the copyright to the content, by obtaining a screenshot of the artwork and selling the fakes as their own. Scammers impersonate NFT marketplace staff, trick users into signing false transactions, or gain access to digital wallets. Indeed, bots scrape artists' online galleries and create collections with auto-generated texts, ready for sale. In 2022, out of more than 480 million minted NFTs, some 390,000 have been identified as stolen.[623] Millions have been lost, and image recognition and other tools have now been invented to help recover the stolen goods. So—still not perfect.

*

Pat had held one of the greatest fakes of all time: that so-called Vermeer confiscated by the Monuments Men. Goering had the painting, "Christ with the Woman Taken in Adultery" hanging behind his desk. It was Hans Van Meergeren's seventeenth Vermeer forgery. Like Hitler, he was a frustrated artist, and a consummate crook. The war offered a perfect confluence of events to support his practice. Museums had hidden their work or had it shipped elsewhere, making comparisons difficult. It also helped that there were only thirty-five paintings identified as original Vermeers. Critic Abraham Bredius, known as the "Pope of Vermeers," circulated a theory that Vermeer once made a series of religious paintings that somehow went missing, and was thrilled to authenticate Van Meergeren's "Christ and the Disciples at Emmaus'.[624] After that review, further forgeries were a snap to sell. When asked at his trial why "The Blessing of Jacob," his fifth Vermeer was so sloppy, Van Meegeren said "they sold just the same," and asked why he sold the fakes at such a high price, he said: "I could hardly have done otherwise. Had I sold them for

Pat inspects fake Vermeer, 1945

low prices, it would have been obvious they were fake." One of his forgeries set a record for the highest price of any artwork ever auctioned. After the war and accused of collaboration, he painted another fake Vermeer for the Dutch court in order to prove that he was indeed a forger and should be allowed to escape execution. The Dutch loved him because he portrayed himself as a patriot, duping the evil Goering in exchange for over a hundred Dutch paintings. The court overlooked the $30 million he made for himself as well as his loving inscription on a book he'd given to Hitler. He died at fifty-three, before serving a single year in jail, of an illness due to the depredations of high living.[625] One of his paintings hung unattributed at the Museum Boijmans until 1984 because the director refused to accept that it wasn't genuine.[626]

The occasional forgery continues to shock museumgoers. In 2018, twenty works in a Modigliani exhibition in Italy were discovered to be fakes.[627] Artists like the very successful Posin brothers of Berlin, who paint copies for high prices, bring up the question of why it is acceptable to copy great paintings, but not to fake them.[628] In *Forged: Why Fakes are the Great Art of Our Age,* my friend Jonathan Keats points out that in Roman times craftsmanship was esteemed over authenticity, and a truly fine copy might even be signed by the person who copied it.[629]

Why should authenticity increase the value of an artwork? The aesthetic experience is the same.

*

Readers are always asking whether the novel or film is true, and true stories are touted in the opening credits in order to garner extra cachet. Why does truth have such power? Isn't it enough that a film or a novel is convincing? We want the story of the murder required for the club run by the Arizona punk to be a lie. Certainly Steve did. Are stories just lies with satisfactory endings? Or are stories the tweaking of memories and anecdotes to make meaning out of the chaos of our lives? What about George Washington's lies? The fairytale cherry tree aside, he was an expert in forgery and trickery during the Revolutionary War, starting with "this land is my land because (close your eyes) nobody is living here."[630]

John Steinbeck said "A story has in it neither gain or loss. But a lie is a device for profit or escape. I suppose if that definition is strictly held to, then a writer of stories is a liar – if he is financially fortunate."[631] He should know. He wrote *Grapes of Wrath* in one hundred days without more than a single interview, relying so heavily on Sanora Babb's notes for her novel *Whose Names Are Unknown* that Babbs could not publish her book for sixty-five years—and she certainly had not given him permission to use those notes.[632] He lied when he put forward that *Grapes of Wrath* was his own.

While Dickson "worked on a novel" (which reminds me of the journalist's joke: "I'm writing a novel," to which a second journalist replies: "Neither am I"), Pat taught journalism at the University of Hawai'i as she had in Arizona, and, similar to the work she did for the Scottsdale Arts Center, wrote the text for the 20th anniversary of the Hawai'i State Foundation on Culture and the Arts catalog, featuring 125 of the 4,000 pieces of art collected by the foundation, "one of the most comprehensive public-owned art collections in the US."[633] After another bout of cancer, she put on a two-day statewide pageant for the bicentennial of Cook's discovery. It was a very political event, given the outcome of Cook's welcome—his death at the hands of native Hawai'ians unhappy with the meeting. "Gov. George Ariyoshi has appointed an unpaid coordinator of the Cook bicentennial" was how the *New York Times* credited her.[634]

*

She again moved from house to house, until she settled on one so unobtrusive you seemed to park in a closet, but its kitchen opened onto an infinity pool and the Hawai'ian sky.

*

"I have no doubt that once you get past the first year that you will steadily improve, as you did in high school," writes Dickson to Steve. The letter finishes with a P.S.: "Send your civ essay."[635] Perhaps the syndicated columnist lent a hand to his severely dyslexic stepson? Dickson must've felt very frustrated to have to father a stepson with such a handicap. Steve could never read fast enough, write or spell well, but eventually Dickson was right: Steve was almost fifty when he received his master's degree.

*

Shortly after our return from our round-the-world tour, my ex leapt onto the stage of the American Museum of Natural History and did the male counterpart of the hula, Pukapuka-style, with a rather shocked female Cook Islander dancing a demo. He knew the moves: Pukapukan men aggressively scissor their legs toward the swaying hips of their partners. Maybe it was a friendly gesture—we New Yorkers welcome you—or maybe it was a gesture of dominance. The audience did clap.

He and I had been running the New York Anthropology Film Center, the venue being our living room in a loft on 31st street, the seating discarded pews from a local church, as casual as the folding chairs at Film Forum that Karen Cooper had begun a few years earlier. I programmed a premiere of Warrington Hudlin's "Barber Shop" alongside classics by Robert Flaherty and whatever I could borrow from the New York Public Library. By then, anthropologists were giving cameras to their subjects, hoping they could pierce the cultural veil themselves. Did that tack provide more truthful insights than sequences edited by an impartial outsider? Moviegoers debated such questions after screenings and the venture turned into the Margaret Mead Film Festival.

Eventually my ex replaced me with a Bahian. He'd always had a penchant for that part of Brazil and loved the music. During one Mardi Gras in New York, he located a celebration in a nightclub, determined that the musicians wore white pants, changed into his own, and brought along his bongo. He played into the early morning with the thirty-piece band, and then demanded payment. After all, he'd worn the pants.

Like the Nuer soldier who wanted to be recognized by his shoes.

*

I was made a visiting professor at the University of Hawai'i and we tried out living there, but Pat seldom invited my boys over to swim, and our few visits were fraught with dealing with her difficult lover. After Dickson died, he'd bought half the house and moved in, saying it was to ensure that Pat had money but he seemed to have his eye more on the Chagalls than her, since he kept a woman in a house down the street. There were other disenchantments: the traffic on the island was unbelievable: you spent more time with the windows rolled up against the exhaust than enjoying the weather. As a family, we experienced a form of racial prejudice where being white—unless you were a descendant of the missionaries—was not good. The poet and my colleague, Haunani Kay-Trask, was straightforward: "I could kick/Your face, puncture/Both eyes./You deserve this kind/Of violence./No more vicious/Tongues, obscene/ Lies./Just a knife/Slitting your tight/Little heart."[636] At the end of my contract, we returned to New York.

*

Terese welcomed at the
University of Hawai'i, 1992

On the unknowability of all parents: they are never your peers.

*

Jay writes that when he was a reporter during the AIDS epidemic, he wrote a first-person piece for the newspaper and drew a parallel between deciding to be there for his sick friend, although he was scared of getting the disease, and his unwillingness to even visit his father while hospitalized and dying of alcoholism because he so abhorred his father's addiction. He did not tell his mother he was writing the piece, and it ended up on the front page. She was not pleased.[637]

*

Tim Burton's film *Big Fish* dramatizes how a son feels when his father tells wild tales about his life. The craziness of the stories delights his audiences—all but his son, who's embarrassed by the obviousness of his father's fabrications, feels lied to, and wonders why the truth isn't enough. The aging parent has the advantage of clarity that comes with time, making stories easier to craft, and all the witnesses gone. Pat doesn't go into surreal grandiose details like those in *Big Fish*, when, for example, his father arrives at his girlfriend's college by cannon and plants thousands of daffodils outside her dorm. No, her stories are mostly factual, if her sons bothered to check. Do children feel threatened when a parent talks about what he or she has accomplished? Is there an implicit command to measure up? In *Big Fish* the son tells his father a story while the father is dying, a story equal in power—his own.

*

Confabulation can be a symptom of memory disorder. Made-up stories fill any gaps in a story subconsciously, as a way to conceal memory loss. A person invents just enough to make sense of the story. Doctors call these "confabulations of embarrassment." Anything more elaborate is "fabulous confabulation."

*

It's one thing to embellish your own career, and another to do it to your offspring's. When Pat, with maternal pride, insisted on saying that one of the boys "had put himself through Harvard" when he had only completed a single course, he said "it made me feel as if she were denigrating what I had accomplished."[638]

*

Six months into our second attempt to live in Hawai'i, I was standing in a new friend's kitchen with my copy of *Vogue* splayed open across her table. This is my first novel, I said, so proud to see *Cannibal's* garish orange cover surrounded by a fabulous review. I had spent fifteen years writing and rewriting it.

My friend was a military wife with a couple of kids, her husband flew helicopters on maneuvers, we had bonded over the mutual loneliness of being new people in a new place. Her family lived in the Philippines and mine in Nebraska, which might as well have been the Philippines when it came to distances in the US. That's nice, she said, turning the *Vogue* page without reading the review so as to see more clothing and handbags, then she turned the page back. Breath held, I hoped she'd read it this time, but she just began leafing the other way. Where'd you get this magazine? she asked. It's not bad.

Had she never seen *Vogue* or was she just pretending not to know how great it was to have a full-page review in such a slick magazine? So it wasn't the *New York Times*. I remember *Very good* was her eventual answer but whether that referred to my sudden fame or the magazine was unclear. She fanned through the rest of the pages while we sat at her table and drank some guava-flavored kid's drink. I was consumed by an enormous àche to return to New York where what I did meant something.

Cannibal is a roman a clef about my expedition to Sudan. It took so long to finish because I had to transform myself from a poet into a fiction writer as well as process the trauma of being in such a difficult place with such a difficult person. I don't know whether my ex ever read it. He had such resistance to finishing anything that only a portion of the Sudanese footage he shot was ever screened, albeit at the American Museum of Natural History a few months before his Pukapukan dance performance. I was thrilled when Pat bought a half dozen copies of my novel, and my sister-in-law's thirteen-member Honolulu book club made it a bestseller for a week, actually more of a sign of how many books are bought on that island, but for me, partially ameliorating *Vogue*'s apparent obscurity there.

I had to get back to New York.

*

On or about the day of my *Vogue* review, Steve came home from his job counting dialysis patients while they sat medicated in the dark in their La-Z Boys, a feat required by Medicare billing and the size of his sister-in-law's father's practice, and agreed to apply to NYU's Interactive Telecommunications Program, which offered two years of retooling in new media. We would figure out the funding, I said, no stranger to loans, familial and otherwise. My elder son, age ten, had hated being dragged away from his schoolmates in New York. He was all for moving back, but the younger, only two and happy in his world of playdates and water, hid a chorizo under his pillow in protest.

Or maybe he just loved chorizos.

My mother! said Steve.

She will miss you, I said. But she missed you before.

*

Just before we left, Pat had a second stroke. I brought the children in to say goodbye to her. She was strapped to her bed and her eyes kept rolling, and she couldn't talk. But she pulled through after a month in rehab.

The third time we lived in Hawai'i, Pat was gone.

22

Polio?

Jay's wife Cindy nursed Pat through her final illness. Although they had lived most of their married lives near Pat, it wasn't until her second and final stroke Cindy said that she got close to Pat's true physical and emotional self. Given the damage done by polio, Pat had learned how to distract people's attention from her physical problems by putting out an energy that was always attractive, intelligent, and engaging, Cindy said, but kept people away. She felt polio had disfigured her—and that her two sisters were far more attractive. She "met people out here," Cindy said, indicating an arm's length.[639]

*

Polio? What polio? Great Uncle Lloyd doesn't remember his sister having polio. He's walking with a cane now but did he have polio? No one in the family says so. He took up sailing as a sport at Princeton—so what. He winks.

How am I supposed to understand that?

See, here are the family pictures, he says. Everyone straight as string.

I see three girls in laced-up shoes, wearing knee-high white socks, no one on crutches. But later I find a photo with a nine or ten-year-old Pat at the front of a line of girls, her half-paralyzed face much in evidence. Her friend Edith kept a newspaper clipping about her acting as mayor of Berchtesgaden whose last paragraph notes that "frail" Pat was "a victim of polio when she was a child, for years she was unable to walk."[640] A 1943 interview in the *San Francisco Chronicle* with the same reporter is titled: "Handicaps, Threats Didn't Stop Her: Patricia Lochridge is a Correspondent."[641] This piece observes that 27-year old Pat suffered "infantile paralysis in her childhood" and achieved a top spot in her profession despite the tenet that "no reporter is better than his legs." The reporter, a friend, states that "we did not ask how in seven years she had completely overcome that handicap." Where did the figure seven years come from? In 1936, she was bicycling through Europe.

*

In Texas' pioneer days, any sign of weakness meant the family and its wagon had to be left behind. Perhaps Pat inherited the instinct to show no pain or impairment, or was it a more basic drive? Dogs are set upon by other dogs if they whimper.

*

In the 1950s, the last time polio was a scourge in the U.S., families considered contracting the disease shameful. In order to catch it, you must have associated with the wrong people or gone "slumming." The irony is that polio actually becomes dangerous when sanitation is good. People living in poorer neighborhoods develop antibodies, since you can gain immunity by ingesting the virus in small doses. But if you caught the disease and became disabled, wealthy or not, you were considered damaged and treated with less respect. Disabled family members were often put into asylums back then and left there for the rest of their lives.[642]

Pat shrewdly used the diagnosis to her advantage. Her 1995 interview for *The Women Who Wrote the War,* she reveals "the fact that she had come down with polio when young had cemented the friendship [with FDR]."[643]

It's only the family that denies it.

*

FDR's outrageous cousin Alice Roosevelt Longworth had polio in childhood, but the family did not disclose it. Her stepmother had insisted she wear special leg braces and shoes as a child and forced her to do physical therapy to strengthen her legs. This regimen did not endear her stepmother to Alice, and although Alice was able to walk without braces as an adult, perhaps their discord was why all mention of her polio was buried. Alice also apparently connected the humiliations of disability with social class, stating that she felt "like a tenement child...deformed with my legs."[644]

*

In an attempt to explain his mother's personality, Jay emails me a link to "After the Cure," an essay in the *Washington Post* by Elizabeth Evitts Dickinson about her polio-stricken mother who spent a year in the hospital with polio as a child. She recovered so well she danced the ballet and became a poster child for the March of Dimes. The woman told a reporter that she was determined "to live her life so that no one would notice she'd ever been sick." But she never fully recovered, writes her daughter, as "polio . . . paralyzed more than her body."[645] The author believed that the early experience of isolation and abandonment—her parents were allowed to visit only on Sundays—severely affected her psyche. Her mother rarely hugged her, or held hands, or kissed her.

*

Although Pat was not named queen of the March of Dimes, she waded in waist deep snow up to Hitler's Eagle's Nest.

Do you remember your mother kissing you or holding your hand? I ask Steve.

No. Only the maid gave us hugs. I thought she didn't hug me because she didn't love me.

*

Pat's "great personal friend," as she refers to FDR in her letters, founded the March of Dimes.[646] That's why his face is on the dime. FDR bought Georgia's Warm Springs' resort because it relieved his symptoms, and eventually those of many others. He led therapy sessions himself occasionally, and patients called him "Uncle Rosey."[647] Although sometimes he couldn't help but reveal his handicap, he refused to be wholly identified as a cripple—is this the reverse of propaganda?—and became a powerful symbol of an individual's persistence in coping with the disease. "Every time I hear your voice on the radio and read about your attitude toward physical handicaps . . . I am strengthened and my courage is renewed," writes one of his admirers.[648]

To support the clinic, he hired Carl Byoir (at the same time Byoir was polishing Germany's image), who organized Birthday Balls across the country in his honor to raise money to combat the disease, the first time philanthropy was open to everyone. Walter Winchell provided the catchy slogan: "Dance so that a child might walk." Six thousand balls were held in 1934, and they raised over a million dollars, nearly twenty million in today's money. After three successful seasons, Byoir moved on, but the groundwork was laid for the mailbags full of dimes that poured into the foundation's office.[649]

Twenty years later, Winchell almost stopped the push for a national polio vaccination by warning that Salk's cure "may be a killer," suggesting on TV, radio and newspaper that the vaccine was live. Perhaps he was being extra cautious with regard to the lives of children, but he did reflect the anti-vaccine movement popularized by the DAR, the American Legion and other right-wing organizations that persists today, and flourished during the Covid-19 pandemic. Only once he was right. A single batch was indeed not properly inactivated, and ten children died, having contracted polio—out of 1.8 million.[650]

*

Although FDR worked hard to obscure his disability—he made seven speeches in seven towns in a day during his campaign for president—he was, in part, defined by it, admired and remembered for it. But the press took great pains to overlook it. At the Philadelphia Municipal Stadium in 1936, after being nominated for a second term, his braces slipped as he was moved behind the speaker's platform. He fell into the mud and pages of his speech scattered. While his aides collected the papers and helped him to stand, Pat's colleague Robert Trout, who was providing on-the-spot reporting, said not a word.[651]

*

Researchers today believe that FDR's symptoms might have been Guillain-Barré syndrome, and not polio. Polio paralyzes limbs unevenly and doesn't move up the body, as happened with Roosevelt, and the intense pain he felt when people touched his paralyzed legs isn't commonly seen in the disease. In addition, it's very unusual for an adult to have been stricken.[652] However, what Pat suffered was most likely polio, having caught it as a child. The disease has many similarities to Covid. Sometimes with mild flu-like symptoms, its serious effects are often sudden: one morning you wake with a headache and an hour later you can't walk.

Like Covid, quarantine was tried for polio, and masks. Few children went out during the polio epidemic, the baseball bats were piled up, bikes were left in the yard, and kids ran away from other kids. Like Covid, polio infection is spread through proximity, and it was thought to be especially virulent in water. Swimming pools were shut down. Like Covid, polio still has no cure, just vaccination—which the majority of Covid anti-vaxxers have had. Like Covid, the disease attacks many organs. Joni Mitchell, who contracted polio at age nine, writes: "If it eats the muscles of the heart, it kills you; if it eats the muscles that control the flexing of your lungs, you end up in an iron lung; if it eats the muscle of your leg, it withers." She began to sing and write songs while in the hospital for polio in her spine.[653]

What people in the 1950s remember most about those in the hospital are the children encased in iron lungs. Since RFK Jr. insists on re-testing the efficacy of the vaccine, Steve's wearable iron lung might be timely.

*

If you play hide and seek in the dark, you won't get polio, said Mrs. Wilson.

I was nine and skeptical. The babysitter was relatively new, unused to babysitting the seven of us.

She went inside. We slapped at bugs under the porch light until I turned it off and said into the dark: Let's watch TV instead.

You're it, said my brother, and the others from the porch corners. For talking.

I didn't count or close my eyes but they went away to hide anyway. Except for the littlest with her wet diapers. I carried her next to base and put her down. Then I did this jig we had to know for the school musical, and someone cleared his throat as if he were waiting.

Game over, I shouted and climbed base, not a very big tree. Polio.

Not fair, said some hidden player.

I hated babysitters worse than baby sisters, like the one on the ground crying, wanting up. From where I was, I could see Mrs. Wilson with her legs crossed in front of the TV with a doctor show on and our bowl of popcorn half-snacked up. In six short years I could be Mrs. Wilson too. I almost had breasts, my shorts were that short, I knew about babies. I climbed down.

The baby's wet, I said, loud into the dark. You guys scared her, I have to take her in.

I knew they wouldn't stay out without me, even if the boys shouted *It, It* to each other. Polio was everywhere.

The sitter switched channels to news as soon as we settled in front of the TV. Bedtime, she said.

No. We have consensus, I said. It was a word I'd picked up just then on the news. It sounded like something everybody wanted.

She laughed at my *consensus* and left to find a diaper. We moved toward some suitcases, the ones stacked in the corner with the winter clothes supposed to be soon turned to summer. We unstacked the suitcases, threw out the clothes. The boys were as quick as movie robbers. The second littlest was already sitting in a trunk when Mrs. Wilson came back, all the suitcases pretty much empty. Mrs. Wilson looked at the mess and shut the trunk on him. In the dark you won't get polio, she said, and picked it up and carried it to the door.

It's fun, said the second littlest after some silence, so anybody who could fit climbed into the others. Then there were five cases by the door, except for me holding the baby who said Click, click with her tongue.

Okay, said Mrs. Wilson, and she went into the kitchen for a bottle in the cabinet that she kept refilling with water after she poured some in a Coke. For polio, she said when I asked what it was.

I let everybody out of the suitcases since they wanted to switch, everybody but the last sister since the lock on that suitcase stuck pretty much always. After a while, after we tried a bobby pin and then a nail and then a paper clip—or rather me, since the others started watching TV again—the lock finally came loose with Dad's hammer, and my sister popped out.

Mrs. Wilson turned up with the new noise and said, Give me the baby, who, of course, wanted her own bottle and was now crying. Then Mrs. Wilson couldn't find the nipple and the baby hated the cup that was still filled with what Mrs. Wilson had been having so she said, If you play chute, you don't get polio either.

Chute? Or Shoot? We didn't know which until she'd wrapped the baby in some of the thick winter things lying around from the suitcases and tossed her down the laundry chute. At the bottom of the chute, in the basement, sat a huge mound of dirty clothes, a lot of wet diapers mostly, so the baby, who was quite quiet for a while, Mrs. Wilson's intention, broke nothing. Of course then we all wanted a turn. I think one of the boys sprained his wrist but he knew better than to say so in front of Mrs. Wilson and went to bed right away, like the rest of us.

Consensus? asked Mrs. Wilson. Then, in the dark, she told a story about a house very much like ours that had someone walking around it and around it, putting his face in the windows, and then coming in, and he had polio.

Boring, I said.

So go to sleep, said Mrs. Wilson, and snapped the gum that she wouldn't share but that Dad had left for us. It's nothing, but my brother has it, said Mrs. Wilson. Then she breathed in all our faces and said, Don't let the bugs bite.

Mom, I said in the morning. Besides, she wouldn't give us the gum.

Mom laughed. You know how many sitters would sit with all of you, or at what price? Anyway, I've heard she's going to have one of her own.

*

In the mid-fifties, I stood in line in the hot sun with the whole school to drink from paper cups filled with the vaccine. For one classmate, it was too late, and Skippy—named after his gait on crutches—became a weatherman, a great occupation for someone who was good at watching.

Like a journalist.

*

Just as FDR de-stigmatized polio by showing the public in 1934 that the disease did not compromise their president, the result of Dickson's public relations work with the Seeing Eye School was that the blind didn't have to sit in dark rooms forever.[654] This was partially accomplished by Dickson's firm placing an episode called "The Seeing Eye" on the Dupont radio show "The American Cavalcade," and Dickson being an "alert and clever young man" when discussing the phenomenon at the posh Burlingame Club in San Francisco.[655] [656] His second wife Ruth must have been a supporter. She wrote *A Friend in the Dark* in 1937, a few years before they met, *Valiant Comrades* in 1943, and *Brave Companions* two years later, all about seeing eye dogs. Dickson's book *Dogs Against Darkness* followed hers in 1946, with a big German Shepherd on the cover. It must've been pretty good—Hedda Hopper, the gossip columnist, sent a fan letter.[657]

As soon as Pat divorced Dickson, she rescued a German Shepherd, a dropout from the Air Force military police school, and not a candidate for blind school. "A sweet and wonderful watch dog, I think," she describes him in a letter.[658] According to Steve and his brothers, the dog bit everyone in sight until it was given away to be employed as a guard for a used car lot.

Or it could also have gone the way of Woofy and Skipper, never to return from their supposed psych evaluation.

23

Silence

Steve's father Henry lived to age ninty-three. His last big adventure was a three-hour bus trip from Boulder, where Henry had taken over his mother's apartment, to the small town in Nebraska where Steve and I were visiting my parents. My father was still farming but his days as district judge were over, and he was home more often, and my mother was happy to hear that Henry had brought a flask. Henry did not greet his grandsons, and barely his son. He had recently displayed his dislike of me and the threat of feminine accomplishment, when he termed Sarah Lawrence "a school for typists" after I proudly announced I had landed a job there. He couldn't have been that ignorant; he spent his cocktail hours with heads of corporations on Shelter Island. Twenty years later, however, I discover that the college offered extracurricular courses in typing and stenography in 1942 to prepare them for war work.[659] My chagrin, however, remains untriggered. He also told Steve that we could never hope to be accepted on the island because I bleached my hair. Never mind that the matrons of Shelter Island knew the color charts far better than I. Steve's first wife, a Guatemalan/Chinese graphic artist, fared even less well. She was forbidden to visit at all. They divorced after seven years.

I was glad Henry did not talk to me.

*

Did Pat resent me for giving up on Hawai'i that first time, and supporting Steve's returning to graduate school in NYC? I think she saw that as progress for him, and she had a great fondness for New York, having spent her late adolescence in Forest Hills and worked in the city for so many years. She understood exactly why we wanted to return but not everyone did. Hawai'i! Paradise! I wanted New York, and if Steve had to go back to school for us to move, so be it. I think Pat understood that I too needed to keep my career going. She had been forced to change her own trajectory for Dickson and corrected it only after he could no longer support them. Eventually Dickson was relegated to an apartment inside her Hawai'i house, and buried, appropriately enough, in the Punchbowl Cemetery. When I told her we were moving back to New York, she said nothing, which is about as eloquent a statement as a mother-in-law can make.

*

Like Jay, I remain very curious about the rightful owner of the Cranach. Among the various possibilities, the National Gallery says it may be the one that was sold by Chemnitz businessman Hans Wilhelm Vogel's widow to industrialist Robert Allmers for 20,000 marks ($160,000 today) in 1935.[660] A large Jewish community had flourished in Chemnitz for 125 years, and other Cranachs were "sold" by wealthy Jews during Hitler's era like nylons, in the hope of being spared.[661] Chemnitz was also at the center of the Nazi's forced labor program, and most of its Jewish factories had been taken over by the Nazis.[662] Two of the Jewish industrialists in Chemnitz were art collectors: David Leder and Dr. Arthur Weiner, who was murdered in 1933.[663]

Wilhelm Vogel's widow had been asking 32,000 marks for the painting. But before feeling sorry for the poor cheated widow, consider that the Vogel's had been Nazis since 1933, and that Wilhelm Vogel's son, Hans Hermann, not only owned a textile and paper factory, but was president of the German Research Institute of the Textile Industry, member of the board of directors of the International Labor Office in Geneva, Presidential member of the Association of German Employers' Association, and Chairman of the Chemnitz Chamber of Industry and Commerce. One of his friends was in the SS.[664] Perhaps the discrepancy between the asking and the sales price of the Cranach was due to it being overpriced? Although the Vogels were Jewish, they spent no time in concentration camps. At least two of their drawings have been proven to have been purchased under duress, not sold.[665]

How would the Cranach end up in Hitler's living room? Robert Allmers was a leading German industrialist, someone who shifted with the political winds early on in the Third Reich.[666] Also a Nazi by 1933, and from 1926 to 1945 president of the Reich Association of the German Automobile Industry (RDA), he was surely involved in the Nazi's industry-wide practice of using slaves, which included Porsche, Audi, BMW, and Mercedes. In 1937, the same year that Allmers donated a luxurious yacht to Goering and his new bride, the painting was photographed in Hitler's private collection.[667] Another present from Allmers? Hitler received many lavish birthday presents from his top brass, and thousands in 1937, his favorites being looted artwork.[668] Or it could be the painting Hitler spent his *Mein Kampf* royalties on.[669] The dimensions are never quite right, like the truth.

How could a painting shrink or shift size? The receipt for the sale of the Cranach to E. A. Silberman in 1962 shows different dimensions, before framing and after. The painting had been transferred to masonite board that year, and the National Gallery theorizes that provenance may have been removed at that time.[670]

The Vogel family might know the truth. They either bought, possibly at a forced sale, or seized the painting from someone else's collection. Contacted via the Chemnitz Museum, they aren't answering. After Vogel died in 1941, his daughter, Walpurg von Dewitz, a member of Deutsches Frauenwerk, a women's Nazi group, sold Hitler more of the family's collection for 50,000 marks, a reasonable amount of money. When the war was over, the first vote during the Soviet occupation of Chemnitz was the transfer of war and Nazi criminals' businesses to the people, and the Vogel company, and what was left of the family's collection, were taken.[671]

The fact is, despite the National Gallery having posted information about the Cranach's lack of provenance online for the last fifteen years, no one has come forward to claim it. Perhaps the immediate family perished in the gas chambers—but wouldn't some surviving relative have noticed a 15th century nude woman 32" x 21" hanging in the family's parlor and wonder what happened to it? This was a masterpiece. Or was only the poor branch of the family left, the ones who were never invited to visit? Scenarios present themselves.

*

In the early eighties, we drove down to Florida to watch a rocket launch. Or that's what we said we were doing. My mother wanted me to check up on her uncle, a widower who had been married to a very wealthy woman whose grandfather had been mayor of New York and whose family had once owned all the sugar in the world. A robber baron. My mother suspected their attorney of foul play: he owned the company that provided the round-the-clock care that had kept her and his now deceased wife sedated for a decade. We were to casually drop by the house, as if a three thousand mile car trip was something we undertook to entertain our four-year-old for the weekend. I had met Uncle Edward twice as an adult.

After spending the pre-dawn hours cramped in the car parked at the beach, eating peanuts and oranges, we received the news that the rocket launch had been indefinitely postponed. Bedraggled and exhausted, we arrived at Uncle Edward's house to make light conversation and discovered, after dinner, that his phone was bugged. You could hear someone breathing on the other end. We stayed just a few days. The phalanx of medical staff could not tell us what my uncle was suffering from, only that he would surely be dead soon. The attorney estimated a year. A year later, the bulk of Uncle Edward's $69 million estate went to a not-for-profit for crippled racehorses. There being no such animal as a crippled racehorse—their armature can't support a broken leg—the foundation, headed of course by the attorney, legitimized his position by designing the "super racehorse."

My mother, my uncle's primary heir, hired lawyers to fight the will but there was more than one, interlocking and impossible to break. Or so she said. It must not have been so impenetrable because all my siblings and myself had to sign a document saying we would not sue. We suspected that the truth was that the attorney had threatened to expose the homosexual leanings of my uncle and his lesbian wife. Being a very conservative Catholic, my mother decided to let the money go. But who could be harmed by the truth? My mother, torn between her shame and $69 million, chose to avoid the shame.

*

"Becoming really dead," argues American historian Thomas Laqueur, "takes time."[672] Hitler was said to have fled Germany by plane to Denmark and then to Argentina by submarine. Others had him relocating to Munich, Hanover, or Hamburg, living under assumed names and disguised by plastic surgery. In reality, the changes would have had to have been less from plastic surgery than a revolver. Some survivors of the Holocaust wanted him alive to render punishment, and some wanted him dead, dead, dead. A 1955 CIA memo declassified in 2017 from the agency's base in Caracas, Venezuela, stated that the co-owner of the former *Maracaibo Times* met someone who "strongly resembled and claimed to be Adolf Hitler." He used the name Adolf Schüttelmayor and felt certain he could not be arrested for war crimes committed more than ten years ago. But the CIA boss didn't endorse the sighting.[673]

Some 9,000 Nazis did escape to South America, aided by Argentine Cardinal Antonio Caggiano and the Austrian Bishop Alois Hudal, who issued Vatican identity papers, allowing them to obtain forged Red Cross passports. The Nazis then made their way along "ratlines" that smuggled them out of Europe. Argentina's Juan Perón was particularly welcoming. Only two prominent Nazis, Klaus Barbie, and Adolf Eichmann, were ever caught, and only the latter was executed. Most lived out the rest of their lives under the South American sun.[674]

*

According to *Off the Record*, Pat was in Buenos Aires on October 12, 1945 on her search for Hitler's cronies. Five days later, Juan Perón would be released from prison. In the midst of sporadic rebel shooting at around two in the afternoon, she decided to walk across the park to the Plaza for lunch. World War II had been over for two months but as soon as she heard a machine gun blast, she hit the ground. What she saw when she lifted herself off the dirty wet street was that her new suit was ruined, and the grinning face of the gunman. She walked over to him and slapped him across the face and then shook him. He was too surprised to shoot at her again. She complained that she never did get lunch. "And believe me, when I picked myself up, I was exceedingly annoyed that I'd gotten through the Pacific and I'd gotten through Europe and here I came to beautiful Buenos Aires and I was under gunfire but this time in my gray flannel and no one made any apologies."[675] [676]

Steve had never heard this story before, but he had never had the curiosity to read the book.

Two years after that trip, she mentions in an interview that the visit to South America was a "vacation assignment."[677] As I mentioned earlier, in a letter home, she said she was looking for post war job opportunities for women in Latin America. In another interview, she was searching for Hitler.[678] Either you're on assignment or you're on vacation—but for four months? And witnessing three revolutions—was that a coincidence? She dined and danced with many embassy people, met with the CIAA, a propaganda organization headed by Nelson Rockefeller, and wore her hat made from Goering's military sashes in Guatemala.[679] She explained to Steve in 1995 that Hitler had told one of his favorite men to go to southern Argentina and carry on, but "it turned out that he hadn't gotten through, he had been killed."

She published nothing.

*

Stepmother Janet rises from the dead to make a cameo in the National Film Board's *A Return to Memory*, a two-hour 2024 documentary about the women who made the National Film Board, after most of the qualified men had been drafted. The ambiance in the women's workplace is described in the film as "people in strange costumes with film cans on their heads, singing and humming. Ideas seemed to fly through the air."[680] One of the directors says "The only way you could tell whether the film board could afford anything was Janet's little black book." Near the end of the film, Red Burns, the founder of NYU's Interactive Communications Program, Steve's alma mater, tells how, at the tender age of sixteen, she hung around the Film Board for so long that they gave her a start. She modeled the NYU program after the NFB.

You owe Janet, I say. It's a long and tortured path back to her, but there it is.

Red Burns was great, says Steve.

*

At a family reunion in Nantucket, I ask Steve's relatives about Pat's life. She was a very accomplished woman, says her now 101-year-old brother Lloyd. Steve's cousins didn't really know her. Ask the cousin who's not here, who's a little older, they tell me. I leave a message on his phone. She was a force, he says. Everyone was afraid of Dickson.

What about Dickson? I ask Uncle Lloyd.

He was a nice man, says Uncle Lloyd. Then he goes silent.

*

Steve and I married in 1981. We hired our upstairs neighbors to play their white baby grand on Henry's front lawn beside the Long Island Sound. How did they haul it out there? I remember very little—being delighted that the garden club would do the flowers because Steve was an ex-member—and choosing chicken cacciatore as a main course. Pat's letters register the event with mind-boggling wedding detail for what apparently never concerned me. She seemed to enjoy the logistics, and for once, I enjoyed all of it: the Royal Souvenir pamphlet we wrote to commemorate our ceremony coinciding with Diana and Charles', my four-year-old son presenting the ring with more gravity than the Justice of the Peace, the polka the pianist broke out for my father, who, as it turned out, didn't know the dance, and the fact that after we left, guests found the champagne that Henry had hidden, drank it up and set fire to the bulkhead.

*

In 1970, posing as fishermen, Vladimir Gumenyuk and two other KGB agents pitched a tent over the site where Hitler's bones had been buried twenty-some years earlier on Russia's Magdeburg base. The Russians were handing over the base back to the East German government but first they had to get rid of the bones. After the digging efforts failed to produce anything, they realized they had pitched the tent in the wrong place. After moving it and digging another five feet down, they found the rotting remains of Hitler buried in a wooden crate. They lit a fire to make soup, and then a second one to burn Hitler's bones.

"We wasted the whole canister of gasoline on him," said Gumenyuk in a 2010 interview. The only surviving member of the KGB trio, he explained that they were supposed to have burned the bones the night before, but it was illegal to make outdoor fires in Germany, a detail overlooked by their superiors. They had to wait until morning when the smoke was less noticeable. Afterwards, they chucked what ashes remained into a rucksack and drove to a cliff beside an unidentified river to scatter them. Not even Gumenyuk's wife knew what they'd done.[681]

*

But what about the forty-seven gallons of gas that burned throughout the afternoon and into the Berlin evening of April 30, 1945 as reported by the *Washington Post*?[682] Didn't that do the trick?

*

The willingness of people to follow leaders appealing to the most degenerate of human impulses is evergreen. Hitler is not dead, he is just silent.

24

Truth to Fit

Imperious still, Pat sits propped in her bed set up on the patio surrounding the pool she built that forces a perspective of chlorinated water over the far edge, one that meets the ocean so without a seam you swim into it with your eyes, swim without the cliff that separates your perspective from one water to the next. Three of her sons watch the encroaching clouds in that trick perspective, hear her lover bang the door that he owns half of, and drink a little wine. They would've given her vodka through a tube if she had one.

But the tubes are gone, she drinks only sips of water.

Steve calls after our family's Christmas. Not that she can talk to him. She had to blink to affirm the document in which she decreed that for her, starving was the way to go. One blink for no, two for yes, and repeated on numerous occasions thereafter. Jay's wife came up with this Morse code before Steve left for home after his two-week vigil. Jay tested her blinking even further, scientifically even, double bind, by asking if she loved him—two blinks—and whether he was the second to youngest, questions she could easily answer, to establish a baseline.

The blinks have to be close together, not a blink, and then a blink.

The palms rustle. You can't have a woman in a sickbed outside in Hawai'i without palms. The palms rustle with geckos fleeing the sudden light of the coming and going of the clouds, palms far from where Steve calls, happy not to bear the grief of her dying and the grief given him by this lover of hers. The lover has also posed questions to her, the answers to which he says belie her clear mind, the blinking not right, not right at all, says the lover. Doesn't she love him more than her children? One blink. She has changed that clear mind of hers. He waits and waits for the next. Maybe all those two-timing years with that woman down the road, who had so many lifts that her kept quality confused even the lover sometimes when they all met in the grocery store, convinced Pat to at last reject him.

Since he owns half the house, the brothers can't keep him out under legal circumstances of title and deed. Instead they change locks and keep guard and sleep in shifts. The lover tried to cut off the ambulance with his car when they moved her home from the hospital, and tried to bribe the hospice workers to let him in as they walked to their cars, giving jewelry to the cute R.N. from the mainland with hot pink lipstick, although they wonder how clear his motivations were with that one.

Having had another devastating stroke, she has been dying for three weeks. Eating nothing and sipping water is a three-week torture, for the sons mostly, since they are told that hunger disappears quickly. Steve has terrible dreams while he waits with them the first two weeks, and in his insomnia easily falls prey to my pleas to return for our own holiday, if only for the presents. Does he want to watch this to the very end? Does he want another run-in with the lover accusing him, the eldest, of being the mastermind of her slow murder? It won't be long now, his brothers keep telling him over the phone, but it is, day after beautiful Hawai'ian day.

Except for this rogue storm that is rising, has risen, a storm with the promise of thunder and lightning, rarer than tsunamis welling up from mid-ocean—is it the weather or the lover rustling those palms? Is he, with the determination of his daily bench-pressing, scaling their mutual wall and sliding down a palm to make it rustle? You can hear it under the first low thunder.

The electricity goes out and the second son does not flick on the flashlight—he wants to see the lightning rip across the black, a phenomenon strange at the equator. In the two hours before midnight all of them have spent getting a little high in the dark with the wine and the quiet of their mother's outdoor bedside, not even eating, no, not even the youngest, the burliest, eats in her presence to validate her decision, and even the clouds have held themselves off while the bay slides over the side of the equator the way the pool water does to the bay, that pool now so full of lightning in reflection.

Jay engineers a toast before the sprays of light and the booming obliterate all sight and sound. For kindness and mercy. Hear, hear, shout the others, hoping she can hear, that her single blink and then half of another signifies two this time and forever. Then Steve calls and cries on the phone. He remains torn between his non-equatorial home and hers, although the third son reassures him his mother is holding up, doing as well as can be expected, is still there, and doesn't hang up, he leaves the phone on the tray table where his brother can hear the thunder at least, their cheers and their glasses coming together and the palms rustling so loudly.

In the post-storm light, the clouds part and the moon shines radiant—there's an actual shaft of light from the sunset—the second son notices, lifting Pat's one hand over the other, that she isn't blinking, that her stare has slipped over the pool's edge into the ocean.

She's gone out in style, hers. An achievement when you're eighty-three and paralyzed.

They forget Steve in all that happens afterward. At dawn a housekeeper replaces the receiver.

*

He says he still feels torn. He admits that the only time he remembers having his mother's full attention was after he recorded Basil Bunting's interview in Cumbria for the Ezra Pound Voices & Visions program ten years earlier, when his mother took the train with him to Edinburgh. They talked about nothing important, and played poker, and of course he lost.

A woman who could keep the truth close.

*

Lee Miller's son had no idea of his mother's achievements until after she died in 1977. Her modeling for the cover of *Vogue*, her work as a top photographer, her relationships with Man Ray, Picasso, Dorothea Tanning and her 60,000 photographs—he had to discover all on his own. "I had known my mum as a useless drunk."[683] He valiantly attributed his neglect as a child to her struggle with flashbacks, insomnia, anxiety, addiction and a huge emotional disconnect from the world—PTSD acquired from her wartime experiences. "I could never get the stench of Dachau out of my nostrils," said Miller.[684] Sigrid Schultz, the first female foreign bureau chief of a major U.S. newspaper who'd interviewed both Hitler and Goering, published only one book—of recipes. Like Pat, correspondent Helen Kirkpatrick had her brush with McCarthy. She resigned from the *Post* when her reports about him were too severely rewritten and became

Public Affairs Officer at the US State Department in Washington, rising to be considered for Assistant Secretary of State for Public Affairs. She didn't take the job, understanding that Americans weren't ready for a woman.[685]

*

When I was nineteen, I spent six months as McGill's rare manuscript curator. The director was undergoing a mid-life crisis and felt that someone who was foolish enough to put Mensa on her skimpy resume could do the job as well as all the twits who studied library science as if it were something you did with test tubes and lab coats.

I did wear white gloves. I drew them on daily, drew as they said in those old books I'd read so few of, to peer into the incunabulum, which is the term for an early printed book, usually one printed before 1501. You opened a specimen as if it harbored arthritis in the hide of whatever animal that bound it, having pages you could only peek at, a spine that you could not crack, nor, horror! pages flattened to examine the print inside. The print in the one I was to research was Latin anyway, and although I'd had three years of it, the book's blocks of print so thick and black discouraged me from even beginning to translate. Where was my teacher when I needed her, Miss Mustache of the prairie with her high button shoes? I sniffed the book for clues—bacon? Maybe the binding was pigskin? Exactly when did pigs die for books? I imagined one flayed in the bloody and cruel 16th century, its organs spread out on the ground like a table of contents.

Classes over for the year, my pre-law, pre–med, pre-everything first husband left Montreal to find construction work. Ironworking is an itinerant trade, though unionized, and the jobs moved with the waves of building. My probationary library wages weren't sufficient to afford our apartment alone. Rather than move, I found a second job at night, wearing a long black cape to sell roses to tourists in the old part of Montreal. One night I sold my entire bouquet, and resold it after it was rejected by its recipient, thrown down in the slush.

During the day I stared at the incunabulum. Research was interesting but very slow. You don't classify incunabula by author or subject matter but through typographic clues to the printer and location and period. The head of the department encouraged me, took me to a book auction where I felt I was a rose seller impersonating a manuscript curator, and of course I was permitted to bid on nothing. When the husband wrote that construction work in Vancouver was booming, one brewery after another, I weighed this adventure on another coast against my nascent career as a book detective (and book warden, since I spent most of my time making sure that researchers didn't steal the Blake illustrations, using a thread to cut oh so slowly against a page and then slipping the plate into a notebook). Being young and foolish, I chose Vancouver.

Two years later, the husband drove off for the weekend with another woman and did not return.

Now I see myself as an impostor and Pat as my incunabulum, the history inside the covers nearly asemic, which means a script that allows the reader to assign his own meaning.

*

Henk De Berg, author of *Trump and Hitler: A Comparative Study in Lying*, asserts that the extremist language used by Trump and his followers is understood as authentic because in everyday speech we too dip into hyperbole, for example, "My mother-in-law is worse than Hitler."[686]

In Trump's case, it's hyperbole come true.

*

Pat's lover threatens her sons with a lawsuit for homicide, and writes about it in a letter to Pat's friend Edith. By proceeding according to Pat's living will, written four years earlier after her first stroke, and allowing her to starve (after having endured, by his own count, five medical emergencies including two more strokes in her last years), the boys "engineered her death" because they wanted her money. "Their excuse: mercy!" writes the bereaved lover.[687]

*

Was Pat a liar, with all that word's pejorative weight? The truth, as I have tried to establish both theoretically and in practice, is various, and hard to determine. Why are there 142 synonyms for lying? All those shades of gray. What about hyperbole? We're all guilty of that. Honestly, says the liar, it's the truth. People lie because they're afraid of the consequences, they feel guilty or full of shame or want to manipulate a situation. If you keep one thing secret, what else are you not telling? Whenever police suspect an informant is lying, they have them tell their story backwards.

Scientists say you can tell how smart your child is by how early they start lying.[688]

*

Courtesy of Governor Ron DeSantis, Florida schoolchildren are taught the lie that slaves benefited from slavery by learning a trade, never mind that many Africans already knew a trade and those who benefited from this knowledge, either known or learned, were the slavers, not the slaves. God forbid that white children should peer through the whitewash of politics and feel guilt, or that black children, their genes bearing the trauma of brutal oppression, know where that trauma came from.

*

Displayed with all the Hawai'ian art Pat had commissioned or pur-chased was the Chagall that the lover had coveted. It was found after her death to have been clipped from an art magazine, the original sold long ago to support Dickson. But the lover got his revenge. His girlfriend writes in his obituary a few years later that she was his "lady friend" during all those years he spent with Pat.[689]

*

Only once did Pat cross me. In the midst of one of her medi-cal emergencies, she held an impromptu meeting with her boys about her will, and I ventured an opinion. She spoke sharply and requested that I "see what was on television." I left in a huff, hurt. Much later, having experienced similar situations with regard to my father, I now understand. In-laws have their own agendas and can hardly grasp the complexities, let alone the strength, of a family's psychodynamics and history. The subject of a legacy is difficult enough in this death-denying culture.

*

When I returned from my long trip around the world via Sudan and the South Pacific, I was surprised that so few wanted to hear about my adventures. Talking about one's travels is as boring as retelling a dream. Or is it the traveler's gender, the fact of a woman being too adventurous or too smart or too lucky? Every time I mention I've lived in Sudan and South Pacific, there is a pause in the conversation, and if I begin to elaborate, the talk is invariably re-routed to more believable, or at least more domes-tic topics.

Surely Pat had that experience. Let me tell you about the time I ransacked Hitler's hideaway.

25

Belief

I think why you and your brothers never believed your mother was not so much because her stories were unbelievable but because your disbelief allowed you to set out on your own. You boys were never going to govern a postwar German town or its contemporary equivalent.

That's a possibility, says Steve. In the family she was the success, unlike both of my fathers. She couldn't put herself forward too much, however, or Dickson would be angry, consciously or unconsciously. It could have caused tension with Henry too.

No one likes a successful woman, even today, I say.

*

We are fond of telling the story that we met on an answering machine, but really a biographer was the matchmaker. Her partner was developing a film on Muhammed Ali with Steve and they invited both of us to dinner. Not knowing I'd been set up, I brought along a friend from Vancouver. Steve was then just-divorced and still dazed by the experience. A year later, hearing my voice on their answering machine—that's what those machines were good for!—Steve asked me out. But then he postponed the date to spend the weekend at Three Mile Island just after the nuclear meltdown, replacing the sound recordist who was pregnant. A hot date.

*

I am leaning forward, close to Steve's moving lips, how salty they will taste! when the boom quivers. A tiny very black cloud is racing toward us, a rag thrown out of an empty sky. Take these, Steve says, grabbing the tiller and tossing life jackets toward the biographer and her boyfriend. It makes one motion, Steve's hand catching the boom, and the other, flinging the last jacket to me. The rest is all about scramble: the boat and its sudden speed—a crazy speed—and the darkness of the water moving so fast under it, making the boat shiver and sing. Then it tips, the boom goes silly, and the wind raps and rips at the unhappy sails.

How do you get this jacket on?

The boyfriend has no idea.

We're thrown clear, then we thrash to get back to the boat. It's turned turtle. Water pours down all around, a hard rain falls from a sky where the lightning's so bright the air fills with diamonds. I'm terrified of the deep water and it's raining so hard I can hardly breathe—and my jacket's not quite on, I've dissolved into saltwater and air while Steve shouts so calmly from so far away, This boat's unsinkable!

It's early in the relationship.

The biographer is smiling. She had been talking about the new film the guys are now planning, Muhammed Ali having signed with someone else, the definition of *schmatta*, whoever's book deal, but who knows what now—too much thunder. For once she's saying nothing, there's just this curious smile. Her boyfriend's not panicked either, no, he's holding onto the thin rail that runs along the edge of the upside-down boat and sticking his free hand up and waving it as if he's on a bucking horse, and Steve—Steve's swimming around, finding overboard things in all this dark and rain and lightning.

My hands claw at the railing.

Is this like in Africa? the biographer asks, smiling wider.

Waves pull at my fingers as if they will pop off at the knuckle. I returned from my Sudanese expedition only a few years earlier—survived is the better word. She is writing about Africa, a bio so removed from being there she had to learn Karen Blixen's Danish to understand it.

I nod, a very small motion. Yes.

Steve dives for the cooler of hors d'oeuvres and drinks, he retrieves a shoe, he shouts, All right? to everyone and then again louder, to me.

The guttural that grips my throat causes Steve to grab my suit bottom and haul me up and onto the hull. I cling flat to it, shiver, and close my eyes. There's so much lightning, its flashing cuts right through.

Nothing like this ever happens to me, shouts the biographer. She's not smiling now, she's beaming. Her boyfriend yells in agreement. The storm blows into a pause, and the three of them swim and kick more or less in a direction, not one I know but Steve, Steve has instinct, Steve directs them, Steve sees something out of the black and then white of the whitecaps. I don't kick, that would be loosening my grip on the hull, my whole-body grip, until at last the mast impales itself in sand or at least land looms up and the boat stops, impaled or not.

The rain stops too. Gray tailings of cloud slide across the sky.

The two of them stand beside the rescued cooler while Steve swims around to pry me off the boat bottom, finger by finger. Okay, I say. I'm okay. Steve staggers ashore with me in his arms, mermaid heavy. All of us hug each other while leftover lightning lights up the spit we've washed up on, water on all sides, an island of gravel relief.

Then Steve's back into the waves like the storm is nothing, securing something to the deep. The boyfriend dives in too—he's wet anyway, and new sheets of rain split the beach from the water. The biographer and I wrap ourselves and our jackets together into one beach towel, oh yes, we cling to each other while the rain slants down again in serious shafts, in jackets that do not at all block the cold despite the entwining towel. We chatter—our teeth, not our speech—and do not look at each other or into the rain but down, we say Wow, what was that? when another thunder shakes us, more lightning from where? until we are crouched as near to the pebbles as we can fold ourselves. To me we are ants in God's eyes, that Nuer saying, meek under the Sudanese thousand-mile horizon that broods and weeps black and terrible for months at a time, a sky the same color as all that water under the boat.

The biographer unwraps herself to open the now rescued cooler. We better get it ready for the guys, she says.

I can't answer her, I can't consider how shaken up the champagne must be now while she pokes around its foil for the wire.

Champagne, sour cream, caviar, and stuffed eggs.

I packed the eggs.

She packed romance food, not picnic, pure bookish romance foodstuffs I don't even know the price of.

Eggs? she'd said earlier, with reticent inflection.

Eggs are all about sex, her boyfriend said, coming to my defense. He's very much about sex, being so much younger than the biographer, who's wise enough to bring champagne and not eggs, who's all about ambition and the allure of colonial Africa, but she's the one who said, Wear that tight dress, not that kaftan.

The guys' feet come into view. The biographer has the bottle open, its foam as wild as the shoreline's. I look at the ocean, the very sound of it big. Over it, I hear them pour after the pop, the glug of it. Why don't you take a swig before it's gone? Steve asks.

I sip but I still don't stand.

The biographer uses the sour cream lid as a scoop for the caviar. Still sitting on the gravel, I eat the salty lumps of fish that could be tears in this rain and my shock. I say, Everyone spotted the hippo at the same time on the ferry to Fangak, and ran to one side and the boat tipped. Water roared in through the mesh. Everyone was screaming.

The sun comes out and is blown away, then a gray cool wind whips around us. We've got the boat righted, says the boyfriend instead of *what?* You can't stay there like that, says the biographer. You'll get really cold, says Steve, and my legs unlock at last, and I walk back into the water.

Chest-deep boatside, Steve bends and kisses me on the neck. I wear my previous relationships like a fat towel and have already borne a son—I can be gathered into his arms but the storm will stay. He kisses me again and then he and the boyfriend take me on, half-hauling me over, leg by leg, crotch and breast. Then we do not set sail into the sunset, no, the sail is wet like the towel, we row and we bail.

The biographer bails with the sour cream container, the boyfriend works the ornamental Polynesian longboat paddle—a souvenir I brought along, while Steve uses the regulation oar and I cup my hands. I can really bail, they notice, I have bailed. We bail and row and switch off and sing rowing songs from early piano lessons and Harvard, rounds about rowboats mostly until the sky at last begins to darken on its own. Then Steve says, There's a boat and any bigger boat seeing us in distress in the dusk must stop—the first rule of the sea—and we'll get on and be saved. Otherwise the current, Steve says, could take us to England.

We sing English rowing songs.

The boat is bigger and out for pleasure after the storm. We hail them and wave, and they wave back and motor on.

Steve says Sorry.

Now all of us row like galley slaves. We do not sing. Dark comes for real just as the land arrives, the most expensive shore of Shelter Island, just enough land to quit the boat, tie it to a fancy pier and walk, all drowned in our suits and towel, sore from rowing, to quite a house. What we've shipwrecked into looms three stories of blue glass in front of us, with kitchen paving leading from a pool. The owners are on their way out when we knock, asking to use their phone. Who are we but bathing-suited no ones casing the place, but even in her black single piece suit-and-towel, the biographer has the poise to ask about the influence of Venice in their choice of glass, and soon we have wine in hand, awaiting our rescue.

The owners had spotted that black cloud from their terrace, it ran across the ocean in sprints, there were whirlwinds behind it, you were so lucky, it was the worst squall they'd ever seen.

The boyfriend stretches his arms across the big couch leather and leans back as if all of that luck is his.

The wipers hardly part the rain against the rescue car, where Steve sits right beside me, all the puff out of him, his father driving and so old we don't even speak when he runs the sign at the crossroads. Instead I cover Steve's hand with mine.

The couple aren't married yet so their divorce sits in their future with all the infidelity they will find to go with it, all the money they will make and inherit, the trainers who will put her in a bikini and the apartment they will split in court on the rocks they make for themselves. They are still friends now and then, not so much lovers. Now they want us to go on ahead, to give marriage a try before them.

I do, I say a third time, the charm.

Why do I go into such detail? The biographer turns up at a concert decades later with a new beau, a publisher, and tells the whole story but it is as herself on her first date with the boyfriend and she is the one holding onto the bottom of the boat. There is the rogue cloud and the caviar and the singing in her telling, but all hers while Steve and I stand there listening, still so married, surprised by whose romance she makes so much of.

*

This book is about Pat pointing at Hitler's ashes: Look, the past is dead, long live the past, but carry on. Shoulder yourself. I'm not smearing these ashes over my face. Why didn't Pat write the book about her life after people had repeatedly begged her to? She survived. She had some oil money from her father, I discover, she wasn't entirely bereft at any point.

My son searches the purple flat files and finds more Holocaust photos, but none of Pat.

Maybe Steve doesn't want to find the photo now.

*

The National Archives says Pat has a large FBI file from 1954-55, but they won't release it for 39 months. I'm appalled. Then I read about someone who wants 132,000 pages released and the estimate is 132 years.[690] I'm hoping I already know everything. Given the dates, it seems the FBI investigated her at the same time as they did Dickson, compliments of Ruth the jealous ex-wife, and there's just more of their hotel romance.

I'm right.

*

We gather in Paterson, New Jersey for a Syrian meal with our son's girlfriend's mother and uncle. Long home to immigrants, Paterson is where I once walked for a *Vogue* article on how far you could get out of New York City on foot in a day. Even then the bar where I phoned for a taxi to take me and my aching legs home—25 miles!—was filled with the exotic scent of somewhere else. This time Steve and I and our son and girlfriend and the girlfriend's mother take a minibus full of other immigrant workers, one of them coughing, with the pandemic announcements just days away, to await the uncle at a Paterson restaurant. He delivers cases of soda for cash in the tri-state area, a job with just enough macho independence and irregular hours that no one is surprised he's not there to meet us. Our son's girlfriend, with her genie smile and dark sad eyes, waves away his absence and we two mothers gossip about politics and whether my son should cut off his curls. The girlfriend is celebrating our meeting with the uncle, her putative father, her own father having abandoned the family and established another in Europe, a father who turned her away at the door when she tried to visit. She's also celebrating her nascent shaman practice, having finished a long course of study almost as hard, she says, as Bard. My son orders drinks and hor d'oeuvres which we gobble, then we finally order meals. The uncle saunters in as we finish. The hour is late. He gives us no excuse but is deferential to me in particular, toasting my status as mother-in-law. I'm willing to be toasted at this point, you might say I need to be toasted. Then he begins to order. We are fully prepared to smile through his meal but then he orders in Arabic for all of us all over again. Plates arrive and keep coming. We struggle through the first round to be polite, while he doesn't touch his. He orders more. We say No, it will be a waste. Eat, he commands, you must eat. We say, after he insists that our waiter bring more, we can take it home, we can't eat another bite. My husband tries valiantly anyway, rising to the challenge, as it were, but this is enough, it is too much. The uncle commands our son's girlfriend to leave the table with him, and she returns in tears. Mother-in-law, she says, you must eat. I see her sorrow, her helplessness before this faux father she loves for claiming her as his daughter, the culture that forces this humiliation, and I nibble, I don't walk out into the late night of Paterson to find a taxi to return us. The uncle looks on approvingly.

*

With regard to our second son, I receive an email from a young woman who graduated from the same undergraduate writing program as mine in Canada, who won a prize named after my professor who invited her for dinner and told her she reminded him of me. So we meet and I'm flattered: she's bright and restless and fearless, the qualities I remember being useful. I never wore shorts so short nor rode a bike so far from uptown, but I imagine I could have. I give her all the contacts I can summon. Days later, I tell her since she's so much like me, maybe she'd like to meet my son. It's logical: why wouldn't he like his mother at her age? A perfect match. She says she laughed out loud, receiving my email. Okay, says my son, she can come to my party. Like his grandfather Henry, he likes to give parties. When she arrives, she's with someone else and with one glance at that someone it's clear, says my son, that he has no chance. Would I have done that—used a human shield to protect myself from the machinations of a mother-in-law? Perhaps. Our son says the couple had a good time.

*

Since I hated being confined to hotel reservations even on our honeymoon, we arrived at the Zona Rosa in Mexico City with nowhere to stay, and two heavy suitcases in the days before wheels. We circled several blocks in the heat, dragging the bags, and decided on a hotel only after I spotted a beautiful interior staircase. Weeks later, Pat telephoned us, having received our postcard, to tell us that that was where she spent her honeymoon, and Steve's father's mother too.

So did he marry his mother or what?

*

At the end of his life, my father had intermittent dementia. This caused a great deal of stress for him and eight years of litigation for us while he made all kinds of legal complications. One of the more minor conflicts arose after the local library solicited him—along with so many other seniors—for money. They showed him a brochure of the proposed new facilities with his name photoshopped across the front: Svoboda. After he'd promised a considerable amount, more than all the other donors put together, the library was built—with someone else's name over the door. He hadn't died soon enough to claim the honor. Apparently the brochure ruse is common.

Truth gets harder and harder to distinguish as you age. You believe anyone—after all, people were honest before, there's history.

*

The making of a memoir is all about digging up the truth. I suppose there's plenty of aged interviewees getting even with the dead, recasting the past, but mostly a memoir consists of putting together a puzzle from clues a/k/a verifiable facts and suppositions deduced from those facts. You're basically writing to the contours of what you don't know. The mysteries.

*

My therapist says the personality is never steady, that the truth of who one is is less like a portrait than a collection of symptoms like a cold.

Wouldn't you know it—a virus, I say.

And every time you encounter someone, the personality adjusts. It's the Heisenberg principle of identity, shining a light on it, you change it.

So my attempts to capture my mother-in-law are doomed?

You capture your mother-in-law, probably not Steve's mother. Probably not his brother's wife's mother-in-law.

No one will be satisfied with my memoir.

*

Steve hoists the flag in front of our beach house, and an osprey screams. He is not pulling out her tail feathers or teasing her babies, those enormous vaudevillian chicks with scrawny necks, but he might as well be. The osprey is annoyed because every day he hoists and lowers that flag.

Unwarranted patriotism, remarks our guest, the very young girlfriend of Steve's collaborator with wonderfully mascaraed eyelashes tipped in pink.

She doesn't know Steve as well as I fear he'd like, but she is correct. At least Steve does not salute.

The osprey screams again, sinks to the sand and snatches her beau's jacket, lifts it off the beach with double wing beats— the desperation of a mother to forage—and flies to the isthmus where a nest sits atop a forty-foot telephone pole.

The beau screams back. The coat holds his cell phone, that object the beau has clung to all afternoon, footnoting every statement and selfie-authenticating every other wave.

We scout the poison ivy-plagued isthmus that surrounds the nest. Neighbors appear with rakes and broom sticks too short.

There is talk that the Conservancy has a camera and we'll be arrested if we disturb the osprey. As middle-aged as we and the neighbors are, it is foolish to even contemplate climbing, though the beau, being youthful, takes it under consideration. The bird is still struggling with the jacket, one arm dangling from the nest like the remains of a sacrificial victim.

It's not that funny, he says.

His date is bent double with laughter, her bikini-top under various transparent bits of cloth slipping just enough. Then she straightens and does what no other birdbrain has thought of: telephones his phone.

There! Cast off into the thinly-bushed.

It is another hour before I offer the conciliatory oysters Steve's dredged up and opened.

You raise the flag every day? she asks, lipstick awry, lips licking.

My father had a house across the water, a big one he kept after the divorce, Steve says. Over there. He points into the sheen. It had a flagpole.

The girl says her father left her mother too, sounding very *Oh poor thing.*

The beau says his father never even noticed him.

Steve points his knife at him, but he's watching the girl. My grandfather came once for a month to look after us, he says, and every morning my brother and I brought out the flag. It was in the fifties when people were still into their country. I was eight years old. We learned to fold it, we carried it back inside—always taking turns. That's me, over there—then.

Steve gestures across the water where no one can see anybody, just more osprey poles and masts.

Steve about to fold the flag, 1955

Overhead another osprey screams. It could be the same one. The girl takes the beau's hand, not so much as if it's handy but more that it's free, and says she hopes the media picks up the bird story on her Facebook page.

Verizon would have collected big, he says, still frowning.

She's shaking her head, which shakes her very evident breasts.

I'm thinking how easily seduced Steve is, but I am wrong.

He's still watching the horizon.

*

We attend a Directors Guild of America screening of *Lee*, the masterfully told feature starring Kate Winslet about the photo-journalist Lee Miller's war time experience. At the end of the film, Lee's interviewer, who has been oddly intimate through-out, almost flirtatious, reveals that he's her son by saying that he always thought he was the problem, that he was the one who made her so unhappy. That's disappointing, she replies, pausing to puff on a cigarette. Steve cried during that scene, identifying with Lee's son, especially when he's shown with her memorabilia and iconic photographs, all of which he knew nothing about until after Lee's death. He wants at last to ask her questions, but she is gone. But isn't this the way all children feel after their parents die? Steve doesn't answer me. Instead he speaks with the director Ellen Kuras who immediately understands his belated grief and his misunderstanding of his mother's distance and promises to give him Lee's son's contact information.

He wasn't the problem.

*

In a July 14, 1983 letter, when Joseph Riznik, a colleague from OWI and the Overseas Press Club, begs her to write her mem-oirs, she writes that she'd rather put together a book of her husband's writings, "his very creative letters to the four boys over the years." Given that Dickson has recently died, it seems, with "very creative," she wanted the boys to remember him for his words, and not his actions. And perhaps it reflected that she realized she was not such a good mother. Rather than discount-ing herself, it smacks more of remorse.

What do you know about your mother-in-law? At first, you are totally naive. You were attracted to the son, not the mother—in fact, thrown in competition with her but that is revealed later, when your crème brûlée fails to impress. A few years later, holding a baby, you think: she's been through this herself and now what? or you're doing this childrearing for her too, or this creature looks or acts just like her, please love him. The decades fly and soon you're spooning gruel into her mouth, tucking her into bed, loved despite you having shoved your way into her life, the woman who delivered your husband, who had to give him up.

What do you know about anyone anyway? Why is your sister, with whom you spent fifteen formative years, frowning over her birthday cake? Or even knowing your own mother, grounded, as it were, in the cemetery and not likely to pop up and dress you down again, would if she could, you think, blinking over a nice note she once sent, not an apology, no, not quite, for something that hurt, but nice, nonetheless. To know what's in the mind of a Sudanese or the CIA operative requires even more extrapolation: you plus everything you've read or seen or smelled or slept next to, a wider net of knowing.

The woman my son is now sharing his apartment with has turned down his proposal, saying maybe next year. How could she? Such a sweetheart, my son. She's a Midwesterner, and a content provider, like me. Maybe he is actually looking for someone like his mother but my motto: marry in passion; repent at leisure, isn't hers. Could she be an improvement?

*

Godwin's Law: "As an online discussion continues, the probability of a reference or comparison to Hitler or to Nazis approaches 1," derives from Mike Godwin's moral outrage with people making trivial analogies with the Holocaust.[691] Sure, both Hitler and Trump have messianic stares, theatrical inclinations—even their tantrums are staged—and the uncanny ability to appear populist. Passing similarities? Now Trump's rapid-fire directives have plunged the government into a chaos like Germany's just prior to Hitler's takeover. Couple that chaos with the inevitable high unemployment, institutional impotence (see: judicial system), national division, and those messianic stares that appear to lead the way out—not trivial.

*

The cover of Pat's last article for *Women's Home Companion* falls in line with the postwar propaganda: a mother cradling a child. Published two months after Steve's birth, Pat's contribution, however, is not in the least maternal. "Look Who's in the Movies Now" is a lively look at location scouting in New York City.[692] She relates an anecdote about extras costumed as nuns shocking policemen, then goes into its challenges: the unions, the permissions, the difficult negotiations. After inspecting some sixty cold water flats, the location scout finds the perfect rundown tenement but the tenant refuses to allow filming. "I don't want murders in my house."

Thirty-two years later, I'm amusing my three-year-old in the car while waiting for Steve to finish Polaroiding what he's hoping is a typical family house somewhere in a tree-lined New Jersey town not too far from principal shooting. He's photographed twenty of them so far, from all angles, the results stapled into presentation folders for the director. Are we buying what he's selling? I'm not the perfect possible mate, already mated, with a child, and he's been divorced too. No wonder we choose to renovate a floor-through in the trashed Lower East Side.

Steve doubts that his mother knew about his stint of location scouting—and he knew nothing about his mother's article. She ends it with the location scouts assuring shopkeepers that they'll rename their store for the shoot to keep away "bobbysoxers [who] come not to buy, but to stand where Frank Sinatra once stood." Fifty-five years later, Steve launches HollywoodUSA, a location app that allows you to find exactly where Sinatra stood.

*

Knowing is a familiarity that lasts. A trait becomes expected. She wouldn't say that, that's not her handwriting. That collection of electrons buzzing around the location of the mother-in-law suggests you'd better say Hi if you want her to smile back. Repeatability, that bugaboo of the restless, creates trust, the core of knowing in this wobbly world of situational ethics. I know my mother-in-law would not lie—unless she had to.

I don't know.

*

Our tiny cottage has already stood on the beach well over a hundred years, sheltering generations of oyster shuckers and water lovers like us. The water level has risen, the hurricane season has become ever more fierce, and severe winter tides now lap the underside of the cottage. The climate crisis is not a matter of belief. We decide we must sell the cottage, no matter how wonderful, hoping there's a family of climate-deniers who will enjoy the view and the tilted Murphy bed, with funds to raise the house high enough above the water that the waves from the next big storm will run under it, not into it. For a while.

They will learn the truth soon enough. Truth must be learned.

Acknowledgements

Stephen Medaris Bull, of course, Jay Hartwell who scanned the overwhelming collection of Hartwell papers, Lloyd Lochridge, Jr. for taking my call, and the entire wonderful Lochridge family. My sons, Felix and Frank and their beloveds, Zayn and Rachel.

Historiographer Bertrand Roehner, always generous with his statistics, Lauren Goss, Special Collections Public Services Librarian at the University of Oregon, for access to the Ruth Adams Knight papers; John Frederick, University of Victoria Special Collections for access to the Edith Iglauer papers; Yeshiva University Museum and Janet Kaplan, who commissioned the poem; Olivier Lalancette at the National Film Board of Canada, Franklin D. Roosevelt Library, Women Writing Women's Lives Forum and my beloved BIO writing group of Rachel Greenfield, Humera Afridi, Sarah Dorsey, Kari Miller, Iris Jamahl Dunkle, Mary Chitty, William Ashcraft and especially Wanda Little Fenimore who educated me in the art of footnotes. My therapist, who suggested I remove one word.

A very special thanks to my long-suffering readers Molly Giles, Margaret Laxton, Jenny Hyslop, Gay Walley, Katherine Arnoldi, Mike Sadava, my wonderful publicist Cassie Mannes Murray, and my agent Margaret Sutherland Brown. Thanks to the entire OR crew for their faith in me. I am also extremely grateful for residencies at the MacDowell Colony, the Hermitage, the Rowlands Writers Retreat, the New York Public Library's Allen Room, and the Greater Victoria Public Library James Bay Branch's Quiet Room.

Thanks also to the editors who published fictionalized versions of the material, including "Polio" in *Many Lights in Many Window*, ed. Laurel Blossom, Milkweed Editions, 1997, reprinted in *Trailer Girl and Other Stories*. Counterpoint, 2001, the collection reprinted by Bison Books, 2009; "Capsized Craft" in SOUTHWORD, Issue 15, February 2009 and shortlisted for the Sean O'Faolain Short Story Prize 2008; "The Stroke of Midnight" in *Brooklyn Rail*, November 2007, reprinted in *The Long Swim*, U. of Massachusetts Press, 2024; and "Kosciusko Bridge" in *The Literarian*, Center for Fiction, https://centerforfiction.org/fiction/kosciusko-bridge/ also reprinted in *The Long Swim*, University of Massachusetts Press, 2024; "At the Horizon" a/k/a "Osprey Prey" in *Identity Theory*, February 4, 2020, http://www.identitytheory.com/section/fiction/, and "Crows and Taxis: Writing to the South Sudan" in *Rumpus*, January 14, 2011, https://therumpus.net/2011/01/14/crows-and-taxis-writing-to-the-south-sudan/.

About the Author

A Guggenheim fellow, **Terese Svoboda** is the author of 24 books. She has won the Bobst Prize in fiction, the Iowa Prize for poetry, an NEH grant for translation, the Graywolf Nonfiction Prize, a Jerome Foundation prize for video, the O. Henry award for the short story, and a Pushcart Prize for the essay. She is a three-time winner of the New York Foundation for the Arts fellowship, and has been awarded Headlands, James Merrill, Hawthornden, Hermitage, Yaddo, MacDowell, Rowland, VCCA, Bogliasco, and Bellagio residencies. Her opera WET premiered at LA's Disney Hall.

Endnotes

1   Edward Bliss, Jr., *Now the News: The Story of Broadcast Journalism* (Columbia University Press, 1992), 1–2. "She was the first woman at CBS to work solely in News."

2   Patricia Hartwell, interview by Joe Rossi, August 6, 1990, 153, Tape Nos. 20-15-1-90 and 20-15-1-90, Center for Oral History, University of Hawai'i at Mānoa, https://hdl.handle.net/10125/21086.

3   Chris Brooke, "Women Tell More Fibs than Men... Honestly!," *The Daily Mail*, June 4, 2015, https://www.dailymail.co.uk/news/article-3110136/Women-tell-fibs-men-honestly-Four-five-say-tell-lie-daily-basis.html.

4   Patricia Hartwell, interview by Steve Bull, 2 tapes, May 22, 1995, Steve Bull Private Papers.

5   Patricia Hartwell to family, September 6, 1945, Patricia Hartwell Private Papers.

6   Judith Mackrell, *The Correspondents: Six Women Writers on the Front Lines of World War II* (New York: Doubleday, 2021), 343.

7   Melissa Wiley, "Rare Interviews with Hitler's Inner Circle Reveal What Truly Happened on 'The Day Hitler Died,'" *Smithsonian Magazine*, November 16, 2015, https://www.

smithsonianmag.com/history/rare-interviews-adolph-hitler-inner-circle-smithsonian-channel-180957283/.

8   Jeremy Noakes and Geoffrey Pridham, eds., *Nazism, 1919-1945*, vol. 4, The German Home Front in WWII (Exeter Press, 1998), 624–26.

9   Caroline Sharples, "The Death of Nazism? Investigating Hitler's Remains and Survival Rumors in Post-War Germany," in *Interdisciplinary Perspectives on Mortality and Its Timings: When Is Death?*, ed. Shane McCorristine (London: Palgrave Macmillan, 2017), 93. https://doi.org/10.1057/978-1-137-58328-4.

10 Carolyn Edy, "Trust but Verify: Myths and Misinformation in the History of Women War Correspondents," *American Journalism* 36, no. 2 (April 3, 2019): 242–51, 242, https://doi.org/10.1080/08821127.2019.1602420.

11 Nancy Caldwell Sorel, *The Women Who Wrote the War* (New York: Arcade, 1999), 23.

12 Patricia Hartwell, Interview by Steve Bull.

13 Patricia Hartwell, Invitations: Accepted; 1941 I - L, September 3, 1941, Anna Eleanor Roosevelt Collection, Container 35, Franklin D. Roosevelt Presidential Library and Museum.

14 Mitchell C. Chaney, "A Life of Serving," State Bar of Texas accessed January 29, 2025, https://www.texasbar.com/AM/Template.cfm?Section=articles&Template=/CM/HTMLDisplay.cfm&ContentID=40421.

15 *Independent* (Long Beach, CA), December 15, 1959, Newspaper Clipping, Patricia Hartwell Private Papers.

16 "Isaac Patton Lochridge," ancestry.com, accessed February 19, 2025, https://www.ancestry.com/genealogy/records/results?firstName=isaac&lastName=lochridge.

17   *Austin Statesman,* October 18, 1916, ancestry.com;
     June Downey, interview by Jay Hartwell, Jay Hartwell
     Notebook [1999-2000], Jay Hartwell Private Papers.

18   *N.W. Ayer & Son's American Newspaper Annual and
     Directory* (Philadelphia, PA: N.W. Ayer & Son, 1918),
     927, https://hdl.handle.net/2027/ien.35556000550954;
     Lloyd P. Lochridge, "The Austin Statesman," The
     Portal to Texas History, December 23, 1913, https://
     texashistory.unt.edu/ark:/67531/metapth1448645/.

19   Patricia Hartwell, interview by Joe Rossi, 152.

20   Patricia Hartwell, interview by Joe Rossi, 151.

21   William Kaufman, "Snow White and Grumpy,"
     Columbia Magazine, Fall 2006, https://magazine.
     columbia.edu/article/snow-white-and-grumpy.

22   Patricia Hartwell, interview by Joe Rossi, 152; Patricia
     Lockridge to Bill Birnie, September 17, 1943, Patricia
     Hartwell Private Papers.

23   Patricia Lochridge, "Radio Girl" (1939), Patricia
     Hartwell Private Papers.

24   "Press: Small-Town News," *TIME,* July 26, 1937.

25   Fleur Feighan, "Hartwell Show Opens Sunday,"
     Scottsdale Daily Progress, Newspaper Clipping, n.d.
     [1971], Patricia Hartwell Private Papers.

26   Lloyd Pampell Lochridge to Patricia Lochridge, December
     2, 1938, Patricia Hartwell Private Papers.

27   Patricia Hartwell to Steve Bull, December 25, 1972,
     Patricia Hartwell Private Papers.

28   Jay Hartwell, *Hawai'ian People Today Na Mamo*
     (Honolulu: Islander Group, Inc., 1996).

29   CBS paycheck, 1939, Patricia Hartwell Private Papers.

30   Gerd Horten, *Radio Goes to War: The Cultural Politics
     of Propaganda during WWII* (Berkeley: University of
     California Press, 2002), 30.

31   Patricia Hartwell, interview by Steve Bull, 1995.

32   Patricia Hartwell, interview by Joe Rossi, 152.

33   Eleanor Carroll to Patricia Hartwell, April 17, 1941, Patricia Hartwell Private Papers.

34   Patricia Lochridge, "Radio Girl."

35   Zilfa Estcourt, "Handicaps, Threats Didn't Stop Her Pat Lochridge is a War Correspondent," *San Francisco Chronicle*, August 17, 1943, Newspaper Clipping; Mary Cherry Allen, "She was the First Woman Correspondent in the Pacific," *The Post,* June 2, 1949, Newspaper Clipping; Patricia Lockridge to Bill Birnie, September 17, 1943. Patricia Hartwell Private Papers.

36   United States Department of Justice, Federal Bureau of Investigation, Identification and Personnel for Employment of United States Citizens, Patricia Hartwell, September 8, 1943, 81.

37   Marion Tuttle Marzolf, *Up from the Footnote: A History of Women Journalists* (New York: Hastings House, 1977), 137.

38   Marion Narvis, "Woman War Correspondent Will Cite Gravity of Pacific Conflict," *Honolulu Advertiser,* n.d. [1944], Newspaper Clipping, Patricia Hartwell Private Papers.

39   Patricia Hartwell, interview by Joe Rossi, 153.

40   Patricia Lochridge, "Radio Girl."

41   "Meet the Ladies," *Broadcasting Magazine*, March 1, 1940, https://www.worldradiohistory.com/Archive-BC/BC-1940/1940-03-01-BC.pdf.

42   Patricia Hartwell to "Mother, Peg et al," August 9 [no year], (on Warner Bros. stationery), Patricia Hartwell Private Papers.

43   Patricia Hartwell, interview by Steve Bull.

44   Allan M. Winkler, *The Politics of Propaganda: The Office of War Information, 1942-1945* (New Haven: Yale University Press, 1978), 36.

45   Archibald MacLeish, Speech (March 19, 1942), Official File 4619, box 2, folder OFF, January-March, 1942, Franklin D. Roosevelt Presidential Library and Museum.

46   Edmunds Stevens, "War Correspondent: Thrills, Danger, and Boredom," *Christian Science Monitor*, June 11, 1943, quoted in Carolyn M. Edy, *The Woman War Correspondent, the U.S. Military, and the Press, 1846-1947* (Lanham, Maryland: Lexington Books, 2017), 56.

47   Gene Witzeman, "Journalist Finds Teaching a Challenge," *Arizona Republic,* February 11, 1970, Newspaper Clipping, Patricia Hartwell Private Papers.

48   Ed Sullivan, "Little Old New York," *Daily News*, March 22, 1943, newspapers.com. For the report "Nazi Slave Labor Society" see *OWI Preliminary Inventory. Special Foreign Relations*, RG 208, Jan 1943-Sept 1944, #351.

49   "Our Photo Flashes," *Edwardsville Intelligencer,* October 21, 1943, Newspaper Clipping, Patricia Hartwell Private Papers.

50   "Timeline: FDR Day by Day," Pare Lorentz Center for FDR Presidential Library, https://www.fdrlibrary.org/timeline

51   Philip Hamburger to Mr. Davie, April 14, 1943, box 5, folder 3, Edith Iglauer Papers, University of Victoria Special Collections and University Archive.

52   Patricia Lochridge, "Startling Facts about Black Market Revealed by Shopping Tour of Nation," *Woman's Home Companion,* February, 1944, quoted in *Tipton Daily Tribune*, January 14, 1944, newspapers.com.

53 Patricia Lochridge to Louis Ruppel, March 1, 1944; Marceline Townsley, "Speaking of People," *Sunday American Statesman*, February 6, 1944, Newspaper Clipping. Patricia Hartwell Private Papers.

54 Robert Trout to Patricia Lochridge, March 10, 1944, Patricia Hartwell Private Papers.

55 Sorel, *The Women Who Wrote the War,* 120.

56 Patricia Hartwell to family, August 9 [1944], Patricia Hartwell Private Papers.

57 Patricia Hartwell, interview by Joe Rossi, 155. Also "Mother of Two: She was the First Woman Correspondent in Pacific," *Queens Post*, 1949, Newspaper Clipping, Patricia Hartwell Private Papers.

58 Zilfa Estcourt, "Handicaps, Threats Didn't Stop Her Pat Lochridge Is a War Correspondent."

59 Edy, *The Woman War Correspondent*, 86.

60 "Dickey Chapelle, Photojournalist - Image Essay," Wisconsin Historical Society, accessed January 29, 2025, https://wisconsinhistory.org/Records/Article/CS3953.

61 Carolyn M. Edy, *The Woman War Correspondent,* 143–49.

62 Wilda M. Smith and Eleanor A. Bogart, *The Wars of Peggy Hull: The Life and Times of a War Correspondent* (El Paso, TX: Texas Western Press, 1991), 245.

63 Anne Sebba, *Battling for News: The Rise of the Woman Reporter* (London: Sceptre, Hodder and Stoughton, 1994), 152–54.

64 Martha Gellhorn, "Only the Shells Whine," *Collier's*, July 17, 1937, General Research Division, New York Public Library Digital Collections, https://digitalcollections.nypl.org/items/c2724c7c-9e09-596e-e040-e00a180661ef.

65   Patrick Garrett, *Of Fortunes and War: Clare Hollingworth, First of the Female War Correspondents* (London: Two Roads Books, 2017), 16.

66   Peggy Hull, column in Cleveland Plain Dealer, August 20, 1944, quoted in Sorel, *The Women Who Wrote the War*, 294.

67   "The Press: Cartwheel Girl," *TIME*, June 12, 1939, https://time.com/archive/6761718/the-press-cartwheel-girl/.

68   Leila J. Rupp, *Mobilizing Women for War: German and American Propaganda, 1939-1945*, Princeton Legacy Library (Princeton, NJ: Princeton University Press, 1978), 70.

69   Pat Lochridge, "Flight for Life," *Woman's Home Companion*, January 1945, 6.

70   Patricia Hartwell, interview by Steve Bull.

71   Lochridge, "Flight for Life."

72   Lochridge, "Flight for Life."

73   Mary Cherry Allen, "She Was the First Woman Correspondent in the Pacific," *The Post*, June 2, 1949, Newspaper Clipping, Patricia Hartwell Private Papers.

74   Patricia Hartwell, interview by Steve Bull.

75   Of Slavish descent, the Wends were at the time subject to Hitler's extermination policies. Irene Van Winkle, "Comparettes, Nimitzes Powerfully Shaped Hill Country History," *West Kerr Current*, January 15, 2009, https://wkcurrent.com/comparettes-nimitzes-powerfully-shaped-hill-country-history-p1718-71.htm.

76   Patricia Hartwell to Louis Ruppel, March 1, 1944, Patricia Hartwell Private Papers.

77   Patricia Hartwell, interview by Steve Bull.

78   Patricia Hartwell to Peg Grubb, February 26, 1945, Patricia Hartwell Private Papers.

79   "Mrs. Bull Married to D.J. Hartwell: Former Patricia
      Lochridge, Who Was War Correspondent Becomes
      Author's Bride," *New York Times*, August 7, 1953,
      ProQuest Historical Newspapers.

80   "Finland to receive a railway wagonload of food aid
      from Denmark," and "Uruguay to Aid Finland," The
      Finnish Defence Forces 1999, accessed January 29, 2025,
      archived from the original https://puolustusvoimat.fi/en/
      perustietoa/talvisota_eng/timer-30.html on June 14, 2007.

81   John Lloyd and John Mitchinson, *The Second Book of
      General Ignorance* (London: Faber and Faber, 2011), 76.

82   Summary of Antti Matikkala, *Kunnian ruletti—
      korkeimmat ulkomaalaisille 1941-1944 annetut
      suomalaiset kunniamerkit* (The Roulette of
      Honour—the Highest Finnish Orders to Foreigners
      1941–1944), Academia.edu, accessed January 29,
      2025. https://www.academia.edu/32832483/Kunnian_
      ruletti_korkeimmat_ulkomaalaisille_1941_1944_
      annetut_suomalaiset_kunniamerkit_The_Roulette_
      of_Honour_the_Highest_Finnish_Orders_to_
      Foreigners_1941_1944_?auto=download.

83   Andrew Breiner, "Thérèse Bonney: Curator, Photographer,
      Syndicator, Spy," Library of Congress Blog, September
      17, 2021, https://blogs.loc.gov/kluge/2021/09/thrse-
      bonney-curator-photographer-syndicator-spy/. Later, in
      what she called her "truth raids," Bonney photographed
      children in Europe that would influence the founding of
      UNICEF.

84   "Order of the White Rose," Wikipedia, accessed January
      25, 2025, https://en.wikipedia.org/wiki/Order_of_the_
      White_Rose_of_Finland.

85 T. J. Park, Review of Kristopher C. Erskine, "American Public Diplomacy with Chinese Characteristics: The Genesis of the China Lobby in the United States, and how Missionaries Shifted American Foreign Policy between 1938 and 1941," H-Diplo, April 4, 2019, https://networks.h-net.org/node/28443/discussions/3956166/h-diplo-article-review-846-park-erskine-%E2%80%9Camerican-public.

86 Robert Farley, "When a China Propaganda Campaign Infiltrated the United States," *The Diplomat*, June 25, 2019, https://thediplomat.com/2019/06/when-a-china-propaganda-campaign-infiltrated-the-united-states/.

87 Benjamin Denison, "Stay Out of the Regime Change Business," War on the Rocks, June 16, 2020, https://warontherocks.com/2020/06/stay-out-of-the-regime-change-business/.

88 "How Trump's Presidency Has Affected Diplomacy," *Weekend Edition Sunday* (NPR, October 25, 2020), https://www.npr.org/2020/10/25/927564364/how-trumps-presidency-has-affected-diplomacy.

89 Patricia Lochridge to Dickson Hartwell, May 26, 1950, Patricia Hartwell Private Papers.

90 Martha Gellhorn, Virginia Cowles, and Sandra Whipple Spanier, *Love Goes to Press: A Comedy in Three Acts* (Lincoln: University of Nebraska Press, 1995), 25.

91 Dickson Hartwell and Andy Rooney, Eds., *Off the Record, the Best Stories of Foreign Correspondents* (Garden City, NY: Doubleday, 1952), 203.

92 William V. Pratt, "What Makes Iwo Jima Worth the Price," *Newsweek*, April 2, 1945, 36.

93 Sorel, *The Women Who Wrote the War*, 306. For decades the famous photo was suspected of being a staged PR

stunt, but recovered film shows the first time the soldiers were interrupted by a Japanese grenade.when they tried putting the flag up. "Iwo Jima Feb. 23, 1945 First Flag Raising: An Eyewitness Account by Radioman Raymond Jacobs," Headquarters Marine Corps, accessed February 14, 2025, https://www.hqmc.marines.mil/Portals/61/ Enclosure%209%20(PFC%20Jacobs%20Statement). pdf?ver=2016-08-24-094525-887.

94 Joseph Alexander, "The Battle of Iwo Jima: A 36-Day Bloody Slog on a Sulfuric Island," *Military Times*, February 17, 2018, https://www.militarytimes.com/ news/2018/02/17/the-battle-of-iwo-jima-a-36-day-bloody-slog-on-a-sulfuric-island/.

95 Patricia Lochridge, "Solace at Iwo," *Woman's Home Companion*, May 1945.

96 Alexander, "The Battle of Iwo Jima."

97 John Walker, "The Battle of Iwo Jima: Red Sun, Black Sand," Warfare History Network, January 2013, https:// warfarehistorynetwork.com/article/the-battle-of-iwo-jima-red-sun-black-sand/.

98 Alexander, "The Battle of Iwo Jima."

99 Julia Edwards, *Women of the World: The Great Foreign Correspondents* (Boston MA: Houghton Mifflin, 1988), 152; Doris Weatherford, *American Women during World War II: An Encyclopedia* (New York, NY: Routledge, 2010), 107, https://doi.org/10.4324/9780203870662.

100 "She's More of a Woman than Ever," *Cincinnati-Enquirer*, April 27, 1945, newspapers.com.

101 Patricia Hartwell, Untitled manuscript, quoted in Mary Jane Bragg, "27th Council of Alums, Students Discuss College Women's Role," *Wellesley College News*, February 23, 1957, Patricia Hartwell Private Papers.

102 Patricia Hartwell, interview by Steve Bull.

103 Lochridge, "*Solace* at Iwo," 116.

104 Robin Richardson, Inter-office memo, The Collier-Cromwell Publishing Company, April 30, 1945, Patricia Hartwell Private Papers.

105 Edwards, *Women of the World*, 179.

106 Richardson, Inter-office memo.

107 "Residents of the Town of Dachau Were Forced to View the Atrocities in the Dachau Camp after It Was Liberated," Scrapbookpages Blog (blog), January 14, 2013, https://furtherglory.wordpress.com/tag/patricia-lochridge/.

108 Patricia Lochridge, "Are Germans Human?," *Woman's Home Companion*, July, 1945, 5.

109 Frank Luther Mott, *A History of American Magazines* (Harvard University Press, 1957), 763–772.

110 Patricia Lochridge, "V.D. Menace and Challenge," *Woman's Home Companion*, March, 1944, 129–31. The magazine received so many letters after her VD article that "the secretary rushes out to the john to wash her hands – just won't take my word for it you don't catch either s. or g. that way," Patricia Hartwell to Louis Ruppel, March 1, 1944, Patricia Hartwell Private Papers.

111 "Abortion is an Ugly Word," *Woman's Home Companion*, March, 1947, 4.

112 Patricia Lochridge to family, April 29, 1945, Patricia Hartwell Private Papers.

113 Patricia Lockridge to Bill Birnie, May 20, 1945, Patricia Hartwell Private Papers.

114 Estcourt, "Handicaps"; Allen, "She Was the First Woman Correspondent in the Pacific."

115 Mackrell, *The Correspondents*, 296.

116 Rachel Cooke, "Women at war: Lee Miller exhibition includes unseen images of conflict," *The Guardian,* September 19, 2015, https://www.theguardian.com/artanddesign/2015/sep/19/lee-miller-a-womans-war-exhibition-imperial-war-museum-second-world-war-dachau-hitler.

117 Lochridge, "Are Germans Human?"

118 Glen Jeansonne, *A Time of Paradox: America from Awakening to Hiroshima, 1890–1945* (Lanham, MD: Rowman & Littlefield, 2007), 235.

119 Harold Marcuse, *Legacies of Dachau: The Uses and Abuses of a Concentration Camp, 1933-2001* (Cambridge: Cambridge University Press, 2008), 421 fn45.

120 Lee Miller in *Lee Miller's War,* ed. by Antony Penrose (London: Thames & Hudson, 2005), 163.

121 "Dachau - Historical Film Footage," *Holocaust Encyclopedia,* United States Holocaust Memorial Museum, accessed January 29, 2025, https://encyclopedia.ushmm.org/content/en/gallery/dachau-films.

122 Lochridge, "Are Germans Human?"

123 Margaret Bourke-White, *Portrait of Myself* (New York: Simon & Schuster, 1963), 258.

124 Carolyn Burke, *Lee Miller: On Both Sides of the Camera* (London: Bloomsbury, 2006), 249.

125 Marcuse, *Legacies of Dachau,* 423 fn54.

126 Sorel, *The Women Who Wrote the War,* 359. See also the film *Zone of Interest* (2023) dir. Jonathan Glazer about the Auschwitz commandant and his family.

127 Lochridge to Birnie.

128 Caroline Moorehead, *Martha Gellhorn: A Twentieth Century Life* (New York: Vintage Books, 2004), 283.

129 Lochridge, "Are Germans Human?"

130 "Independence," United States Holocaust Museum, accessed February 4, 2025, https://www.ushmm.org/genocide-prevention/countries/south-sudan/case-study.

131 Center for Preventive Action, "Civil War in Sudan," Global Conflict Tracker, updated March 26, 2025, https://www.cfr.org/global-conflict-tracker/conflict/power-struggle-sudan.

132 Eliott Brachet, "War in Sudan: Death strikes at every corner in devastated Khartoum," *Le Monde*, November 11, 2024, https://www.lemonde.fr/en/le-monde-africa/article/2024/11/11/war-in-sudan-death-strikes-at-every-corner-in-devastated-khartoum_6732461_124.html#.

133 Areesha Lodhi, "After a year of war in Sudan, what is the situation now?," *Al Jazeera*, April 11, 2024, https://www.aljazeera.com/news/2024/4/11/why-did-war-break-out-in-sudan-a-year-ago-where-does-it-currently-stand#.

134 Michelle Nichols and Maggie Michael, "Ethnic killings in one Sudan city left up to 15,000 dead, UN report says," *Reuters*, January 20, 2024, https://www.reuters.com/world/africa/ethnic-killings-one-sudan-city-left-up-15000-dead-un-report-2024-01-19/.

135 "Victim Tells of Torture in Sudan's Ghost Houses," *Dabanga*, March 7, 2011, https://www.dabangasudan.org/en/all-news/article/victim-tells-of-torture-in-sudan-s-ghost-houses.

136 Marcuse, *Legacies of Dachau*, 55.

137 Marcuse, 423 fn56.

138 Marcuse, 423 fn57–58.

139 Mackrell, *The Correspondents*, 336.

140 Michele Midori Fillion, dir. *No Job for a Woman: The Women Who. Fought to Report WWII*. Women Make Movies, 2011.

141 Moorhead, *Martha Gellhorn*, 246.

142 Nancy Sorel to Patricia Hartwell, April 8, 1995, Patricia Hartwell Private Papers.

143 Marilyn Shulman, "A Perspective on Journalist's Experience of Post-Traumatic Stress Disorder: An Exploratory Study" (Master of Arts, University of Johannesburg, 2012), 66.

144 Patricia Hartwell, interview by Steve Bull.

145 "The Nazi Conspiracy and the German People," quoted in "World War II Liberation Photography," United States Holocaust Memory Museum, accessed January 29, 2025, https://www.ushmm.org/collections/the-museums-collections/about/photo-archives/world-war-ii-liberation-photography.

146 Bonny Ibhawoh, "Do truth and reconciliation commissions heal divided nations?," The Conversation, January 23, 2019, https://theconversation.com/do-truth-and-reconciliation-commissions-heal-divided-nations-109925.

147 Matt Soniak, "Whatever Happened to Hitler's Body?," Mental Floss, June 23, 2011, https://www.mentalfloss.com/article/28058/whatever-happened-hitlers-body].

148 Michael Ruane, "Hitler shot himself 75 years ago, ending an era of war, genocide and destruction," *Washington Post,* April 30, 2020, https://www.washingtonpost.com/history/2020/04/30/hitler-suicide-bunker-eva-braun/.

149 David R. Blumenthal, *The Banality of Good and Evil: Moral Lessons from the Shoah and Jewish Tradition* (Washington, DC: Georgetown University Press, 1999), 180.

150 Theresa Ast, "German Civilian Knowledge of the Concentration Camps," Hub Pages, December 13, 2013, https://hubpages.com/education/Waht-Did-Most-

Germans-Know-About-the-Nazi-Concentration-Camp-System-Part-II.

151 Lochridge, "Are Germans Human?"

152 Despina Stratigakos, "Where Did Adolf Hitler Live? The Homes of the Führer and How They Were Used as Nazi Propaganda," HistoryExtra, August 2, 2018, https://www.historyextra.com/period/second-world-war/where-did-adolf-hitler-live-berlin-munich-home-germany-nazi-propaganda/.

153 Elizabeth May Craig, "Hitler's Mountain," *Press Herald*, August, 1945, Newspapers.com.

154 Mackrell, *The Correspondents*, 319.

155 Patricia Lochridge to family, May 20, 1945, Patricia Hartwell Private Papers.

156 Patricia Lochridge to family, June 13, 1945, Patricia Hartwell Private Papers.

157 Patricia Lochridge to family, May 20, 1945, Patricia Hartwell Private Papers.

158 Dickson Hartwell and Andy Rooney, Eds., *Off the Record*, 234.

159 Patrick Garret, *Of Fortunes and War: Clare Hollingworth, First of the Female War Correspondents* (London: Two Roads Books, 2017), 149, 199.

160 Mackrell, *The Correspondents*, 320.

161 Mackrell, 325.

162 Leonard Miall, "Obituary: Helen Kirkpatrick Milbank," *The Independent,* January 7, 1998, https://www.the-independent.com/news/obituaries/obituary-helen-kirkpatrick-milbank-1137424.html.

163 Virginia Leimert, "Woman Correspondent Shows Souvenirs of Her Exploits," *Chicago Daily News*, 1946; Patricia Lochridge, "I'll Never Forget," *Woman's Home*

Companion, September, 1945; Patricia Hartwell to family, June 13, 1945. Patricia Hartwell Private Papers.

164 Mackrell, *The Correspondents*, 319.

165 Patricia Hartwell, interview by Steve Bull.

166 Henry Wager Halleck, *Halleck's International Law, or, Rules Regulating the Intercourse of States in Peace and War* (C. K. Paul & Company, 1861), 64.

167 "Background to Protection of Cultural Property," US Committee of the Blue Shield, 2018, https://uscbs.org/1863-lieber-code.html#:~:text=.

168 Daile Kaplan, email message to author, July 17, 2020.

169 Terry Frieden, "TV employee charged with smuggling Iraqi art," *CNN.com/Law Center*, April 24, 2003, http://edition.cnn.com/2003/LAW/04/23/sprj.nilaw.antiquities/index.html.

170 Margaret Bourke-White, *Portrait of Myself* (New York: Simon & Schuster, 1963), 163.

171 Davis Malakoff, "American Soldiers Saved Great Art. They Also Stole Some," *Slate*, February 7, 2014, https://slate.com/culture/2014/02/monuments-men-movie-tells-story-of-german-looting-american-soldiers-looted-too.html.

172 Caroline Sharples, "The Death of Nazism? Investigating Hitler's Remains and Survival Rumours in Post-War Germany," in *Interdisciplinary Perspectives on Mortality and its Timings*, ed. Shane McCorristine (London: Palgrave MacMillan, 2020), https://doi.org/10.1057/978-1-137-58328-4_6.

173 Anthony Beevor, *Berlin: The Downfall 1945* (New York: Viking-Penguin Books, 2003), 399.

174 Merrill Fabey, "Here's How the First Fact-Checkers Were Able to Do Their Jobs Before the Internet,"

TIME, August 24, 2027, https://time.com/4858683/fact-checking-history/.

175 Fabey, "Here's How."

176 Shane Croucher, "Why Has Mark Zuckerberg Copied Elon Musk," *Newsweek*, January 9, 2025, https://www.newsweek.com/why-has-mark-zuckerberg-copied-elon-musk-2011447.

177 Nancy Bernard, "Not If I Can Help It: Relentless Antifascist Martha Gellhorn," Medium, October 25, 2018, https://medium.com/@nancy.bernhard/not-if-i-can-help-it-relentless-antifascist-martha-gellhorn-9443c2524de2.

178 Lawrence K. Altman, "The Feud," *New York Times*, November 27, 2007.

179 David Lesjak, "World War II: Interview with Lester Leggett About the Mission to Capture Hermann Göring," Historynet, January/February 2006, https://www.historynet.com/world-war-ii-interview-with-lester-leggett-about-the-mission-to-capture-hermann-goring.htm.

180 Franz Walchhofer and Gottfried Steinbrecher, *The Capture of Hermann Göring in Altenmarkt,* quoted in Christoph Awender, Axis History Forum, May 29, 2002, https://forum.axishistory.com/viewtopic.php?f=5&t=3334&sid=e9fc9a67eaf0039b1df1da81ede9557b: "Hermann Göring and his Adjutant left the car and went to the west while two US military vehicles closed from the east in the front a Jeep with a machinegun, behind a limousine."

181 Patricia Hartwell, interview by Steve Bull.

182 Heinrich Fraenkel and Roger Manvell, *Goering: The Rise and Fall of the Notorious Nazi Leader* (New York: Skyhorse, 2011), 325 fn26.

183 David Lesjak, Historynet.: "General Stack said, 'Take as many pictures as you can, because there's not going to be any newspaper people here . . . That's why years later a lot of controversy came up over the picture of Göring standing in front of the Texas flag. It was said it was taken at Fischhorn. I maintain it was not [the Texas flag picture], because we would have known if any press photographers came up there on that first night."

184 Harryk, "Göring Apprehension/Arrest by 36th Texas Div. May 45," November 26, 2006, 3:45 pm, comment on Axis History Forum, https://forum.axishistory.com/viewtopic.php?t=56461.

185 Virginia Leimert, "Woman Correspondent Shows Souvenirs of Her Exploits," *Chicago Daily News*, 1946, Patricia Hartwell Private Papers.

186 Patricia Lochridge to family [1945], Patricia Hartwell Private Papers.

187 Leonard Rapport, *Rendezvous with Destiny: A History of the 101st Airborne* (Lucknow Books, 2015), 740.

188 Patricia Lochridge to Bill Birnie, May 20, 1945, Patricia Hartwell Private Papers.

189 Patricia Hartwell, interview with Steve Bull.

190 Louis Ruppel to Patricia Lochridge, April 3, 1944, Patricia Hartwell Private Papers.

191 Patricia Lochridge, "Our Shocking Accident Wards," *Collier's, March* 12 and 19, 1949, accessed January 29, 2025, https://www.dougcomicworld.com/inventory/INVENTORY-Collier'sSite.html.

192 "Louis Ruppel." Prabook. https://prabook.com/web/louis.ruppel/1079289#google_vignette and several entries in "Franklin D. Roosevelt "Day by Day Project,"

http://www.fdrlibrary.marist.edu/daybyday/daylog/june-10th-1934/.

193   Patricia Lochridge to family [1945], Patricia Hartwell Private Papers.

194   Melaney Moisan, *Tracking the 101st Cavalry* (Brooklyn, NY: Wheatfield Press, 2011), 306.

195   Moisan, *Tracking*, 307.

196   Moisan, *Tracking*, 313.

197   Rapport, *Rendezvous with Destiny*, 741.

198   Kenneth D. Alford, *Hermann Göring and the Nazi Art Collection: The Looting of Europe's Art* (Jefferson, NC: McFarland, 2012), 137.

199   Patricia Lochridge to her mother, 1945, Patricia Hartwell Private Papers.

200   "High-ranking Nazi Hermann Göring is captured by the U.S. Seventh Army," History.com, November 16, 2009, https://www.history.com/this-day-in-history/herman-goering-is-captured-by-the-u-s-seventh-army.

201   "Hermann Göring Press Conference, Augsburg, Germany, 5/14/1945," posted January 30, 2015, by WWII Public Domain, YouTube, https://www.youtube.com/watch?v=jNZs5IXQ0Tc.

202   Brian B., "Tony Scott to Direct Emma's War," Movieweb., June 12, 2003, https://movieweb.com/tony-scott-to-direct-emmas-war/#:~:text=Ridley%20and%20Tony%20Scott's%20studio%2Dbased%20Scott%20Free,Nicole%20Kidman%20is%20on%20board%20to%20topline.

203   Dickson Hartwell and Andy Rooney, Eds., *Off the Record*, 162.

204   Edwards, *Women of the World*, 131.

205 John Cassidy, "Donald Trump's Big Lies at the Commander-in-Chief Forum," *New Yorker*, September 8, 2016, https://www.newyorker.com/news/john-cassidy/donald-trumps-big-lies-at-the-commander-in-chief-forum.

206 "Clifford Geertz: Work and Legacy," Institute for Advanced Study, accessed February 14, 2025, https://www.ias.edu/clifford-geertz-work-and-legacy.

207 "Joint Report with Allied Leaders on the Potsdam Conference," Harry S. Truman Library & Museum, August 2, 1945, https://history.state.gov/historicaldocuments/frus1945Berlinv02/d1380.

208 Patricia Lochridge, "I Governed Berchtesgaden," *Woman's Home Companion*, August 1945, 4.

209 Patricia Hartwell, interview by Steve Bull.

210 Lochridge, "I Governed Berchtesgaden," 4.

211 Mackrell, *The Correspondents,* 311.

212 Antony Beevor, "An Ugly Carnival," *Guardian,* June 4, 2009, https://www.theguardian.com/lifeandstyle/2009/jun/05/women-victims-d-day-landings-second-world-war.

213 Rapport, *Rendezvous with Destiny,* 751.

214 Rapport, *Rendezvous with Destiny,* 279; Lochridge, 'I Governed Berchtesgaden," 4.

215 "Only Jew Remaining in Berchtesgaden Placed on American Military Government Staff," *Jewish Telegraph Agency*, July 23,1945, https://www.jta.org/1945/07/23/archive/only-jew-remaining-in-berchtesgaden-placed-on-american-military-government-staff.

216 Philip Hamburger, "Beauty and the Beast," *New Yorker,* May 1, 1995, 70, https://www.newyorker.com/magazine/1995/05/01/beauty-and-the-beast.

217 Having accomplished so much, it does seem that she worked more than a single day. She asserts that she governed for the full week in at least two sources: Stewart Fern, Notes for Wellesley Tribute, 1999, personal collection, 2, and Patricia Hartwell, interview by Steve Bull.

218 Lochridge, "I Governed Berchtesgaden."

219 Sarah Wildman, "The Revelations of a Nazi Art Catalogue," *New Yorker,* February 12, 2016, https://www.newyorker.com/books/page-turner/the-revelations-of-a-nazi-art-catalogue.

220 Lynn H. Nicholas, *Rape of Europa: The Fate of Europe's Treasures in the Third Reich and the Second World War* (New York: Vintage, 1995), 328; "How the Monuments Men Discovered & Returned the World's Treasures," *Craters and Freighters*, August 14, 2014, https://www.cratersandfreighters.com/2014/08/how-the-monuments-men-returned-their-treasures/#:~:text=.

221 Jim Ring, *Storming the Eagle's Nest: Hitler's War in the Alps* (London: Faber & Faber, 2013), 295.

222 Louise Fox and Cindy Dowling, *Daughter of the Reich: The Incredible Life of Louise Fox* (United Kingdom: Exisle Publishing, 2015), 139; Henrick Eberle and Matthias Uhl (eds.), *The Hitler Book: The Secret Dossier Prepared for Stalin*, trans. Giles MacDonogh (London: John Murray, 2005; first published in German 2005), 12.

223 David Irving, *Göring,* (United Kingdom: Parforce, pdf., 1989),748, https://archive.org/details/IrvingDavidGoeringABiographyEN2002846S.

224 Kenneth D. Alford, *Hermann Göring and the Nazi Art Collection* (Jefferson, NC: McFarland, 2012),140.

225   Russ Loving, *Fat Boy and the Champagne Salesman: Göring, Ribbentrop, and the Nazi Invasion of Poland* (Bloomington, IN: Indiana University Press, 2022); Hartwell, interview by Steve Bull.

226   Patricia Lochridge to Louis Ruppel, June 26, 1945, Patricia Hartwell Private Papers.

227   Dietrich Maerz, "Dietrich Maerz on Goring's Grand Crosses," Fake Nazi VIP Memorabilia, December 5, 2020, https://wcstumpmilitaria.blogspot.com/2020/12/dietrich-maerz-on-gorings-grand-crosses_5.html.

228   W.D. Stump, "The Göring Surrender Medals," Great War Forum, 2002, https://www.greatwarforum.org/topic/84043-blue-max/.

229   Noel Kearney, "Goering's-Medals," Flkr, August 9, 2013, https://www.flickr.com/photos/ei-njk/9468740085.

230   Alford, *Hermann Göring and the Nazi Art Collection*, 135.

231   Richard Brooks, "National gallery admits painting may be looted," *The Sunday Times,* November 26, 2006, reposted on Elginism, November 27, 2006, https://www.elginism.com/similar-cases/national-gallery-admits-painting-may-be-looted/20061127/596/.

232   Kylie Holloway, "The Man Who Sold an Art Forgery to the Nazis...and Almost Got Away With It," Museum Hack, November 19, 2019, https://museumhack.com/anniversary-forgery-meegeren/.

233   Erroll Morris, "Bamboozling Ourselves (Part 4)," *New York Times,* June 1, 2009, https://archive.nytimes.com/opinionator.blogs.nytimes.com/2009/06/01/bamboozling-ourselves-part-4/.

234   Alford, *Hermann Göring and the Nazi Art Collection,*141.

235   Leimert, "Woman Correspondent Shows Souvenirs of Her Exploits."

236 Patricia Lochridge, "I'll Never Forget."

237 William Hastings Burke, "Albert Göring, Hermann's anti-Nazi brother," *Guardian,* February 20, 2010, https://www.theguardian.com/lifeandstyle/2010/feb/20/albert-goering-hermann-goering-brothers.

238 Alford, *Nazi Plunder,* 53.

239 Alford, *Hermann Goring and the Nazi Art Collection,* 140.

240 Thomas Mashberg, "Returning the Spoils of World War II, Taken by Americans." *New York Times,* May 6, 2015, Section C, 1, https://www.nytimes.com/2015/05/06/arts/design/returning-the-spoils-of-world-war-ii-taken-by-our-side.html.

241 Adam Markovitz, "Clooney Talks 'The Monuments Men,'" *Entertainment,* August 12, 2013, https://ew.com/article/2013/08/12/george-clooney-monuments-men-2/.

242 Kevin Lang, "The Monuments Men History vs. Hollywood," History Hollywood, February 7, 2014, https://www.historyvshollywood.com/reelfaces/monuments-men.php.

243 Matt Goldberg, "George Clooney Struggling with THE MONUMENTS MEN Tone Could Be another Reason for Delay," Collider, October 23, 2013, https://collider.com/george-clooney-monuments-men-delay-tone/.

244 Fortson Beth, "The Lost Paintings – The Schloss Art Collection," The Unwritten Road, National Archives, November 17, 2015, https://unwritten-record.blogs.archives.gov/2015/11/17/the-lost-paintings-the-schloss-art-collection/.

245 Hector Feliciano and Alain Vernay, *The Lost Museum: The Nazi Conspiracy to Steal the World's Greatest Works of Art* (New York: Basic Books, 1997) 253.

246 Margaret Bourke-White, *Portrait of Myself* (New York: Simon & Schuster, 1963), 164.

247 Kenneth D. Alford, *Nazi Plunder Great Treasure Stories of World War II* (Boston: Da Capo Press, 2000), 55.

248 Martin Bailey, "Growing evidence that Göring seized National Gallery's Cranach from its pre-war owner," *The Art Newspaper,* December 31, 2006, https://www.theartnewspaper.com/2007/01/01/growing-evidence-that-goring-seized-national-gallerys-cranach-from-its-pre-war-owner.

249 Catrin Lorch and Joerg Hantzschel, "Munich's Looted Art Bazaar," Lootedart.com, June 25, 2016, https://www.lootedart.com/RWFWSS249591.

250 Daniela Späth, "Unsolved Nazi Mystery," *Deutsche Welle,* March 20, 2014, https://www.dw.com/en/conspiracies-swirl-in-1939-nazi-art-burning/a-17510022.

251 "Harry Vernon Anderson (1902-1983)," Monuments Men and Women Foundation, accessed February 7, 2025, https://www.monumentsmenfoundation.org/anderson-maj-harry-v.

252 Jay Hartwell, email to author, September 14, 2020.

253 Dickson Hartwell and Andy Rooney, Eds., *Off the Record*, 64.

254 Phillip Knightley, *The First Casualty. The War Correspondent as Hero and Myth-Maker from the Crimea to Iraq* (Baltimore MD: Johns Hopkins University Press, 2004), 102.

255 "Censorship in WWII," *Censorship in the Humanities,* September 21, 2010, https://censorshipissues.wordpress.com/2010/09/21/censorship-during-ww2/.

256 Michael Sweeney, *Secrets of Victory: The Office of Censorship and the American Press and Radio in World*

War II (Chapel Hill: University of North Carolina Press, 2001), 25.

257 John Steinbeck, *Once There Was A War* (New York: Penguin Classics, 2007), xiii.

258 Steinbeck, *Once There Was A War*, xvii.

259 Carol Schultz Vento, "Censorship and WWII," Defense Media Network, July 13, 2014, https://www. defensemedianetwork.com/stories/censorship-and-world-war-ii/.

260 Patricia Lochridge, "I saw the wounded come home," *Woman's Home Companion*, May 1944, 22.

261 Lochridge, "I saw the wounded come home," 48.

262 Bertrand M. Roehner, "Relations Between Allied Forces and the Populations of Germany and Austria," Institute for Theoretical and High Energy Physics, University of Paris, UPMC Working Report, Version of April 14, 2009, 40, https://www.lpthe.jussieu.fr/~roehner/ocg.pdf.

263 Roehner, "Relations Between Allied Forces," 41.

264 Patricia Lochridge to family, June 3, 1945, 2, Patricia Hartwell Private Papers.

265 Patricia Lochridge to Mother, Dad and Lynn, April 18, 1945, Patricia Hartwell Private Papers.

266 "Frances Potter Lochridge," Dignity, accessed February 7, 2025, https://www.dignitymemorial.com/obituaries/austin-tx/frances-lochridge-8211289.

267 "Press Conference, 4 PM, July 14, 1942," R. Ernest Dupuy Papers, 1943-1945, Wisconsin State Historical Society, Madison, Wisconsin as cited in Edy, *The Woman War Correspondent*, 58, 59.

268 Martha Gellhorn and Virginia Cowles, *Love Goes to Press: A Comedy in Three Acts* (Lincoln NE: University of Nebraska Press, 1995), 76.

269   Betty Houchin Winfield, *FDR and the News Media* (New York: Columbia University Press, 1992), 172.

270   "Remembering Pearl Harbor: Censorship," *Hawaii Tribune Herald*, December 7, 2016, newspapers.com.

271   Cris Gearhart, "Censoring the Weather During World War II," National Weather Service Heritage, accessed February 7, 2025, https://vlab.noaa.gov/web/nws-heritage/-/censoring-the-weather.

272   Hart Crane to Charles Harris, December 2, 1923, Box 1, Series 1, 1923, Hart Crane and family papers, Special Collections and Archives. Kent State University, https://www.library.kent.edu/special-collections-and-archives/hart-crane-and-family-papers.

273   Franklin Ashley, "James Dickey, The Art of Poetry No. 20," *Paris Review*, Issue 65, Spring 1976, https://www.theparisreview.org/interviews/3741/the-art-of-poetry-no-20-james-dickey#.

274   Henry Hart, *James Dickey: The World as a Lie* (New York: Picador, 2001), 243.

275   Maria Hummel, "James Dickey: The Sheep Child," Poetry Foundation, Aug 27, 2007, https://www.poetryfoundation.org/articles/68914/james-dickey-the-sheep-child.

276   Edward Byrne, "James Dickey: "The Firebombing," One Poet's Notes, September 26, 2007, http://edwardbyrne.blogspot.com/2007/09/james-dickey-firebombing.html.

277   Paul Hendrickson, "On James Dickey and the Truths That Matter," Literary Hub, December 7, 2020, https://lithub.com/on-james-dickey-and-the-truths-that-matter/.

278   Dickson Hartwell to Patricia Lochridge, October 9, 1945, Patricia Hartwell Private Papers.

279 Patricia Lochridge to family, June 2, 1945, Patricia Hartwell Private Papers.

280 "Return to Austin," *Austin American Statesman,* December 30, 1939, 22, Newspaper Clipping, Patricia Hartwell Private Papers.

281 Zilfa Estcourt, "Handicaps." See also Mary Cherry Allen, "She Was the First Woman Correspondent in the Pacific."

282 Patricia Lochridge to her mother, [September?] 1945, Patricia Hartwell Private Papers.

283 "Display Ad 81," *New York Times*. November 22, 1946, 19, newspapers.com.

284 Anton Joachimsthaler, *The Last Days of Hitler: The Legends, the Evidence, the Truth,* Trans. Helmut Bögler (London: Brockhampton Press, 1999), [1995],169.

285 Adam Lusher, "Adolf Hitler really is dead: scientific study debunks conspiracy theories that he escaped to South America," *Independent*, May 21, 2018, https://www.independent.co.uk/news/world/europe/adolf-hitler-debunked-escaped-south-america-skull-fragment-woman-teeth-jawbone-scientific-study-journal-nazis-russians-european-journal-of-internal-medicine-a8360356.html.

286 Henry Bull to parents, August 23, 1945, Patricia Hartwell Private Papers.

287 Scott M. Cutlip, *The Unseen Power: Public Relations: A History* (New York: Routledge, 1994), 542.

288 Dickson Hartwell to Patricia Hartwell, [Feb 1953], Patricia Hartwell Private Papers.

289 United States Department of Justice, Federal Bureau of Investigation, Identification and Personnel for Employment of United States Citizens, Patricia Hartwell, September 8, 1954, 6.

290 "Annual Report of the Consultant in Mental Hygiene 1935-1936," Wellesley College, 1936, Patricia Hartwell Private Papers.

291 "Divorce Given Mrs. Hartwell," *Palm Beach Post*, August 4, 1953, 3, newspapers.com.

292 "Legacy Inventory," Ruth Adams Knight Collection, Special Collections and Archives, University of Oregon Library, 1-4.

293 "UN Aide Hartwell Divorced," *Miami Herald*, August 4, 1953, 5-D, newspapers.com.

294 United States Department of Justice, Federal Bureau of Investigation, Identification and Personnel for Employment of United States Citizen, Patricia Hartwell, September 8, 1954. 2-3.

295 Lisa Fogarty, "What Getting a Divorce Was Like Every Decade Since the 1900s," *Redbook*, April 11, 2017, https://www.redbookmag.com/love-sex/relationships/g4275/divorce-throughout-history/?slide=5.

296 V. J. Schweizer, "Divorce: More than a century of change, 1900-2018," National Center for Family & Marriage Research, Bowling Green State University, 2020, https://www.bgsu.edu/ncfmr/resources/data/family-profiles/schweizer-divorce-century-change-1900-2018-fp-20-22.html.

297 Margarita Tartakovsky, "A Glimpse into Marriage Advice from the 1950s," Psych Central, February 27, 2012, https://psychcentral.com/blog/a-glimpse-into-marriage-advice-from-the-1950s/.

298 Fleur Feighan, "Hartwell Show Opens Sunday"; Patricia Lochridge to Dickson Hartwell, December 1, 1944, Patricia Hartwell Private Papers.

299 "South Miami Writer Weds N.Y. Newspaperwoman," *Miami News*, August 8, 1953, newspapers.com.

300 Dickson Hartwell, "Beware of Your Dog," *The Berkshire Eagle*, August 4, 1953, 17, newspapers.com.

301 Ann Lochridge, interview by Jay Hartwell, Jay Hartwell Notebook [1999-2000], 36, Jay Hartwell Private Papers.

302 Krysia Diver, "Journal Reveals Hitler's Dysfunctional Family," *The Guardian*, August 4, 2005, https://www.theguardian.com/world/2005/aug/04/research.secondworldwar.

303 Alice Miller, "Adolf Hitler: How Could a Monster Succeed in Blinding a Nation?" The Natural Child Project, accessed February 10, 2025, https://www.naturalchild.org/articles/alice_miller/adolf_hitler.html.

304 Jane Stevens, "Donald Trump Is the Product of Abuse and Neglect," Bounce Coalition (KY), July 30, 2020, https://www.pacesconnection.com/g/bounce-kentucky/blog/donald-trump-is-the-product-of-abuse-and-neglect-his-story-is-common-even-for-the-powerful-and-wealthy.

305 June Downey, interview by Jay Hartwell.

306 Jay Hartwell, email message to author, September 14, 2020.

307 Kai Willführ, "Stepparents Are Not Always Evil," Max-Planck-Gesellschaft, November 12, 2013, https://www.mpg.de/7593752/stepparents.

308 Memorandum for Theobold Englehardt Jr., February 15, 1953, Patricia Hartwell Private Papers.

309 Satoshi Kanazawa, "Why Are Stepparents More Likely to Kill Their Children?," *Psychology Today*, January 9, 2011, https://www.psychologytoday.com/ca/blog/the-scientific-fundamentalist/201101/why-are-stepparents-more-likely-kill-their-children; Martin Daly and Margo Wilson, "Child Abuse and Other Risks of Not Living with Both Parents," *Ethology and Sociobiology*

6, no. 4 (January 1, 1985): 197–210, https://doi.
org/10.1016/0162-3095(85)90012-3.

310 Yvonne Roberts, "'The Fear of Every Step-Parent Is That
They Really Are a Monster,'" *The Guardian*, June 29,
2005, https://www.theguardian.com/lifeandstyle/2005/
jun/29/familyandrelationships.children.

311 Miriam Ascarelli, *Independent Vision: Dorothy Harrison
Eustis and the Story of The Seeing Eye* (West Lafayette,
IN: Purdue University Press, 2010), 89.

312 Lyle Therese A. Hilotin-Lee, "Child Abuse Background
and History," Findlaw, May 25, 2023, https://www.
findlaw.com/family/child-abuse/child-abuse-background-
and-history.html.

313 "Corrections," *New York Times*, March 29, 1981,
ProQuest Historical Newspapers.

314 Leonard Engel, "Columbia VFW Cheers Slogan of No
Cashee! No Fighter!," Columbia Spectator Archive, Vol.
LIX, March 23, 1936, https://spectatorarchive.library.
columbia.edu/?a=d&d=cs19360323-01.2.6&srpos=
1&e=-------en-20--1--txt-txIN-leonard+engel+%22columb
ia+VFW%22------.

315 "Nye Committee Report, 1936," in U.S. Congress,
Senate, Special Committee on Investigation of the
Munitions Industry, (ed.), Munitions industry, Report of
the Special Committee on investigation of the munitions
industry, United States Senate, pursuant to S. Res. 206
(73d Congress) a resolution to make certain investigations
concerning the manufacture and sale of arms and other
war munitions, (Washington: G.P.O., 1936), 3-13. https://
www.ruhr-uni-bochum.de/gna/Quellensammlung/09/09_
nyecommitteereport_1936.html.

316 Ronald H. Bailey, "Serious Fun: Veterans of Future Wars," HistoryNet, accessed February 6, 2025, https://www.historynet.com/serious-fun-veterans-of-future-wars.htm. Originally published in the February 2015 issue of *World War II.*

317 April C. Armstrong, "War is Imminent," The Veterans of Future Wars Mudd Manuscript Blog, September 30, 2015, https://blogs.princeton.edu/mudd/2015/09/war-is-imminent-the-veterans-of-future-wars/.

318 "Education: Future Veterans," *TIME,* March 30, 1936, http://content.time.com/time/subscriber/article/0,33009,931382-2,00.html.

319 Donald W. Whisenhunt, *Veterans of Future Wars: A Study in Student Activism* (New York: Lexington Books, 2010), 43.

320 Chris Rasmussen, "'This thing has ceased to be a joke': The Veterans of Future Wars and the Meanings of Political Satire in the 1930s," *Journal of American History* 103, no. 1 (June 2016), 103, https://www.jstor.org/stable/48560052.

321 Susan Hamson, "The Veterans of Future Wars," *Cabinet Magazine,* Spring 2004, http://www.cabinetmagazine.org/issues/13/hamson.php.

322 "Women in the Third Reich—Photograph," *Holocaust Encyclopedia*, quoted from United States Holocaust Memorial Museum, Washington, DC., accessed February 6, 2025, https://encyclopedia.ushmm.org/content/en/gallery/women-in-the-third-reich-photographs.

323 Whisenhunt, *Veterans of Future Wars,* 40.

324 "VFW Gives History Worthy of Records," *Wellesley College News,* April 16, 1936, 9, Wellesley College Digital Repository, https://repository.wellesley.edu/object/wellesley10904?search_api_fulltext=.

325 Whisenhunt, *Veterans of Future Wars,*118.

326 Patricia Hartwell, interview by Joe Rossi, 154.

327 Thomas R. Davies, "Internationalism in a Divided World: The Experience of the International Federation of League of Nations Societies, 1919–1939," *Peace & Change, a Journal of Peace Research*, March 8, 2012, https://onlinelibrary.wiley.com/doi/10.1111/j.1468-0130.2011.00744.x#:~:text=.

328 "15,000 Take Pledge to Work for Peace," *New York Times*, September 7, 1936, 17, https://www.nytimes.com/1936/09/07/archives/15000-take-pledge-to-work-for-peace-brussels-delegates-acclaim.html.

329 Mackrell. *The Correspondents,* 71, 81.

330 Helen Kirkpatrick to Lyle Kirkpatrick, September 10, 1931, Helen Paull Kirkpatrick Papers, Box 1, Sophia Smith Collection, Smith College Special Collections, Northampton, MA.

331 Mackrell. *The Correspondents*, 78-79.

332 Patricia Lochridge to family, May 12, 1945; Patricia Lochridge to Bill Burnie, May 12, 1945. Patricia Hartwell Private Papers.

333 Marc Malkin, "Taika Waititi's Mom Explains Why She Told Her Son to Make 'Jojo Rabbit,' *Variety*, January 31, 2020, https://variety.com/2020/film/news/taika-waititi-mom-robin-cohen-jojo-rabbit-1203488959/.

334 Kit Ramgopal, "Survey finds 'shocking' lack of Holocaust knowledge among millennials and Gen Z," NBC News, September 16, 2020, https://www.nbcnews.com/news/world/survey-finds-shocking-lack-holocaust-knowledge-among-millennials-gen-z-n1240031.

335 Patricia Lochridge, "Vultures on the Home Front," *Woman's Home Companion*, August 1944, 35.

336 Lochridge, "Vultures on the Home Front," 35.

337 Patricia Lochridge, "Good and Different," *Woman's Home Companion*, June 1947, 38.

338 United States Department of Labor, *Infant Care*, Washington, DC 1922, National Library of Medicine Digital Collections, https://collections-us-east-1.awsprod.nlm.nih.gov/bookviewer?PID=nlm:nlmuid-1285103R-bk.

339 Kendra Cherry, "Biography of Psychologist Harry Harlow," Very Well Mind, March 23, 2020, https://www.verywellmind.com/harry-harlow-biography-1905-1981-2795510.

340 Matthew Impelli, "Portland Dads with Leaf Blowers Join Wall of Moms to Blow Back Tear Gas from Police," *Newsweek,* July 22, 2020, https://www.newsweek.com/portland-dads-leaf-blowers-join-wall-moms-blow-back-tear-gas-police-1519673.

341 Patricia Lochridge, "The Mother Racket," *Woman's Home Companion,* July 1944, 72-73.

342 Estcourt, "Handicaps."

343 Olivia Little, "A quick recap of Moms for Liberty's really rough year," Media Matters for America, September 6, 2024, https://www.mediamatters.org/moms-liberty/what-i-saw-moms-liberty-summit-diminished-and-desperate-group. See also "Media Matters for America" video, accessed April 14, 2025, https://www.mediamatters.org/media/4008037.

344 Decca Muldowney and Kelly Weill, "Florida Mom Behind Amanda Gorman Book Ban Has Proud Boy Links," *The Daily Beast*, May 25, 2023; RSN.org, April 14, 2025, https://www.rsn.org/001/florida-mom-behind-amanda-gorman-book-ban-has-proud-boy-links.html.

345 Jaclyn Peiser, "N.H. governor slams conservative group's $500 reward for reporting critical race teachings: 'Wholly inappropriate,'" *The Washington Post*, November 19, 2021, https://www.washingtonpost.com/nation/2021/11/19/moms-for-liberty-new-hampshire/.

346 Kelly Weill, "Far-Right Group Wants to Ban Kids From Reading Books on Male Seahorses, Galileo, and MLK," *The Daily Beast*, September 24, 2021, https://www.thedailybeast.com/far-right-group-wants-to-ban-kids-from-reading-books-on-male-seahorses-galileo-and-martin-luther-king-jr/.

347 Debra Hale-Shelton and Austin Gelder, "Secret Moms for Liberty audio captures threatening rhetoric targeting a school librarian," *Arkansas Times*, June 16, 2022, https://arktimes.com/arkansas-blog/2022/06/16/secret-moms-for-liberty-audio-captures-threatening-rhetoric-targeting-a-school-librarian/.

348 Henry Robinson Luce, *Fortune*, February, 1958, 190, https://books.google.ca/books?redir_esc=y&id=3Zz3snJsTAsC&focus=searchwithinvolume&q=henry+bull.

349 "Hula Hoop," The Strong National Museum of Play, accessed April 15, 2023, https://www.museumofplay.org/toys/hula-hoop/.

350 "How to get rich in your own basement," *House & Gardens*, May, 1950, Newspaper Clipping, Henry Bull Private Papers.

351 "Toys in Space," Google Arts & Culture, accessed April 15, 2025, https://artsandculture.google.com/story/toys-in-space-smithsonian-national-air-and-space-museum/cgXxkg5p2YrIKA?hl=en.

352 William J. Broad, "Pentagon is said to focus on ESP for wartime use," *New York Times,* January 10, 1984,

Sec. C, 1, https://www.nytimes.com/1984/01/10/science/
pentagon-is-said-to-focus-on-esp-for-wartime-use.html.

353 "Whee-lo." Wikipedia, accessed May 6, 2025, https://
en.wikipedia.org/wiki/WHEE-LO#:~:text=Cultural%20
References.

354 "Nine historical polling results that might surprise you,"
Roper, April 17, 2015, https://ropercenter.cornell.edu/
blog/nine-historical-polling-results-might-surprise-you.

355 Martin Pengelly, "Aide tried to stop Trump praising
Hitler – by telling him Mussolini was 'great guy,'"
Guardian, March 12, 2024, https://www.theguardian.
com/books/2024/mar/12/mussolini-trump-hitler-john-
kelly-jim-sciutto-book?link_id=.

356 Statista Research Department, "The Holocaust - Statistics
& Facts," Statista, July 3, 2024, https://www.statista.com/
topics/9066/the-holocaust/.

357 "Results of Lawsuits Regarding the 2020 Elections,"
Campaign Legal Center, accessed April 15, 2025, https://
campaignlegal.org/results-lawsuits-regarding-2020-
elections.

358 Sarah Fortinsky, "One-third of adults in new poll say
Biden's election was illegitimate," *The Hill*, January 4,
2024, https://thehill.com/homenews/campaign/4384619-
one-third-of-americans-say-biden-election-illegitimate/.

359 Madison Czopek, "2024 election results don't prove
2020 stolen election claims. Voters' choices can change,"
Politifact, Poynter Institute, November 4, 2024, https://
www.politifact.com/factchecks/2024/nov/06/dinesh-
dsouza/2024-election-results-dont-prove-2020-stolen-elect/.

360 "*The Invention of Lying* Official Trailer," posted June 22,
2016, by Rotten Tomatoes, *YouTube*, 2:16, https://www.
youtube.com/watch?v=RhRnmyBjOLs.

361 Gellhorn and Cowles, *Love Goes to Press*, 12.

362 Patricia Lochridge to family, May 12, 1945, Patricia Hartwell Private Papers.

363 Francine Uenuma, "Journalist Virginia Irwin Broke Barriers When She Reported from Berlin at the End of WWII," *Smithsonian,* March 28, 2018, https://www. smithsonianmag.com/history/virginia-irwin-broke-barriers-she-reported-berlin-end-wwii-180968615/.

364 Ray Moseley, *Reporting War: How Foreign Correspondents Risked Capture, Torture and Death to Cover World War II* (New Haven: Yale University Press, 2017), 316.

365 Patricia Hartwell, interview by Steve Bull.

366 Uki Goñi, "Tests on skull fragment cast doubt on Adolf Hitler suicide story," *Guardian,* September 26, 2009, https://www.theguardian.com/world/2009/sep/27/adolf-hitler-suicide-skull-fragment.

367 "Press Accreditation During WWII," No Job for a Woman, accessed April 15, 2025, https://nojobforawoman. com/press-accreditation/#:~:text=America's%20 armed%20forces%20accredited%20127,followed%20 military%20law%20and%20censorship.

368 Walter Shapiro, "Hustling Hitler: The Jewish Vaudevillian Who Fooled the Führer," Yale University Department of Political Science, accessed February 9, 2025, https:// politicalscience.yale.edu/publications/hustling-hitler-jewish-vaudevillian-who-fooled-f-hrer.

369 Meriel Schindler, "On Dr. Eduard Bloch, Hitler's Family Physician (Who Happened to Be Jewish)," Literary Hub, October 18, 2021, https://lithub.com/on-dr-eduard-bloch-hitlers-family-physician-who-happened-to-be-jewish/.

370 Silvia Foti, "My grandfather wasn't a Nazi-fighting war hero — he was a brutal collaborator," Salon, July 18, 2018, https://www.salon.com/2018/07/14/my-grandfather-didnt-fight-the-nazis-as-family-lore-told-it-he-was-a-brutal-collaborator/.

371 David Domina, email to author, December 30, 2021.

372 Nell Prior, "PTSD: Eyes can reveal previous trauma, study reveals," *BBC News,* July 26, 2020, https://www.bbc.com/news/uk-wales-53503289.

373 Leila Levinson, "Concentration Camp Liberators Reveal Their Silent Trauma," Warfare History Network, Spring 2010, https://warfarehistorynetwork.com/article/concentration-camp-liberators-reveal-their-silent-trauma/.

374 Patricia Hartwell interview by Joe Rossi, 156.

375 "Wife Succeeds Husband at UN," *New York Times,* September 14, 1954, 18, https://www.nytimes.com/1954/09/14/archives/wife-succeeds-husband-in-un.html.

376 Patricia Hartwell, interview by Joe Rossi, 156.

377 Maggie Black, *The Children and the Nations* (UNICEF, 1986), 37, http://www.cf-hst.net/unicef-temp/Child-Nation/Child-Nation-M-Black-Ch02-p37-62-milk-fat-bread.pdf.

378 Jennifer M. Morris, *The Origins of UNICEF 1946-1953* (New York: Lexington Books, 2015), 120.

379 Morris, *The Origins of UNICEF,* 115.

380 Judith M. Spiegelman, *We are the Children* (Boston/NY: The Atlantic Monthly Press, 1986), 135, https://archive.org/stream/in.ernet.dli.2015.264447/2015.264447.We-Are_djvu.txt.

381 Patricia Hartwell, interview by Joe Rossi, 160.

382 June Downey, interview by Jay Hartwell.

383 Patricia Hartwell, interview by Joe Rossi, 160.

384 "Landscape with United Nations Headquarters Building," United Nations, accessed April 15, 2025, https://www. un.org/ungifts/landscape-united-nations-headquarters-building.

385 Spiegelman, *We are the Children*, 135.

386 June Downey, interview by Jay Hartwell.

387 Patricia Hartwell, interview by Joe Rossi, 157-8.

388 "Special Exhibits from UNICEF Archives," UNICEF Records and Archives, accessed February 8, 2025, http:// www.cf-hst.net/unicef-temp/cf-hst%20redesign/special-exhibits-gco-roy.htm.

389 Feighan, "Hartwell Show Opens Sunday."

390 Ascarelli, *Independent Vision*, 87-89.

391 "Advertising and Marketing News," *New York Times,* September 22, 1954, 41, https://www.nytimes. com/1954/07/22/archives/advertising-and-marketing-news.html.

392 Dickson Hartwell, "Prince of Press Agents," *Colliers Magazine*, November 22, 1947, 75, https:// whitmanarchive.org/item/encyclopedia_entry651.

393 "Letters: Jul. 21, 1967," *TIME*, July 21, 1967, https:// time.com/archive/6874612/letters-jul-21-1967/.

394 Cutlip, *The Unseen Power*, 255.

395 "Hill & Knowlton Tobacco Tactics," University of Bath, May 22, 2018, https://tobaccotactics.org/wiki/hill-knowlton/.

396 "Wham! Musician Goes Berserk, Sends Jetliner Into Nose Dive," *LA Times*, April 9, 1985, 1, https://www. latimes.com/archives/la-xpm-1985-04-09-mn-27976-story.html.

397 Alexander Griffing, "A Brief History of 'Lügenpresse,' the Nazi-era Predecessor to Trump's Fake News," *Haaretz,* October 8, 2017, https://www.haaretz.com/us-news/ the-ominous-nazi-era-precedent-to-trump-s-fake-news-attacks-1.5438960.

398 Griffing, "A Brief History."

399 Fact Checker, "In four years, President Trump made 30,573 false or misleading claims," *Washington Post,* January 20, 2021, https://www.washingtonpost.com/ politics/2021/01/24/trumps-false-or-misleading-claims-total-30573-over-four-years/.

400 Rachel Leingang and Sam Levine, "Trump's resounding Iowa win shows his 2020 election lie is working," *Guardian*, January 17, 2024, https://www.theguardian. com/us-news/2024/jan/17/trump-2020-lies-voter-impact-2024-election.

401 Daniel Dale, "Fact check: Trump, on a lying spree, made at least 40 separate false claims in two Pennsylvania speeches," *CNN Politics*, October 10, 2024, https:// www.cnn.com/2020/10/19/politics/fact-check-trump-dishonest-weekend-florida-michigan-georgia-wisconsin/ index.html.

402 Carole McGranahan, "An anthropology of lying: Trump and the political sociality of moral outrage," *American Ethnologist* 44, no. 2 (May 2017): 243–248, https:// anthrosource.onlinelibrary.wiley.com/doi/10.1111/ amet.12475.

403 Kate Plummer, "Donald Trump Hires Alina Habba's New Company for Campaign," *Newsweek*, September 26, 2024, https://www.newsweek.com/alina-habba-donald-trump-payments-business-1957821.

404 Ronn Torossian, "Hitler's Nazi Germany Used an American PR Agency," *Observer,* December 22, 2014, https://observer.com/2014/12/hitlers-nazi-germany-used-an-american-pr-agency/.

405 Andrew Rowell, *Green Backlash—Global Subversion of the Environment Movement* (New York: Routledge, 1996), 122.

406 Cutlip, *The Unseen Power,* 273.

407 "Pioneer – Carl Byoir," PR Museum, accessed February 9, 2025, https://www.prmuseum.org/pioneer-carl-byoir.

408 Robertson C. Cameron, Letter to the editor, *Pittsburgh Post-Gazette,* January 7, 1954, 8, newspapers.com.

409 Dickson Hartwell, "Are Trucks Gravediggers," For the Record syndicated column, *Meriden Journal,* December 9, 1953, 16, newspapers.com.

410 Eastern Railroad Presidents Conference v. Noerr Motor Freight, Inc., Oyez, accessed February 15, 2025, https://www.oyez.org/cases/1960/50.

411 Deposition, Eastern Railroad Presidents Conference v. Noerr Motor Freight, Inc, 135, 149, Patricia Hartwell Private Papers.

412 "The Railroad-Trucker's Brawl, Pioneer - Carl Byoir." PR Museum, accessed February 6, 2025, https://www.prmuseum.org/pioneer-carl-byoir.

413 Zack Beauchamp, "The *New York Times'* first article about Hitler's rise is absolutely stunning," *Vox,* March 3, 2016, https://www.vox.com/2015/2/11/8016017/ny-times-hitler.

414 Hedwig Mauer Simpson, "Herr Hitler at Home in the Clouds. High up on his favorite mountain he finds time for politics, solitude and frequent official parties," *New York Times,* August 20, 1939, Section SM, 3,

https://archive.org/details/new-york-times-pro-nazi-pro-hitler-1939/mode/1up.

415 Despina Stratigakos, "Hitler at home: How the Nazi PR machine remade the Führer's domestic image and duped the world," *The Conversation*, September 21, 2015, https://theconversation.com/hitler-at-home-how-the-nazi-pr-machine-remade-the-fuhrers-domestic-image-and-duped-the-world-47077.

416 "Thayer & Eldridge to Walt Whitman, 14 June 1860," in The Walt Whitman Archive, ed. Matt Cohen, Ed Folsom, & Kenneth M. Price, accessed March 16, 2025. http://www.whitmanarchive.org.

417 Rufus W. Griswold, "[Review of *Leaves of Grass* 1855], November 10, 1855," The Walt Whitman Archive, https://whitmanarchive.org/criticism/reviews/lg1855/anc.00016.html#:~:text.

418 Eric Christopher Conrad, "The Walt Whitman Brand" (PhD diss., University of Iowa, 2013), 37, https://ir.uiowa.edu/cgi/viewcontent.cgi?article=5895&context=etd.

419 Conrad, *The Walt Whitman Brand*, 30-31.

420 Conrad, *The Walt Whitman Brand*, 16.

421 Peter Carlson, "Walt Whitman Celebrated Himself, and Made Sure the Public Knew It," History.net, accessed April 15, 2025, https://www.historynet.com/walt-whitman-celebrated-himself-and-made-sure-the-public-knew-it.htm.

422 Horace Traubel, *With Walt Whitman in Camden,* Vol. 2 (New York: Mitchell Kennerley, 1915), July 27, 1888, 45.

423 Walt Whitman letter to Ralph Waldo Emerson, August 1856, Whitman Archive, https://whitmanarchive.org/about/archive/wwa-2000-to-2007/published/LG/1856/poems/35.html.

424 Lisa Hix, "Walt Whitman—Patriotic Poet, Gay Iconoclast, or Shrewd Marketing Ploy?," *Collectors Weekly,* May 3, 2016, https://www.collectorsweekly.com/articles/walt-whitman/.

425 Horace Traubel, "Commentary," Walt Whitman Archive, December 30, 1890, https://whitmanarchive.org/criticism/disciples/traubel/WWWiC/7/med.00007.178.html.

426 "Whitman as His Own Press-Agent," *American Mercury,* December 17, 1929, 483-485, https://whitmanarchive.org/item/encyclopedia_entry651.

427 "Franklin Roosevelt's Press Conference December 17, 1940," Franklin Delano Roosevelt Library, accessed February 9, 2025, http://docs.fdrlibrary.marist.edu/odllpc2.html.

428 Ellen Chesler, *Woman of Valor: Margaret Sanger and the Birth Control Movement in America* (New York: Simon and Schuster, 1992), 63.

429 Emma Goldman, "Living my Life - Emma Goldman," libcom.org., January 8, 2012, https://libcom.org/article/living-my-life-emma-goldman.

430 Candace Falk, "Emma Goldman: passion, politics, and the theatrics of free expression," *Women's History Review* 11, no.1 (2002): 11-26, https://doi.org/10.1080/09612020200200308; Margaret Sanger, "[Ford Hall Forum Address], 1929," The Margaret Sanger Papers Project, accessed February 9, 2025, https://www.m-sanger.org/items/show/1367.

431 Jos. Gibbons, "A 'Heroine of History': Margaret Sanger, revolutionary birth control activist," Blue Stocking Oxford, April 1, 2008, https://blue-stocking.org.uk/2008/04/01/a-heroine-of-history.

432 Chesler, *Woman of Valor,* 6.

433 Jill Lepore, "Birthright: What's Next for Planned Parenthood?," *New Yorker*, November 14, 2011, 46, https://www.newyorker.com/magazine/2011/11/14/ birthright-jill-lepore.

434 Chen Chao-ju, "*Sim-pua* under the Colonial Gaze: Gender, 'Old Customs' and the Law in Taiwan under Japanese Imperialism," in *Gender and Law in the Japanese Imperium*, ed. Susan L. Burns and Barbara J. Brooks (Honolulu, HI: Hawai'i Scholarship Online, 2016), 189–218, https://doi.org/10.21313/ hawaii/9780824837150.003.0008.

435 Patricia Hartwell to Edith Iglauer, June, 1962, box 5, folder 3, Edith Iglauer Papers, University of Victoria Special Collections and University Archive.

436 Graham McInnes, *One Man's Documentary: A Memoir of the Early Years of the National Film Board* (Winnipeg: University of Manitoba Press, 2004), 19, https://archivaria. ca/index.php/archivaria/article/view/12897/14127.

437 "Women in 16mm Film," *Glamour*, Newspaper Clipping, Henry Bull Private Papers.

438 Bryant Rousseau, "Talking to In-laws Can Be Hard. In Some Languages, It's Impossible," *New York Times,* January 9, 2017, https://www.nytimes.com/2017/01/09/ world/what-in-the-world/avoidance-speech-mother-in-law-languages.html.

439 Jamie and Rachel Ellis, interview by Jay Hartwell, Jay Hartwell Notebook [1999-2000], Jay Hartwell Private Papers, 109.

440 "Franziska Katharina 'Fanny' Kronburger Braun," *Find a Grave*, accessed February 9, 2025, https:// www.findagrave.com/memorial/139887128/franziska-katharina-braun.

441 "Wilhelm Friedrich Braun," *Find a Grave*, accessed
     February 9, 2025, https://www.findagrave.com/
     memorial/139887559/otto-wilhelm_friedrich-braun;
     Guido Knopp, *Hitler's Women,* (United Kingdom: Sutton
     Publishing, 2006), 20.

442 "Private Motion Pictures of Adolf Hitler and Eva Braun,"
     Digital Public Library of America, RG 242, Reel 6,
     https://dp.la/item/750f38e5c4dc3884ca307d8f355ff8e0,
     accessed April 30, 2025.

443 "Franziska Braun," *Peoplepill*, accessed February 9,
     2025, peoplepill.com/people/franziska-braun.

444 Patricia Hartwell to Henry Bull, [1981], Patricia Hartwell
     Private Papers.

445 Joseph McCarthy, "Enemies from Within," Speech,
     Wheeling, WV, February 9, 1950, read into the
     Congressional Record, 81st, 2nd, pt 2, 1954-56;
     U.S. Senate, *State Department Loyalty Investigation
     Committee on Foreign Relations*, 81st Congress, February
     19, 1950, *History Matters,* http://historymatters.gmu.
     edu/d/6456.

446 Jennifer Morris, *The origins of UNICEF 1946-1953*
     (New York: Lexington Books, 2015), 120.

447 United States, "Activities of United States Citizens
     Employed by the United Nations," *Hearings before the
     Subcommittee to Investigate the Administration of the
     Internal Security Act and Other Security Laws of the
     Committee on the Judiciary of the United States Senate.*
     83rd Congress, First Session, Part 5, December 22,
     1953, 680.

448 "UN Fires Woman Press Aide. Self Admitted Red,"
     Evening American, January 22, 1953, 6, newspapers.com.

449 United States, Congress, House Committee on Foreign Affairs, "Aid for Children" quoted from Ottawa, IL *Republican-Times*, April 14, 1953; *Mutual Security Act Extension*, Hearing Before the Committee, March-June, 1953, 650.

450 "Subversive Infiltration of Radio, TV, and The Entertainment Industry," *U.S. Congress, Senate, Committee on the Judiciary*, April 28, 1951, 310, https://www.google.com/books/edition/ Mutual_Security_Act_Extension_Hearings_M/ LIbiIHEMwx8C?hl=en&gbpv=1&bsq=unicef.

451 "Raymond Knight," LA Times Hollywood Star Walk, accessed Aug 7, 2025, https://projects.latimes.com/ hollywood/star-walk/raymond-knight/.

452 "Himan Brown," New York Times obituary, accessed Aug 7, 2025, https://www.legacy.com/us/obituaries/ nytimes/name/himan-brown-obituary?id=27799868.

453 Forsyth Hardy, ed., *Grierson on Documentary* (New York: Harcourt, Brace & Co, 1947), 226, accessed April 11, 2025, https://www.worldradiohistory. com/BOOKSHELF-ARH/Education/Grierson-on-Documentary-Hardy-1947.

454 Brian J. Low, *NFB Kids: Portrayals of Children by National Film Board of Canada 1939-1989* (Waterloo: Wilfrid Laurier University Press, 2002). 41.

455 "Norman McLaren's Chinese Odyssey," Culture on Campus: University of Stirling Archives, October 7, 2011, https://archives.wordpress.stir.ac.uk/2011/10/07/norman-mclarens-chinese-odyssey/.

456 Patricia Lochridge to Louis Ruppel, May 18, 1945, Patricia Hartwell Private Papers.

457 Maggie Black, *The Children and the Nations*, 219, https://www.unicef.org/documents/children-and-nations219.

458 Patricia Hartwell, interview with Joe Rossi, 161.

459 Maggie Black, *The Children and the Nations*, 2019.

460 Thomas Doherty, "Revisiting Lindbergh and Winchell Ahead of 'The Plot Against America,'" *Hollywood Reporter*, February 25, 2020, https://www.hollywoodreporter.com/news/revisiting-lindbergh-winchell-plot-america-guest-column-1280950.

461 Walter Winchell, "Scenes of a Columnist's Secretary," *New York Daily Mirror*, July 26, 1944, 12, Newspaper Clipping, Patricia Hartwell Private Papers.

462 Walter Winchell, "On Broadway with Walter Winchell," *Christian Science Monitor*, September 13, 1945, Newspaper Clipping, Patricia Hartwell Private Papers.

463 Walter Winchell, "This and That Off a Well-Worn Cuff," in *Man About Town* column, *Birmingham Herald*, March 15, 1948, 4, newspapers.com.

464 "Top Flight Authors," *Star-Gazette*, March 30, 1953, 2, newspapers.com.

465 "New Type of Column by Top-Flight Authors," *Star-Gazette*, March 30, 1953, 2; *Detroit Free Press*, October 6, 1953, 1, newspapers.com.

466 Rick and Christina Gables, "American Masters Examines How Walter Winchell Wielded 'The Power of Gossip,'" TV Insider, Oct. 19, 2020, https://www.tvinsider.com/953450/american-masters-walter-winchell-the-power-of-gossip/.

467 Dickson Hartwell, "Walter Winchell: An American Phenomenon," *Collier's*, February 28, 1948, 12.

468 Dickson Hartwell with Donald Robinson, "How Walter Winchell Came To Be Written," in *A Guide To Successful Magazine Writing*, ed. Clive Howard and Morton

Sontheimer, (New York: Scribner, 1954),16, google books, https://www.google.com/books/ edition/A_Guide_to_Successful_Magazine_ Writing/55VBAQAAIAAJ?hl=en&gbpv=1&bsq=dickson.

469 "Editorial," *Mansfield Advertiser,* March 3, 1948, 4, newspapers.com.

470 Hartwell with Robinson, "How Walter Winchell Came To Be Written," 17.

471 Patricia Lochridge, "The Role of College Women at This Mid-Century Point," Speech for 27th Council of Alums, *Wellesley News,* February 23, 1950, 5, Patricia Hartwell Private Papers.

472 Frank X. Tolbert, "Note from the Dead Under Window Sill," *Dallas News,* December 6, 1965, newspapers. com; Jason Stern, excerpt from *Plantation Parade: The Ambitions of Two Virginians*, January 11, 2020, https:// bellegrove.net/plantation-parade-the-ambitions-of-two-virginians-excerpt/.

473 Christopher Long, "Ware, Henry (1813–1898)," *Texas State Historical Society Handbook of Texas,* Texas State Historical Association, accessed February 9, 2025, https:// www.tshaonline.org/handbook/entries/ware-henry.

474 Brian Kelly Madaris, "Domingo Medearis," accessed February 10, 2025, https://xpda.com/family/Medearis-Domingo-ind01559.htm.

475 Douglas Martin, "Harvey Matusow, 75, an Anti-Communist Informer, Dies," *New York Times,* February 4, 2002, 87, https://www.nytimes.com/2002/02/04/us/harvey-matusow-75-an-anti-communist-informer-dies.html.

476 Edward Alwood, *Dark Days in the Newsroom: McCarthyism Aimed at the Press* (Philadelphia: Temple University Press, 2007), 66.

477 "Agent Calls Singers Reds," *New York Times,* February 26, 1952, https://www.nytimes.com/1952/02/26/archives/agent-calls-singers-reds.html.

478 Charles Alverson, "Harvey Matusow: I Led Twelve Lives," *Rolling Stone*, August 17, 1972, https://www.rollingstone.com/culture/culture-news/harvey-matusow-i-led-twelve-lives-75024/.

479 Alverson, "Harvey Matusow."

480 Jenni Avins, "That time when 'the Hollywood elite' took on Washington, 70 years ago," *Quartz,* February 25, 2017, https://qz.com/919067/how-it-looked-when-the-hollywood-elite-took-on-washington-70-years-ago/.

481 Jelani Cobb, "The Model for Donald Trump's Media Relations Is Joseph McCarthy," *New Yorker*, September 22, 2016, https://www.newyorker.com/news/daily-comment/the-model-for-donald-trumps-media-relations-is-joseph-mccarthy.

482 Louis Menand, "Joseph McCarthy and the Force of Political Falsehoods," *New Yorker,* July 27, 2020, https://www.newyorker.com/magazine/2020/08/03/joseph-mccarthy-and-the-force-of-political-falsehoods.

483 David Remnick, "What Donald Trump Shares with Joseph McCarthy," *New Yorker*, May 17, 2020, https://www.newyorker.com/magazine/2020/05/25/what-donald-trump-shares-with-joseph-mccarthy.

484 United States Department of Justice, Federal Bureau of Investigation, Identification and Personnel for Employment of United States Citizen, Dickson Hartwell, July 8, 1953, 58.

485 United States Department of Justice, Dickson Hartwell, 88.

486 Walter Winchell, "On Broadway," *Waco News Tribune,* July 15, 1953, newspapers.com.

487 United States Department of Justice, Dickson Hartwell, 122.

488 United States Department of Justice, Dickson Hartwell, 131.

489 Jake Hall, "A Farewell to Sobriety, Part Two. Drinking During World War II," *War on Rocks*, June 5, 2015, https://warontherocks.com/2015/06/a-farewell-to-sobriety-part-two-drinking-during-world-war-ii/.

490 Jo Smith, interview by Jay Hartwell, Jay Hartwell Notebook [1999-2000], 21, Jay Hartwell Private Papers.

491 "Newshawk Flies into Town," *CBS News Bureau*, May 20, 1941, Newspaper Clipping, Patricia Hartwell Private Papers.

492 "King Carol Relies on a Safe Topic," *Times Dispatch*, June 15, 1941, 63, newspapers.com.

493 "Bermuda, 1941," *Paris News*, September 16, 1941, 8, Newspaper Clipping, Patricia Hartwell Private Papers.

494 "Reports on Bermuda," *Bristol News Bulletin*, September 1, 1941, newspapers.com.

495 Patricia Lochridge to family, June 2, 1945, Patricia Hartwell Private Papers.

496 Patricia Lochridge to father, [1944?], Patricia Hartwell Private Papers.

497 Lawrence R. Samuel, "Why do Writers Drink So Much?" *Psychology Today*, January 22, 2018, https://www.psychologytoday.com/us/blog/psychology-yesterday/201801/why-do-writers-drink-so-much.

498 United States Department of Justice, Federal Bureau of Investigation, Identification and Personnel for Employment of United States Citizens, Dickson Hartwell, July 8, 1953; "Overseas Press Club of America Archives," accessed April 30, 2025. https://archive.org/details/opc-archive=.

499 "Overseas Press Club Opens Memorial Fund Campaign," *Albuquerque Journal,* November 21, 1952, 9, newspapers.com.

500 Dwight D Eisenhower, "Remarks Recorded for the Dedication of the Memorial Press Center, New York City," The American Presidency Project, December 13, 1954, https://www.presidency.ucsb.edu/documents/ remarks-recorded-for-the-dedication-the-memorial- press-center-new-york-city. Plaque states "To Patricia Hartwell, in recognition of distinguished service to the club in bringing to reality its dream of a memorial center honoring heroes of the press."

501 "Annual Awards Dinner," *Overseas Press Club of America,* May 7, 1952, Patricia Hartwell Private Papers.

502 Patricia Hartwell, interview by Joe Rossi, 158.

503 Dickson Hartwell to Patricia Hartwell, March 28, 1962, Patricia Hartwell Private Papers.

504 Dickson Hartwell to Patricia Hartwell, March 27, 1962, Patricia Hartwell Private Papers.

505 Dickson Hartwell to Particia Hartwell, March 23, 1962, Patricia Hartwell Private Papers.

506 "Lucas Cranach the Elder, 'Cupid complaining to Venus,'" The National Gallery, March 2008, https:// www.nationalgallery.org.uk/about-us/press-and-media/ press-releases/lucas-cranach-the-elder-cupid-complaining- to-venus#.

507 "Acquisitions," *National Gallery, June 1962-Dec 1964* (London: National Gallery, 1965), 37.

508 "Nazi-looted Artworks To Remain at Pasadena Museum," *Artforum,* May 24, 2019, https://www. artforum.com/news/nazi-looted-artworks-to-remain-at- pasadena-museum-79900.

509 Susan Foster, "Lucas Cranach The Elder," *National Gallery Annual Review*, 2019, https://www.nationalgallery.org.uk/media/30943/national-gallery-annual-review-2018.

510 Charlotte Higgins, "Hitler Owned Painting Now in National Gallery," *Guardian,* March 28, 2008, https://www.theguardian.com/artanddesign/2008/mar/28/art.secondworldwar.

511 Chris Wiley, "When Lee Miller Took a Bath in Hitler's Tub," *New Yorker,* January 9, 2024, https://www.newyorker.com/culture/photo-booth/when-lee-miller-took-a-bath-in-hitlers-tub.

512 Higgins, "Hitler owned painting now in National Gallery."

513 Peter Edidin, "Art and the Nazis, Times Two," *New York Times*, March 29, 2008, https://www.nytimes.com/2008/03/29/arts/29arts-ARTANDTHENAZ_BRF.html.

514 Jay Hartwell, email to author, April 3, 2020.

515 Jay Hartwell, email to author, June 10, 2023.

516 "Holocaust Claims," *New York State Department Financial Services*, accessed February 11, 2025, https://www.dfs.ny.gov/consumers/holocaust_claims.

517 Alexandra Tremayne-Pengelly, "A New York Law Requires Museums to Label Nazi-Looted Art. But Are They Following It?" *Observer,* February 28, 2023, https//observer.com/2023/02/a-new-york-law-requires-museums-to-label-nazi-looted-art-but-are-they-following-it/.

518 Ori Z. Soltes, "Cultural Plunder and Restitution and Human Identity," 15 J. *Marshall Rev*. Intell. Prop. L. 460 (2016), https://repository.law.uic.edu/ripl/vol15/iss3/4/.

519   Hector Feliciano, *The Lost Museum, The Nazi Conspiracy To Steal The World's Greatest Works Of Art* (New York: Basic Books, 1998), 179.

520   Sebastian Smee, "Picasso portrait returned by National Gallery to heirs of Jewish banker persecuted by Nazis," *Washington Post*, April 1, 2020, https://www.washingtonpost.com/entertainment/museums/picasso-portrait-returned-by-national-gallery-to-heirs-of-jewish-banker-persecuted-by-nazis/2020/04/01/7e0704be-7394-11ea-87da-77a8136c1a6d_story.html.

521   Eleanor Roosevelt, "My Day," *The Eleanor Roosevelt Papers Digital Edition*, October 17, 1956, https://www2.gwu.edu/~erpapers/myday/displaydoc.cfm?_y=1956&_f=md003619.

522   "E. & A. Silberman Galleries," *Wikipedia Commons*, accessed February 11, 2025, https://commons.wikimedia.org/wiki/E._%26_A._Silberman_Galleries.

523   Stephen C. Jordan, *Hollywood's Original Rat Pack: The Bards of Bundy Drive* (New Jersey: Scarecrow Press, 2008), 115-6.

524   Jonathan Stempel, "California museum can keep Cranachs looted by Nazis - U.S. appeals court," *Reuters*, July 30, 2018, https://www.reuters.com/article/us-art-nazi-cranach/california-museum-can-keep-cranachs-looted-by-nazis-us-appeals-court-idUSKBN1KK223/#.

525   Sue Merrell, "Grand Rapids Art Museum to Return Stolen Art," *Michigan Live*, April 4, 2008, https://www.mlive.com/grpress/2008/04/grand_rapids_art_museum_to_ret.html.

526   Ray Dowd, "Art Law: Boston Museum of Fine Arts: Sues Heirs of Jews To Keep Stolen Property, Hides Evidence," *Copyright Litigation Blog*, July 20, 2011, https://

copyrightlitigation.blogspot.com/2011/07/art-law-boston-museum-of-fine-arts-sues.html.

527 "Desco da Parto with the Amorous Hunt," Yale University Gallery of Art, accessed April 30, 2025, https://artgallery.yale.edu/collections/objects/43501.

528 Graham Bowley, "The Mystery of the Painting in Gallery 634," *New York Times*, February 8, 2020, https://www.nytimes.com/2020/02/08/arts/met-art-nazi-loot.html.

529 Judith H.Dobrzynski, "Seattle Museum Is Sued For a Looted Matisse," *New York Times*, August 4, 1998, https://www.nytimes.com/1998/08/04/arts/seattle-museum-is-sued-for-a-looted-matisse.html.

530 "Remembering Aristides de Sousa Mendes," *The Jewish Foundation for the Righteous*, April 29, 2011, https://jfr.org/remembering-aristides-de-sousa-mendes/.

531 Felicia R. Lee, "Wildensteins Sued Over Looted Art," *New York Times*, July 28, 1999, https://www.nytimes.com/1999/07/28/arts/wildensteins-sued-over-looted-art.html.

532 Jay Hartwell, email to author, March 27, 2020.

533 Jay Hartwell, email to author, April 12, 2020.

534 Simon Goodman, *The Orpheus Clock* (New York: Simon & Schuster, 2016), 79.

535 Goodman. *The Orpheus Clock*, 93.

536 Goodman, *The Orpheus Clock,*144.

537 Goodman, *The Orpheus Clock,*151.

538 Goodman, *The Orpheus Clock,*191.

539 Goodman, *The Orpheus Clock,*153.

540 Goodman, *The Orpheus Clock,* 269.

541 Goodman, *The Orpheus Clock,*191.

542 Jocelyn Noveck, "Nazi-looted portrait returned to heirs, will be auctioned," *Times of Israel*, March 21, 2018,

https://www.timesofisrael.com/nazi-looted-portrait-returned-to-heirs-will-be-auctioned/.

543 Marvin Alisky, "Arizona's first newspaper, the *Weekly Arizonian*, 1859," *New Mexico Historical Review* 34 (April 1959): 134-143, https://digitalrepository.unm.edu/nmhr/vol34/iss2/5/.

544 Dickson Hartwell to Patricia Hartwell, March 28, 1962, Patricia Hartwell Private Papers.

545 Patricia Hartwell, interview by Joe Rossi, 158.

546 "2 Producers of Mythical Musical Held; Accused of Stealing $39,000," *New York Times*, March 27, 1949, 32, https://www.nytimes.com/1949/04/27/archives/2-producers-of-mythical-musical-held-accused-of-stealing-39000-from.html.

547 Michael Wendland, *The Arizona Project* (Kansas City, MO: Sheed Andrews and McMeel, Inc., 1977), excerpt accessed from https://www.mail-archive.com/ctrl@listserv.aol.com/msg27665.html.

548 Joseph Dalton, "The Lonesome Death of Don Bolles," *Harvard Crimson*, October 1, 1976, https://www.thecrimson.com/article/1976/10/1/the-lonesome-death-of-don-bolles/.

549 Jon Talton, "Phoenix 101: Underworld," *Rogue Columnist*, September 8, 2009, https://roguecolumnist.typepad.com/rogue_columnist/2009/09/phoenix-101-underworld.html.

550 "The Story of Africa," *BBC World Service*, accessed February 11, 2025, https://www.bbc.co.uk/worldservice/africa/features/storyofafrica/9chapter1.shtml; "Modern slavery in Europe and Central Asia," *Walk Free Global Slavery Index*, accessed April 11, 2025, https://www.

globalslaveryindex.org/2018/findings/regional-analysis/
europe-and-central-asia/.

551 Alexander J. Motyl, "Experts' on Ukraine," *World Affairs Journal*, March 21, 2014, http://www.worldaffairsjournal.
org/blog/alexander-j-motyl/experts-ukraine.

552 Lev Golonkin, "Neo-Nazis and the Far Right Are On the March in Ukraine," *The Nation*, February 22, 2019, https://www.thenation.com/article/politics/neo-nazis-far-right-ukraine/.

553 "The rights of Ukrainian prisoners of war from Azovstal must be respected," *Amnesty International USA*, May 17, 2022, https://www.amnestyusa.org/press-releases/the-rights-of-ukrainian-prisoners-of-war-from-azovstal-must-be-respected/.

554 "Ukraine updates: New claims that Russian units fled Bakhmut," *Deutsche Welle,* May 10, 2023, https://www.dw.com/en/ukraine-updates-new-claims-that-russian-units-fled-bakhmut/a-65570676.

555 Rick Friedman, "The Weekly Editor: Education Beat," *Editor & Publisher* (October 6, 1962), Newspaper Clipping, Patricia Hartwell Private Papers.

556 "INGAA Missouri Award Winners," *AHBJ.org*, accessed April 30, 2025, https://ahbj.sabew.org/awards/04012013ingaa-missouri-award-winners./

557 "Weekly Staffer Gets Top Award," *AZ Daily Star,* March 2, 1964, 16; *Kansas City Times*, October 20, 1965, newspapers.com.

558 Patricia Hartwell, "Art in from Capitals," *The Arizonian*, May 11, 1962, Patricia Hartwell Private Papers.

559 Particia Hartwell to Edith Iglauer, Sunday [1962], box 5, folder 3, Editor Iglauer Papers, University of Victoria Special Collections and University Archive.

560 Ian Austen, "Edith Iglauer. Journalist and Bard of Canada, Dies at 101," *New York Times*, March 15, 2019, https://www.nytimes.com/2019/03/15/obituaries/edith-iglauer-dead.html.

561 Edith Iglauer to Patricia Hartwell, July 23,1962, Patricia Hartwell Private Papers.

562 Black, *The Children and the Nations*, 215.

563 Patricia Hartwell to Maurice Pate, July 21,1963, Patricia Hartwell Private Papers.

564 Patricia Hartwell to Maurice Pate, April 20, 1962, Patricia Hartwell Private Papers.

565 June Downey, interview by Jay Hartwell.

566 Patricia Hartwell to Maurice Pate, July 21, 1963, Patricia Hartwell Private Papers.

567 Patricia Hartwell to Edith Iglauer, June 18, 1963, box 5, folder 3, Edith Iglauer Papers.

568 Hartwell to Iglauer, June 18, 1963.

569 Patricia Hartwell to June Downey, July 21 [1963], Patricia Hartwell Private Papers.

570 Patricia Hartwell to John P. Frank, July 5, 1963, Patricia Hartwell Private Papers.

571 "Property Settlement Agreement," July 24, 1963, Patricia Hartwell Private Papers.

572 Jay Hartwell, email to author, May 24, 2020.

573 Patricia Hartwell to June Downey, July 21, [1963], Patricia Hartwell Private Papers.

574 Lloyd Lochridge to Patricia Hartwell, July 8, 1963, Patricia Hartwell Private Papers.

575 Jay Hartwell, email to author, April 12, 2020.

576 Patricia Hartwell resume, 1973, Patricia Hartwell Private Papers.

577 Patricia Hartwell, interview by Joe Rossi, 1995.

578 Patricia Hartwell, "The Acropolis Still Stands," *Arizonian,* 1962, Patricia Hartwell Private Papers.

579 Edward Lebow, "How Dare They?," *Phoenix New Times,* December 10, 1998, https://www.phoenixnewtimes.com/news/how-dare-they-6421490.

580 Lebow, "How Dare They?"

581 Dickson Hartwell to John Marshall, September 8, 1965, Patricia Hartwell Private Papers.

582 "Last Sunset for the *Arizonian,*" *Arizona Republic,* November 25, 1969, 1, newspapers.com.

583 Jonathan Marshall, *Dateline History* (Phoenix, Arizona: Acacia Publishing, 2009), 144.

584 "67 Named to STEP Seminar," *Scottsdale Progress,* Oct 1,1971, 1, newspapers.com.

585 Patricia Hartwell, *The Scottsdale Collection* (Scottsdale, AZ: Scottsdale Fine Arts Commission, 1975).

586 Patricia Hartwell to Dickson Hartwell, March 5, 1973, Patricia Hartwell Private Papers.

587 Patricia Hartwell, interview by Joe Rossi, 160.

588 "A Work of Art for Scottsdale," *Arizona Republic,* February 20, 1972, 16, newspapers.com.

589 Patricia Hartwell, interview by Joe Rossi, 162.

590 Jamie and Rachel Ellis, interview by Jay Hartwell.

591 Chris Page, "Scottsdale Center Marks 30 Years," *Eastvalley.com,* October 6, 2011, https://www.eastvalleytribune.com/news/scottsdale-center-marks-30-years/article_c2cf1632-4a47-5b2b-a97f-3804655c7c69.html.

592 Patricia Hartwell, interview by Joe Rossi, 161.

593   Candace Blomendahl, "Palmer Museum exhibit honors Bicentennial I-80 rest stop sculpture," *York News-Times*, December 2, 2011, https://yorknewstimes.com/news/palmer-museum-exhibit-honors-bicentennial-i-80-rest-stop-sculpture/article_e6a0e335-5a5e-58e1-9efb-9a6a77a8d1d0.html.

594   Mary Lierley, "Nebraska interstate 80 bicentennial sculpture project" (PhD diss., University of North Texas, 1982), 72, https://digital.library.unt.edu/ark:/67531/metadc798206/m1/143/?q=selection%20committee.

595   Katie Kelly, "Can sculpture stand up beside toilets?" *Village Voice,* December, 1975, 106-7, newspapers.com.

596   "Mrs. Anne Svoboda and Linda Howard on the Today Show," September 12, 2020, posted by Stephen Bull, YouTube, accessed February 11, 2025, https://youtu.be/FUyBo9AZlEM.

597   Maggie Wilson, "Around the Valley," *Arizona Republic*, March 6, 1970, 69, newspapers.com.

598   Jay Hartwell, email to author, August 3, 2020.

599   Dickson Hartwell to Patricia Hartwell, [1969]. Patricia Hartwell Private Papers.

600   Dickson Hartwell to Patricia Hartwell, [1969].

601   Patricia Hartwell, interview by Joe Rossi, 160; Maggie Wilson, "Naive Art," Newspaper Clipping, Patricia Hartwell Private Papers.

602   "Phoenix College - Historical Timeline - 1920 - 2015," accessed April 10, 2025, https://www.pc.maricopa.edu/anniversary/95th.html.

603   Maggie Wilson, "From war coverage, UNICEF, Prague: She Turned to Teaching Oriental History," *Arizona Republic*, September 27, 1968, Patricia Hartwell Private Papers.

604 "Franklin D. Roosevelt: Usher Books," *Franklin D. Roosevelt,* microfiche, 1933-1945, Roosevelt Institute for American Studies, Franklin Delano Roosevelt Presidential Library and Museum, accessed April 10, 2025, https://www.roosevelt.nl/en/library/archival-collections/presidential-collections-administrations-2/franklin-d-roosevelt/.

605 Mary Jane Barnett, interview by Jay Hartwell, Jay Hartwell Notebook [1999-2000],144, Jay Hartwell Private Papers.

606 Particia Hartwell to Edith Iglauer, [1972], box 5, folder 3, Edith Iglauer Papers, University of Victoria Special Collections and University Archive.

607 "Kailua Discussion of Tests," *Honolulu Advertiser,* March 22, 1972, 15, newspapers.com.

608 Particia Hartwell to Dickson Hartwell, June 17, 1975, Patricia Hartwell Private Papers; Jamie and Rachel Ellis, interview by Jay Hartwell.

609 G.H, *Outlook*, February 2, 1973, 12, Newspaper Clipping, Patricia Hartwell Private Papers.

610 Maggie Wilson, "Woman coordinates Scottsdale City-owned Collection," *Arizona Republic,* March 2, 1975, newspapers.com.

611 Particia Hartwell to Dickson Hartwell, June 17, 1975, Patricia Hartwell Private Papers.

612 Patricia Hartwell, interview by Joe Rossi, 159.

613 Ian Shank, "How Salvador Dalí Accidentally Sabotaged His Own Market for Prints," *Artsy.net,* April 18, 2017, https://www.artsy.net/article/artsy-editorial-salvador-dali-accidentally-sabotaged-market-prints.

614 Patricia Hartwell, interview by Joe Rossi, 171.

615 Erin K. Hollenbank, "Insights into Identifying Fake Artworks," *PropertyCasualty360*, March 5, 2020, https://www.propertycasualty360.com/2020/03/05/insights-to-identifying-fake-artworks/?slreturn=20200702183915.

616 Laurence Gay, Speech, *Honolulu Advertiser*, June 29, 1977, newspapers.com; "Emil Laurence Gay," *R&V Funeral Homes*, accessed February 11, 2025, https://www.ranfranzandvinefh.com/obituaries/emil-laurence-gay.

617 Tom Kaser, "Drive fights bill to cut funds for local and bought in works of international worth $3 million/ten years after 1% passed," *Honolulu Advertiser*, February 22, 1977, 3, newspapers.com.

618 Momi Cazimero, author, Patricia Hartwell, editor, and Douglas Peebles, photographer, *Retrospective: 1967-87*, (Hawaii: State Foundation on Culture and the Arts), 1987.

619 Patricia Hartwell, interview by Joe Rossi, 178.

620 "Arts and Cultural Production Satellite Account," *Bureau of Economic Analysis*, accessed February 11, 2025, https://apps.bea.gov/regional/arts-and-culture/stateMap.cfm.

621 Patricia Hartwell, interview by Joe Rossi, 172.

622 Pat Ging, "Help for Those who Buy Prints," *Honolulu Advertiser*, February 12, 1978, 43, newspapers.com.

623 Ellen Glover, "NFT Art Theft: What Buyers and Artists Need to Know," Builtin, September 7, 2022, https://builtin.com/articles/NFT-art-theft/.

624 Jonathan Lopez, *The Man Who Made Vermeers: Unvarnishing the Legend* (New York: Houghton Mifflin Harcourt, 2008), 111-115.

625 Peter Schjeldahl, "Dutch Master: The Art Forger who Became a National Hero," *New Yorker*, October 20, 2008, https://www.newyorker.com/magazine/2008/10/27/dutch-master.

626 Jonathan Janson, "Han's Fake Vermeers," *Essential Vermeer 3.0,* accessed February 11, 2025, http://www. essentialvermeer.com/misc/van_meegeren.html.

627 Katherine McGrath, "20 Works in Major Modigliani Exhibition Have Just Been Confirmed," *Architectural Digest,* January 11, 2018, https://www.architecturaldigest. com/story/a-major-modigliani-forgery-scandal-hits-italy#.

628 Michael Glover, "Why is it OK to copy great paintings, but not to fake them?," *The Independent,* January 15, 2018, https://www.independent.co.uk/arts-entertainment/ art/features/tate-royal-academy-leonardo-da-vinci-modigliani-giampietrino-fake-copy-russia-a8160276.html.

629 Jonathan Keats, *Forged: Why Fakes are the Great Art of Our Age* (Oxford: Oxford University Press, 2013), 7.

630 Amy Zegart, "George Washington was a master of deception," *The Atlantic,* November 25, 2018, https:// fsi.stanford.edu/news/george-washington-was-master-deception.

631 John Steinbeck, *Grapes of Wrath* (New York: Penguin Books, 2002), 33.

632 Joy Lanzendorfer, "The Forgotten Dust Bowl Novel That Rivaled "The Grapes of Wrath," *Smithsonian,* May 23, 2016, https://www.smithsonianmag.com/ arts-culture/forgotten-dust-bowl-novel-rivaled-grapes-wrath-180959196/; Iris Jamahl Dunkle, *Riding Like The Wind* (Oakland, CA: University of California Press, 2024).

633 *Honolulu Advertiser,* January 10, 1988, 64; Fleur Feighan, "Hartwell Show Opens Sunday," Newspaper Clipping, Patricia Hartwell Private Papers.

634 Wallace Turner, "Hawaii to Recall Captain Cook's Arrival in Subdued Style," *New York Times,* January 2, 1978, newspapers.com.

635 Dickson Hartwell to Steve Bull, January 8, 1967, Patricia Hartwell Private Papers.

636 Larry Keller, "Hawaii suffering from racial prejudice," *Southern Poverty Law Center*, August 30, 2009, https://www.splcenter.org/fighting-hate/intelligence-report/2009/hawaii-suffering-racial-prejudice.

637 Jay Hartwell, email to author, September 13, 2020.

638 Jeff Bull, interview by Jay Hartwell, Jay Hartwell Notebook [1999-2000], 20, Jay Hartwell Private Papers; Patricia Hartwell to Edith Iglauer, April 20, 1990, box 5, folder 3, Edith Iglauer Papers, University of Victoria Special Collections and University Archive.

639 Jay Hartwell, email to author, April 5, 2020.

640 Zilfa Estcourt, "Lady Ruler—Journalist Patricia Lochridge Writes of Governing Hitler's Home for a Day," *Wellesley News,* Newspaper Clipping, box 5, folder 3, Edith Iglauer Papers, University of Victoria Special Collections; "Jay Hartwell," pdf. 41.

641 Estcourt, "Handicaps."

642 Amy Berish, "FDR and Polio," Franklin D. Roosevelt Presidential Library and Museum, accessed Aug 8, 2025, https://www.fdrlibrary.org/polio.

643 Sorel, *The Women Who Wrote the War*, 334.

644 Stacy A. Cordery, *Alice* (NY: Viking Penguin, 2007) 29.

645 Elizabeth Evitts Dickinson, "After the Cure," *Washington Post*, May 4, 2020, https://www.washingtonpost.com/magazine/2020/05/04/my-mothers-childhood-bout-with-polio-paralyzed-more-than-her-body-ive-spent-much-my-life-trying-understand-that-paralysis/.

646 Dickson Hartwell and Andy Rooney, Eds., *Off the Record*, 35.

647 "Remembering FDR's Holiday Ritual," *Greensboro News & Record,* November 21, 1990, https://greensboro.com/remembering-fdrs-holiday-ritual/article_708973d2-6e57-5a67-8e22-de1ea1a8b7ab.html.

648 Jennifer Wright, *Get Well Soon: History's Worst Plagues and the Heroes Who Fought Them* (New York: Henry Holt and Co., 2017), 243.

649 Scott M. Cutlip, *Fund Raising in the US: Its Role in America's Philanthropy* (New York: Routledge, 1990), 361.

650 Joanne Kenan, "When Elvis Helped to Conquer Polio," *Politico,* December 18, 2020, https://www.politico.com/news/magazine/2020/12/18/elvis-presley-polio-vaccine-confidence-448131.

651 Paul W. White, *News on the Air* (New York: Harcourt Brace, 1947), 179.

652 Beckman, Mary, "Did FDR have Guillain-Barré?" *Science,* October 31, 2003, https://www.science.org/content/article/did-fdr-have-guillain-barr.

653 Andrea Michelson, "8 celebrities who had polio and described their experiences, from paralysis to having their belongings burned," Insider, August 12, 2022, https://www.insider.com/celebrities-who-have-had-polio-2022-8.

654 Miriam Ascarelli, *Independent Vision: Dorothy Harrison Eustis and the Story of The Seeing Eye* (West Lafayette, IN: Purdue University Press, 2010), 88.

655 "The Seeing Eye," *Old Time Radio Downloads,* December 2, 1936, https://www.oldtimeradiodownloads.com/drama/the-cavalcade-of-america/the-seeing-eye-1936-12-02.

656 "Susan Smith Says . . . ," *San Francisco Examiner,* June 16,1936, 25, newspapers.com.

657 "Hedda Hopper Autographs, Memorabilia & Collectibles," History for Sale, accessed February 15, 2025, https://www.historyforsale.com/hedda-hopper-typed-letter-signed-01-10-1940/dc320752.

658 Patricia Lochridge to June Downey, July 21 [1962], Patricia Hartwell Private Papers.

659 "The College During World War II," *Sarah Lawrence College*, accessed February 11, 2025, https://www.sarahlawrence.edu/archives/digital-collections/wwii/background.html.

660 "Cupid Complaining to Venus," National Gallery, accessed February 2, 2025, https://lucascranach.org/UK_NGL 6344.

661 "Art Collection David Leder, Chemnitz/Berlin," Facts & Files, accessed February 11, 2025, https://www.factsandfiles.com/en/projects/art-collection-david-leder/.

662 Peter Gumbel, "70 years after D-Day, some companies still struggle with their dark WWII history," *Reuters,* June 6, 2014, https://finance.yahoo.com/news/column-70-years-d-day-181811724.html?

663 Andreas Platthaus, "His place in his city," *Frankfurter Allgemeine,* May 18, 2021, https://www.faz.net/aktuell/feuilleton/debatten/chemnitz-erinnert-mit-platzbenennung-an-arthur-weiner-17344061.html.

664 "Vogel, Hans Hermann," and "Dewitz, Walpurg von," Proveana. August 3, 2022, https://www.proveana.de/en/person/vogel-hans-hermann and https://www.proveana.de/en/person/dewitz-walpurg-von?term=Walpurg%20Gertrud.

665 Deutsches Zentrum Kulturgutverluste, email to author, August 11, 2023.

666 Paul Erker, *Suppliers for Hitler's War – The Continental Corporation in the Nazi Era*, (Berlin, 2020), 38.

667 "Carinhall—The ruins of Herrmann Görings Villa," Digital Cosmonaut, January 26, 2018, https://digitalcosmonaut.com/2018/herrmann-goering-carinhall/.

668 "Hitler's Birthday Gifts Include a Pair of Giraffes," *New York Times*, April 21, 1937. https://www.nytimes.com/1937/04/21/archives/hitlers-birthday-gifts-include-pair-of-giraffes.html; See also Robert M. Edsel, *The Monuments Men: Allied Heroes, Nazi Thieves, and the Greatest Treasure Hunt in History* (NY: Little, Brown and Company, 2013), 322.

669 "Cupid complaining to Venus," Cranach Digital Archive. National Gallery Library. fn 7, accessed February 15, 2025, http://lucscranach.org/UK_NGL_6344.

670 "Lucas Cranach the Elder, Cupid complaining to Venus." The National Gallery, accessed February 2, 2025. https://www.nationalgallery.org.uk/research/research-resources/national-gallery-catalogues/the-german-paintings-before-1800/lucas-cranach-the-elder-cupid-complaining-to-venus?viewPage=3 2.

671 "Sammlung Hans Hermann Vogel," *Proveana,* "After the war, remaining works owned by the von Dewitz family [daughter of Hans Hermann Vogel] were confiscated and transferred to the Chemnitz Municipal Art Collections, donated or given as a permanent loan," February 2, 2023, https://www.proveana.de/en/collection/sammlung-hans-hermann-vogel; Deutsches Zentrum Kulturgutverluste, email to author, August 11, 2023.

672 Thomas W. Laqueur, "The Deep Time of the Dead," *Social Research, The Body and the State: How the State Controls and Protects the Body*, 78 (2011), 802.

673 Andres Oppenheimer, "Did Hitler escape and move to Colombia? Despite new CIA memo, there's reason to doubt," *Miami Herald,* November 3, 2017, https://www.miamiherald.com/news/local/news-columns-blogs/andres-oppenheimer/article182412061.html.

674 Christopher Klein, "How South America Became a Nazi Haven," History.com, July 27 2023, https://www.history.com/news/how-south-america-became-a-nazi-haven

675 Dickson Hartwell and Andy Rooney, Eds., *Off the Record*, 209.

676 Patricia Hartwell, interview by Joe Rossi, 155.

677 "Search for model dwelling place ends in Midwest city," *Daily Oklahoman,* March 6,1947, 29, newspapers.com.

678 Patricia Hartwell, interview by Joe Rossi, 155.

679 Letter to family, September 10, 1945, Patricia Hartwell Private Papers.

680 Donald McWilliams, dir. *A Return to Memory*, National Film Board of Canada, 2024.

681 Will Stewart, "Russian who 'cremated' Adolf Hitler refuses to reveal where he scattered his ashes," *DailyMail.com*, April 30, 2010, https://www.dailymail.co.uk/news/article-1270108/Russian-cremated-Adolf-Hitler-refuses-reveal-scattered-ashes.html.

682 Michael Ruane, "Hitler shot himself 75 years ago, ending an era of war, genocide and destruction," *Washington Post,* April 30, 2020, https://www.washingtonpost.com/history/2020/04/30/hitler-suicide-bunker-eva-braun/.

683 Hettie Judah, "Lee Miller: the Vogue model turned photographer who captured the horrors of the Dachau concentration camp," Inews, May 1, 2020, https://inews.co.uk/culture/lee-miller-vogue-model-photographer-world-war-two-horrors-dachau-concentration-camp-424122.

684 Carolyn Burke, *Lee Miller: On Both Sides of the Camera* (London: Bloomsbury, 2006), 367, 371.

685 Mackrell, *The Correspondents*, 365, 374.

686 Henk de Berg. *Trump and Hitler: a comparative study in lying* (London: Palgrave Macmillan, 2024), 296.

687 Edith Iglauer, interview by Jay Hartwell, Jay Hartwell Notebook [1999-2000], Jay Hartwell Papers; Stewart Fern to Edith Iglauer, February 15, 1999, box 5, folder 3, Edith Iglauer Papers, University of Victoria Special Collections and University Archive.

688 Eric Barker, "Signs of Lying: Here's What Will and Will Not Help You Detect Lies," *Time*, April 26, 2014, https://time.com/77940/detect-lying/.

689 Kelliann Shimote, "Fern 'saw possibilities and made them happen,'" *Honolulu Star Bulletin*, August 2, 2001, https://archives.starbulletin.com/2001/08/02/news/story19.html.

690 Pat J. Brown, "My FOIA Request Will Outlive Me," *Muckrock*, February 15, 2019, https://www.muckrock.com/news/archives/2019/feb/15/my-foia-request-will-outlive-me/.

691 Mike Godwin, "I seem to be a Verb: 18 Years of Godwin's Law," *Jewcy*, April, 2008, https://www.jewcy.com/arts-and-culture/i_seem_be_verb_18_years_godwins_law/.

692 Patricia Lochridge, "Look Who's in the Movies Now," *Woman's Home Companion*, May, 1948, 7.

Index

A

Airborne Division, 101st, 71, 84, 85, 90
  Leonard Rapport, chronicler, 85
  Lieutenant Colonel Robert S. Smith, 84
  Unterstein art collection, 90, 106, 113
Allen, Paul, 147
Allmers, Robert, 287–288
America First Committee, 138
Anderson, Lindsay, 171–172
Arizonian, The, 237–238, 241, 243, 250–253, 263
Azov battalion, 241

B

Babb, Sanora,
  Whose Names Are Unknown, 268
Barbie, Klaus, 291
Berchtesgaden, 2, 59–60, 66, 73, 75, 84–90, 162, 226, 259, 277
Bernays, Edward, 110

Bernstein, Freeman,
  Hustling Hitler, 160
Better Homes and Gardens,
  article on Hitler, 177
Birnie, Bill,
  editor, *Woman's Home Companion,* 41, 48, 201
Black Lives Matter protests, 137, 141
Bloch, Eduard, 160
Bolles, Don, 239
Bonney, Thérèse, 39
Bourke-White, Margaret, 75, 93
  Dachau, 51, 55
  on "the looting fever," 65
Braun, Eva, 2, 57, 60, 69, 158
  parents,
    Franziska Braun, 192
    Fritz Braun, 192
Brown, Barry, 199
Brown, Hi, 199
Bull, Henry
  family,
    Jeff Bull, 111
    Metta Bull, 186–187

Steve Bull, 112, 117, 122,
143, 187, 189, 195,
219, 286–287, 293–
294, 315
Maggi Magnetics, 143–144, 151
Harvey Matusow and, 207
Roy Green and, 151
Whee-Lo, 143, 145,
151, 207
marriages,
Janet Scellen, 187, 200,
215–216
Pat Lochridge, 107–108,
110–115, 189, 195,
201, 299
Terese Svoboda and, 286–287
Bull, Stephen (Steve), 111, 118,
196, 199, 269, 314, 317, 319
family,
abuse by stepfather, 117,
120, 122, 141, 144–146
children, 120, 134,
140–141, 256, 274,
310–312, 318
Henry Bull and, 112, 117,
122, 143, 187, 189,
195, 219, 286–287,
293–294, 315
Janet Scellen and, 216–217,
292–293
kidnapping by mother, 111,
115, 189, 217
Pat Lochridge and, 6, 56,
106, 117, 132–133,
158–165, 201, 225,
243, 261
relationship with Shawnee
(nanny), 111, 115, 120

film projects,
Kidnap, 115
*Margaret Sanger: A Public
Nuisance,* PBS, 180–
182, 260
Voices & Visions, PBS,
156, 299
WHAM! film shoot,
171–174
Interactive Telecommunications
Program, NYU, 145, 274,
293
Interval Research, 147, 150
Interview with Pat Lochridge
Hartwell, 14, 117, 156,
159, 215, 278
inventions, 147–150, 281
marriages,
first marriage, 286–287
Terese Svoboda, 1, 5, 122,
133–134, 176, 180, 188,
200, 216, 236, 243, 304
honeymoon, 312–313
wedding, 293–294
Scot Gresham-Lancaster and,
150
Three Mile Island and, 305
Burns, Red, 293
Byoir, Carl, 175–177, 279
Carl Byoir & Associates, 110,
168, 176

C
Carter, Jimmy, 146
CBS Radio, 2, 13, 16–17, 20–21,
23, 26, 30, 134, 206, 211,
213, 215
Elmer Davis and, 23

H.V. Kaltenborn and, 17
Louis Ruppel and, 74
Chagall, Marc, 201, 263, 303
UNICEF greeting cards
and, 168
Chapelle, Dickey, 31, 42
Chesler, Ellen, 181
Cohn, Roy, 202
Comstock, Anthony,
Anti-obscenity laws, 179,
182–183
Conrad, Brian, 5
Cooley, Denton A., 70
COVID-19 pandemic, 102, 126,
196, 236, 280–281
Cowles, Virginia,
Love Goes to Press (with
Martha Gellhorn), 41, 103,
154
Craig, Elizabeth May,
description of the Berghof, 59
Cranach, Lucas the Elder
"Cupid Complaining to
Venus," 90, 93–94, 222–
228, 229, 233, 237, 254,
287–289
Crane, Hart, 105
Crawford, Ruth Elizabeth, 197

D

Dachau concentration camp, 31,
48–58, 87, 101, 103, 130,
132, 135, 156, 166, 224, 299
Daughters of the American
Revolution (DAR), 138, 201,
204, 206, 280
Davis, Elmer,
CBS and, 23

Pat Lochridge and, 23–24, 52,
202, 219
United States Office of War
Information (OWI) and,
24–25, 52, 202
De Berg, Henk,
*Trump and Hitler: A
Comparative Study in
Lying,* 301
Dickey, James, 105–106
Dickinson, Elizabeth Evitts,
"After the Cure," 278–279
Downey, June D.,
Pat Lochridge and, 169, 236,
246, 247, 248
Dufy, Raoul,
UNICEF greeting cards and,
168–169

E

Edwards, Julia
*Women of the World:
The Great Foreign
Correspondents,* 47
Edy, Carolyn M.,
*The Woman War
Correspondent, the U.S.
Military, and the Press,* 11
Eichmann, Adolf, 192, 291
Eisenhower, Dwight D., 14, 37,
56, 71, 102, 218

F

Federal Bureau of Investigation
(FBI), 103, 131
investigation of Dickson
Hartwell, 113, 208–211,
242, 243, 310

investigation of Pat Lochridge, 138, 242, 310

Fegelein, Hermann, 192

Finch, Barbara, 31

Flanner, Janet, 4

Foti, Sylvia, 160

G

Geertz, Clifford,
The Interpretation of Cultures, 80

Geller, Uri, 146

Gellhorn, Martha, 12, 47, 70, 175
"Only the Shells Whine," 31
Dachau, 51, 52, 55
Ernest Hemingway and, 79
Love Goes to Press (with Virginia Cowles), 41, 102–103, 154

Goebbels, Joseph, 11, 68, 69, 95, 174

Goering, Hermann, 40, 75, 91, 94, 101, 128, 156, 267, 299
Carinhall estate, 88, 90
differing accounts of arrest, 71–73, 75
Robert Allmers and, 288
suicide, 88
Unterstein art collection, 88, 90, 266
wife, 91

Gold Star Mothers, 126–127, 129

Goldman, Emma, 181, 183

Goldwater, Barry, 237, 239

Gonzales, Bennie,
Scottsdale Arts Center and, 255, 256

Goodman, Simon,
The Orpheus Clock, 233–235

Green, Roy,
Henry Bull and, 151

Gresham-Lancaster, Scot
Steve Bull and, 150

Grierson, John, 187, 199–200

Gumenyuk, Vladimir,
disposal of Hitler's remains, 294

H

Hamburger, Philip, 16, 26, 87, 210

Hammarskjöld, Dag, 57
Secretary General, UN, 167

Hartwell, Cindy, 276, 296

Hartwell, Dickson,
"Railroad Trucker's Brawl" and, 176
advocacy for the blind
"The Seeing Eye," radio program, 284
Dogs Against Darkness, 124, 284
awards,
recipient of bronze star, 11, 123, 221
recipient of Order of the White Rose, 38
death, 10, 190, 271, 287
obituary, 125
Donald Robinson and, 204
FBI investigation, 113, 208–211, 242, 243, 310
Head of Censorship for the Pacific, 38, 42, 96, 114
health issues,

alcoholism, 10, 113, 124,
    215, 221–222, 246
heart attack, 70, 244
    Denton A. Cooley and,
        70
journalism,
    articles,
        "America's Bruised and
            Beaten Children,"
            120
        "For the Record," 153
        "How to get rich in
            your own basement,"
            144
        "How Walter Winchell
            Came to be Written,"
            203
        "Walter Winchell:
            An American
            Phenomenon," 203
    Off the Record (with Andy
        Rooney), 61, 72, 96,
        153, 218, 291
    Overseas Press Club, 153,
        218–219
marriages,
    abuse of stepchildren,
        117, 120, 122, 141,
        144–146
    Pat Lochridge, 38, 107,
        111–116, 122, 131, 144,
        167, 218, 237, 247
    Ruth Adams Knight, 112,
        113, 198, 208–211,
        222, 284, 310
public relations,
    Harold F. Strong Corp.,
        171
    Hartwell, Jobson, and
        Kibbee and, 38, 40,
        52, 171
    ACNPJA and, 40
    Hill & Knowlton, 171,
        175–176
    Robinson/Hannagan,
        Vice President, 171,176
    St. Clair McKelway and, 210
    The Arizonian and, 237–238,
        241, 243, 250–253, 263
    purchase of, 222, 237
    UNICEF and, 111, 209
    Walter Winchell and, 202–
        204, 208, 209, 242, 250
Hartwell, Jay, 17, 101, 159, 169,
    226, 232, 246, 259, 265, 272,
    278, 287, 296, 298
Hayes, Helen,
    "Solace at Iwo," 47
Hemingway, Ernest,
    Martha Gellhorn and,79
Hendrickson, Paul, 105
Hickok, Lorena,
    Eleanor Roosevelt and, 14
Higgins, Charlotte, 225
Himmler, Henreich, 192
Hitler, Adolf, 17, 38, 57, 58,
    60–62, 79, 104, 119, 127,
    155, 160, 200, 224, 266, 278,
    288, 318
    ashes, 1, 4, 63, 69, 81, 83,
        99, 107, 117, 123, 134,
        162, 196, 200, 254,
        261, 310
    Berchtesgaden and, 3, 73
    Carl Byoir and, 175, 177
    depiction in JoJo Rabbit, 130

Eva Braun and, 57, 69, 158,
192
Franziska Braun and, 192
Fritz Braun and, 192
Führerbunker, 2, 68–69, 109
Führermuseum, 93 Moms for
Liberty, 141
New York Times articles on,
177
rumors surrounding death, 66,
108, 109, 152, 158, 290,
294, 299, 303
Hollingworth, Clare, 62, 129
Holocaust Expropriated Recovery
Act (HEAR), 227–228
Hoover, Edgar J., 208, 209
Hoover, Herbert, 167
Hull, Peggy, 31–32

I
Iglauer, Edith,
Pat Lochridge and, 232, 244,
246, 259, 277, 302
Irwin, Virginia, 156

K
Kaltenborn, H.V., 17, 23
Kaye, Danny,
UNICEF and, 207
Kazin, Alfred, 217
Keats, Jonathan,
*Forged: Why Fakes are the
Great Art of Our Age*, 268
Kennedy, Jacqueline, 202
Kennedy, John F., 87
Kennedy, Robert F. (Jr), 281
Kesselring, Albert, 71, 74–75
Kirkpatrick, Helen, 62, 129, 299

Knight, Ruth Adams,
Dickson Hartwell and, 112,
113, 198, 208–211, 222,
284, 310
Hi Brown and, 199
literary career, 112–113, 198,
284
Raymond Knight and, 198
testimony at McCarthy
hearings, 198–199
Ku Klux Klan, 182, 204
Kubala, Paul,
Hermann Goering and, 89

L
Lochner, Louis,
Associated Press, 100
Lochridge, Patricia (Pat),
"Cupid Complaining to Venus"
and, 90, 93–94, 223–228,
233, 254, 287–289
"Railroad Trucker's Brawl"
and, 176
Albert Kesselring and, 71,
74–75
articles,
"Abortion is an Ugly
Word," 48
"Are Germans Human?," 48
"Flight for Life," 34
"Good and Different," 132
"I Governed Berchtesgaden,"
84, 90, 226
"I saw the wounded come
home," 98
"Look Who's in the Movies
Now," 319
"Solace at Iwo," 47

"Startling Facts about
Black Market," 26
"The Mother Racket," 138
"They Call It Passion
City," 37
"VD: Menace and
Challenge," 48
"Vultures on the Home
Front," 130
CBS and, 2, 13, 16–17,
20–21, 23, 26, 30
Cultural Climate and,
10, 264
Daily Intelligencer
newspaper and, 15
Honolulu Advertiser
and, 263
Kansas City Star
newspaper and, 15
Radio Girl, unfinished
memoir, 18
birth, 14
Carl Byoir & Associates and,
110–111, 168, 175–176
Chester W. Nimitz and, 30,
31, 36–37
death, 299
Edith Iglauer and, 232, 244,
246, 259, 277, 302
education,
School of Journalism,
University of Columbia,
15, 18, 244
University of Texas, 15
Wellesley College, 15, 44,
84, 129, 244
Eleanor Roosevelt and, 2, 10,
12, 168, 219

family,
children, 5, 10, 14, 112,
117, 131, 248, 257–
258, 260, 272, 296–299
Franklyn Lochridge, 14, 37,
112, 187, 201, 215, 232
kidnapping of children,
111, 115, 189, 217
Lloyd Lochridge, 4, 14, 15,
16, 310
alcoholism, 215
Vice president of
Standard Oil, 108
Lloyd Lochridge Jr., 13, 70,
101, 248, 276, 293
Steve Bull and, 6, 56, 106,
117, 132–133, 158–
165, 201, 225, 243, 261
Interview with, 14, 117,
156, 159, 215, 278
FBI investigation, 138, 242, 310
Franklin Delano Roosevelt
and, 12, 13, 25
Future Gold Star Mothers,
126, 129
Hartwell Collection and, 258
Hawai'ian Arts Council and,
264
health issues,
cancer, 257, 269
hysterectomy, 257
polio, 2, 276–278
strokes, 197, 275, 276
Hermann Goering and, 71–72,
91
Hitler's ashes and, 1–4, 63,
99, 107, 117, 123, 134,
162, 196, 200, 261, 310

June D. Downey and, 169,
236, 246, 247, 248
Ku Klux Klan and, 204
League of Nations' World
Youth Congress, 129
marriages,
Dickson Hartwell, 38,
107, 111–116, 122,
131, 144, 167, 218,
237, 247
Henry Bull, 107–108, 110–
115, 189, 195, 201, 299
Overseas Press Club
Co-chair, 218
Retrospective:1967–1987, 264
The Arizonian and, 285, 291,
299, 312, 315
firing from, 250–251
UNICEF, 46, 56, 131, 133,
134, 167–170, 194, 223,
236, 246, 258–260
Director of Information,
56, 167, 207
greeting cards and, 168–
170, 201
United States Office of War
Information (OWI) and, 1,
24, 26, 87, 108, 202
University instructor,
Phoenix College, 259
University of Hawai'i, 269
wartime travel,
Berchtesgaden,
mayor of, 2, 66, 75,
84–89, 162, 226,
259, 277
Dachau, 31, 48–58, 130,
132, 135, 156

Eagle's Nest, 31, 47, 59,
201, 279
Guam, 30–31, 34, 202
Hawai'i, 40–42
Iwo Jima, 14, 35, 42–
44, 46
Nuremberg trials, 4
Saipan, 35, 41
South America, 3, 107,
117, 291–292
Woman's Home Companion,
25–26, 34, 44, 47–48, 60,
84, 130, 202, 226, 319
WWII souvenir collection, 11,
60–62, 89, 200, 226
Unterstein collection and,
90, 266

M
Machar, Riek,
Emma McCune and, 76
Terese Svoboda and, 76–78
MacLaren, Norman, 200
MacLeish, Archibald,
United States Office of War
Information (OWI) and,
24, 26
March of Dimes, 278–279
Franklin Delano Roosevelt
and, 278
Marcuse, Harold
Legacies of Dachau,
Pat Lochridge and, 54
Mareng, Mario Jackson, 76
Marshall, Jonathan, 251–252,
262
Scottsdale Progress and,
251–252

The Arizonian and, 251, 252

Marshall, Ru, 251, 262
   biography of Carlos
      Castaneda, 252
   Lenore Marshall and, 251

Matisse, Henri,
   UNICEF greeting cards and,
      168–169

Matusow, Harvey, 207

Maverick, Maury, 127

McCarthy, Joseph, 111, 197,
   201, 202, 205, 206, 207–208,
   211, 299

McGranahan, Carole, 175

McKelway, St. Clair, 210, 252

Mead, Margaret, 80
   Margaret Mead Film
      Festival, 270
   National Anthropological
      Film Center and, 32

Medearis, Domingo,
   Steve Bull and, 206

Mendes, Aristides de Sousa,
   Paul Rosenberg and, 230
   Terese Svoboda and, 230

Miller, Lee, 51, 62, 63,
   224, 299
   Dachau, 49, 55, 224, 299
   "Believe It," 49
   Lee, 316
   Pat Lochridge and, 49

Mitchell, Joni,
   polio, 281

Moisan, Melaney,
   *Tracking the 101st
      Cavalry*, 74

Molotov, Vyacheslav, 39
   Molotov cocktail, 39

Moms for Liberty, 141–142

Monuments Men, the, 90, 92,
   235, 266
   Howe, Thomas, 94
   The Monuments Men, 92, 211

Muldoon, Paul, 160

Munich Putsch, 4

Murrow, Edward R., 2, 17, 20,
   211, 218
   Good Night and Good Luck,
      211
   Overseas Press Club,
      Co-chair, 218
   Pat Lochridge and, 2, 218

Mussolini, Benito, 94, 127, 234

N

National Gallery, the, 223, 226–
   227, 229, 287, 289

Nevelson, Louise,
   Scottsdale Arts Center and,
      254–255

Niemöller, Martin, 104

Nixon, Richard, 240, 256

Non-fungible tokens (NFTs),
   265–266 Norieka, Jonas, 160

Nuer people of Sudan,
   Harvard Film Study Center
      documentary, 6
   in-law customs, 193
   refugees to United States,
      164–165
   Riek Machar and, 76
   songs, 7, 23, 78, 165
      *Cleaned the Crocodile's
         Teeth*, 76, 165
   Terese Svoboda and, 6, 8, 23,
      76, 164–166

The Nuer, E. Evans Pritchard, 80

victims of civil wars, 54, 164–166

Nuremberg Trials, 56

Pat Lochridge and, 4

O

Olsen, Sid,
TIME magazine, 100

Overseas Press Club, 218, 317
Deadline Delayed, 218
Off the Record, 72, 153

P

Pantaleoni, Helenka,
UNICEF greeting cards and, 168

Pate, Maurice, 116, 168, 194, 244, 246, 258

Patton, George S.,
Pat Lochridge and, 49, 87, 194

Price, Byron, 94, 97

Pritchard, E. Evans,
The Nuer, 80

R

Rajchman, Ludwick, 197

Ridge, Lola, 183–184, 251

Riznik, Joseph, 317

Roe *vs.* Wade, 183

Rooney, Andy,
Off the Record (with Dickson Hartwell), 61, 72, 96, 153, 218, 291

Roosevelt, Eleanor, 32, 127, 138, 228
It's Up to the Women, 44

Pat Lochridge and, 2, 10, 12, 168, 219
Woman's Home Companion and, 13

Roosevelt, Franklin Delano, 73, 74, 96, 218
fireside chats, 180
Guillain-Barré syndrome, 280
March of the Dimes, founder, 279
Pat Lochridge and, 12, 13, 25
polio, 279–280, 284
The United States Office of War Information and, 24

Rosenberg, Paul, 232
Aristides de Sousa Mendes and, 230
Georges Wildenstein and, 230

Roy, Jamini, 196
UNICEF greeting cards and, 169

Ruoc, Philip Machar, 7

Ruppel, Louis, 111
CBS Radio and, 74
Deputy Commissioner, Bureau of Narcotics, 74
Pat Lochridge and, 74, 89

S

Sanger, Margaret, 180–183
Ellen Chesler biography, 181
Margaret Sanger: A Public Nuisance, PBS, 180, 260

Scellen, Janet, 238
Glamour magazine profile, 187
Henry Bull and, 187, 200, 215–216

National Film Board, 187,
199, 200, 217, 292–293
Steve Bull and, 216–217,
292–293
Schindler, Meriel,
The Lost Café Schindler, 160
Schloss Collection, 227
Schultz, Sigrid, 62, 299
Scottsdale Arts Commission,
Pat Lochridge and, 250, 254,
259, 262
Scottsdale Town Enrichment Plan
(S.T.E.P.), 253, 254, 262
Scroggins, Deborah,
Emma's War, 76
Sevareid, Eric, 17
Shah, Nilay, 170
Shapiro, Walter,
Hustling Hitler, 160
Shirer, William, 17
Silberman, E.A., 223, 228–
229, 289
Smithsonian National
Anthropological Film
Center, 32
Society of Magazine Writers, 219
Sorel, Nancy,
*The Women Who Wrote the
War,* 55, 117, 121, 278
Steinbeck, John, 48, 97
Sanora Babb and, 268
Stevens, Edmund,
*War Correspondent: Thrills,
Danger and Boredom,* 24
Svoboda far-right movement, 241
Svoboda, Terese,
Aristides de Sousa Mendes
and, 276

Donald Sutherland and,
22–23
family,
children, 115, 120, 134,
140–141, 256, 274,
294, 308, 310–312, 318
death of son Deng,
45–46, 83, 157
father, 83, 120, 121, 155,
188, 239, 243, 286
dementia, 313
mother, 2, 83, 121, 123,
131, 139, 149, 160,
186, 195, 255, 261, 289
alcoholism, 131, 213,
286
Interstate 80
BiCentennial
Sculpture Project,
256, 258
Right-to-Life
organization, 260
film projects,
"Between Word and
Image," MoMA, 1993,
82
"Whitman," PBS, 158,
162, 180
*Margaret Sanger: A Public
Nuisance,* PBS, 180, 260
Real People, 22
To See or Not to See, 82
Voices & Visions, PBS, 22,
81, 156, 162
Henry Bull and, 286–287
KOGA radio and, 20
Margaret Mead Film Festival
and, 270